Ancient Greece

This book examines the development of ancient Greek civilization through a path-breaking application of social scientific theories. David Small charts the rise of the Minoan and Mycenaean civilizations and the unique characteristics of the later Classical Greeks through the lens of ancient social structure and complexity theory, opening up new ideas and perspectives on these societies. He argues that Minoan and Mycenaean institutions evolved from elaborate feasting and that the genesis of Greek colonization was born from structural chaos in the eighth century. Small isolates distinctions between Iron Age Crete and the rest of the Greek world, focusing on important differences in social structure. His book differs from others on ancient Greece, highlighting the perpetuation of Classical Greek social structure into the middle years of the Roman Empire and concluding with a comparison of the social structure of Classical Greece to that of the Classical Maya.

David B. Small is Professor of Archaeology at Lehigh University. A Fulbright fellow, he has conducted research in Greece, Italy, Israel, Honduras, and the United States.

Case Studies in Early Societies

Series Editor
Rita P. Wright, New York University

This series aims to introduce students to early societies that have been the subject of sustained archaeological research. Each study is also designed to demonstrate a contemporary method of archaeological analysis in action, and the authors are all specialists currently engaged in field research.

The books have been planned to cover many of the same fundamental issues. Tracing long-term developments, and describing and analyzing a discrete segment in the prehistory or history of a region, they represent an invaluable tool for comparative analysis. Clear, well organized, authoritative, and succinct, the case studies are an important resource for students, and for scholars in related fields, such as anthropology, ethnohistory, history, and political science. They also offer the general reader accessible introductions to important archaeological sites.

Other titles in the series include:

Ancient Mesopotamia
Susan Pollock

Ancient Oaxaca
Richard E. Blanton, Gary M. Feinman, Stephen A. Kowalewski and Linda M. Nicholas

Ancient Maya
Arthur Demarest

Ancient Jomon of Japan
Junko Habu

Ancient Puebloan Southwest
John Kantner

Ancient Cahokia and the Mississippians
Timothy R. Pauketat

Ancient Middle Niger
Rod McIntosh

Ancient Egyptian Civilization
Robert Wenke

Ancient Tiwanaku
John Janusek

The Ancient Indus
Rita P. Wright

Ancient Inca
Alan L. Kolata

Ancient Central China
Rowan K. Flad, Pochan Chen

The Colonial Caribbean
James A. Delle

Ancient Teotihuacan
George L. Cowgill

Early Medieval Britain
Pam J. Crabtree

Ancient Greece

Social Structure and Evolution

David B. Small

Lehigh University

CAMBRIDGE UNIVERSITY PRESS

CAMBRIDGE
UNIVERSITY PRESS

University Printing House, Cambridge CB2 8BS, United Kingdom

One Liberty Plaza, 20th Floor, New York, NY 10006, USA

477 Williamstown Road, Port Melbourne, VIC 3207, Australia

314–321, 3rd Floor, Plot 3, Splendor Forum, Jasola District Centre,
New Delhi – 110025, India

79 Anson Road, #06–04/06, Singapore 079906

Cambridge University Press is part of the University of Cambridge.

It furthers the University's mission by disseminating knowledge in the pursuit of
education, learning, and research at the highest international levels of excellence.

www.cambridge.org
Information on this title: www.cambridge.org/9780521895057
DOI: 10.1017/9781139034388

First published 2019

Printed in the United Kingdom by TJ International Ltd., Podstow, Cornwall

A catalogue record for this publication is available from the British Library.

Library of Congress Cataloging-in-Publication Data
Names: Small, David B., author.
Title: Ancient Greece : Social Structure and Evolution / David B. Small,
  Lehigh University.
Description: First edition. | London ; New York, NY : Cambridge University
  Press, 2019. | Series: Case studies in early societies | Includes bibliographical
  references.
Identifiers: LCCN 2018043662 | ISBN 9780521895057 (hardback) |
  ISBN 9780521719261 (pbk.)
Subjects: LCSH: Greece–Civilization–To 146 B.C.
Classification: LCC DF77 .S48 2019 | DDC 938–dc23
LC record available at https://lccn.loc.gov/2018043662

ISBN 978-0-521-89505-7 Hardback
ISBN 978-0-521-71926-1 Paperback

Contents

List of Figures		*page* xi
List of Boxes		xiii
Acknowledgments		xv
1	**My Analytical Frame**	**1**
	Social Structure as an Analytical Frame	1
	Complexity Theory	3
	Structure and Scope of This Book	6
	Readings	7
2	**The Ancient Greek Landscape**	**9**
	People, Land, Environment	9
	The Topography	11
	The Seas	13
	Climate	14
	Subsistence	14
	Subsistence and the Environment	15
	Demographics	15
	Readings	16
3	**The Neolithic in Greece**	**18**
	Tell Sites	20
	Were Communities Hierarchical?	27
	Measures of Social Complexity	29
	Readings	29
4	**Developments ca. 3200–2200 BCE**	**31**
	Developments on the Mainland	32
	Measures of Social Complexity	37
	The Cyclades	39
	Measures of Social Complexity	44
	Crete	44
	Measures of Social Complexity	46
	Readings	46

5   The Beginning of Change and the Evolution of a Koine   48
    Crete   48
    Evolution on the Community Level   49
    The Complexity Theory Frame   49
    Evolution on a Different Scale: The Palace Polities and Peak Sanctuaries   50
    The Complexity Theory Window into the Palaces   51
    The West Court   54
    Large Storage Rooms   54
    Central Courtyards   55
    Reception Rooms   59
    Banquet Halls   59
    Residential Areas   60
    Various Cult Facilities   61
    Other Results of Feasting: Houses, "Villas," and a Return to the
        Community-Level Scale   63
    Polity Size and Measures of Territorial Control   66
    Measures of Social Complexity   66
    The Cyclades   67
    Measures of Social Complexity   70
    The Mainland   71
    Measures of Social Complexity   74
    Later Developments and the Creation of an Aegean Koine   74
    Readings   76

6   Changes in the Latter Part of the Second
    Millennium BCE   78
    Charting Social Evolution on the Mainland: Complexity Theory's Frame   79
    Institutions of the Palaces: What the Architecture Tells Us   82
    Record Keeping   87
    Institutions of the Palaces: What the Texts Tell Us   89
    Problems in Understanding Mycenaean Greece   93
    The Palaces Disappear   96
    Measures of Social Complexity   98
    Readings   98

7   The Eleventh to Eighth Centuries: From Collapse to
    Created Chaos   100
    Demographics   100
    Regionalism   101
    New Ways of Feasting   102
    Introduction of Iron   102
    The Return of Literacy   104
    Our Analytical Frame   106
    Aspects of Social Structure before Chaos   107
    Institutions within the House   107
    Religious Ceremonies and Sacrifice   110
    Funeral Practices   112

Contents

Institution of Warfare/Battle 118
Institutions of Leadership and Power 119
Economic Institutions 121
Chaos and Change 122
Community Fissioning: The Start of Greek Settlement
   Expansion 126
Creating the Context for Self-Organization and Phase Transition 129
Early Examples 130
Measures of Social Complexity 131
Readings 132

8 A Brave New World: The New Structure and Characteristics
   of Its Emergence 133
Community Sanctuaries: General Characteristics 135
The Religious Sanctuary 135
Intercommunity Sanctuaries 143
Athletic Contests 145
Other Sanctuaries 149
Warfare/Battle 151
Funerals and Burials 152
Political Institutions 156
Similarities of Internal Political Structure: The Result of the Codification
   of the Epics as an Attractor 157
Additional Institutionalized Public Assembly 158
The Gymnasion 162
Economic Institutions, Principally Markets 162
The Household 163
Another Complexity: Structure within the Ethne 166
Aspects of Emergence 167
Measures of Social Complexity: Community Cohesion, Agency,
   and Political Economy 169
Readings 172

9 Developments after the Rise of Macedon 173
The Historical Context 173
Considerations of Structure 176
Measures of Social Complexity 183
Readings 184

10 The Cretan Difference 185
Azoria and the Different Institutions of Crete 185
A View into the Evolution of the Cretan Polis 196
Measures of Social Complexity 203
Readings 203

11 The Sweep of Things: The Larger Picture of the Evolution
   of Ancient Greece 204

12 Greece Is Not Alone: The Small Polity Evolutionary
   Characteristics of the Ancient Greeks and Other
   Past Cultures   208
      Characteristics of Greek Small Polities   208
      The Classic Maya   209
      Benefits from Employing the Greek Model   216
      Readings   218

   Glossary   219

   Bibliography   225

   Index   267

Figures

2.1 Spread of Greek and Phoenician settlements
    in antiquity   *page* 10
2.2 NASA satellite map of Greece   12
3.1 Franchthi cave   19
3.2 Map of Greece with major sites mentioned in the text   22
3.3 Plan of Neolithic Dhimini   24
3.4 Plan of Neolithic Sesklo   25
4.1 Cycladic "frying pan"   33
4.2 Sauceboat   34
4.3 House of the Tiles at Lerna   36
4.4 Cycladic figurine   40
5.1 Palace of Minos   56
5.2 Minoan Hall system from the palace at Phaistos   61
5.3 Linear A tablet   64
5.4 Kastri/Lefkandi feasting assemblage   68
5.5 House at Eutresis   73
6.1 Santorini (Thera) after explosion   80
6.2 Palace of Nestor at Pylos   84
6.3 Mycenaean kylix cup   86
6.4 Examples of Linear B   88
6.5 Rank-size analysis of Pylian polity   94
7.1 Greek feasting ware for the Iron Age and after   103
7.2 Various regional forms of the Greek alphabet   105
7.3 House at Nichoria   108
7.4 Ceramic centaur from Lefkandi burial   114
7.5 Funeral pavilion at Lefkandi   115
7.6 Areopagos warrior grave   117
7.7 Euboian skyphos   124
8.1 Agora from Megara Hyblaia   134
8.2 Fifth-century temple of Ares in Athens, moved to agora
    in Roman period   136
8.3 Sanctuary of Athena Polias at Priene   138

8.4	Early Iron Age centaur and human statuette	141
8.5	Fifth-century bronze statues	142
8.6	Early temple of Hera at Samos	144
8.7	Sanctuary of Zeus at Olympia	146
8.8	Lekythos with false bottom	153
8.9	Lekythos by the Achilles Painter	154
8.10	Theater at Epidauros	159
8.11	Mosaic of theatrical masks from the villa of Hadrian	161
8.12	House from Olynthos	164
9.1	Map of Hellenistic Greece	174
9.2	Agora of Priene	178
9.3	Philippeion at Olympia	180
10.1	Plan of Azoria	186
10.2	Early hearth temple at Prinias	188
10.3	Cretan Iron Age pithos	190
10.4	Social structure of Iron Age Azoria	194
10.5	Use of ostentatious mortuary feasting material at Iron Age Knossos	201
12.1	Map of Classic period Maya centers	210
12.2	El Palmar	212
12.3	Skyband on elite presentation bench from Las Sepulturas, Copan	214

Boxes

1 Caves Can Be Important: Franchthi Cave   *page* 19
2 The Emblematic Sauceboat   34
3 The Problem with Cycladic Figurines   40
4 The Minoan Hall   60
5 Mysterious Linear A   63
6 A New Feasting Assemblage   67
7 The Mycenaean Kylix Cup   86
8 Our First Centaur?   114
9 A Warrior Grave   117
10 A Greek Temple   136
11 Greek Sculpture: Humans and the Divine in Metal
    and Stone   141
12 Cheating the Dead? The White Ground Lekythos in
    Classical Athens   153
13 Greek Drama   160
14 The Philippeion   180
15 Showing off Your Agricultural Wealth   190
16 Usurping Symbols of Rulership: The Skyband in the
    Elite Compound of Las Sepulturas, Copan   213

Acknowledgments

This book has taken a long time to write, and there are quite a large number of people who have helped with its creation. I would first like to thank my classes in Greek archaeology at Lehigh University. Whether they knew it or not, the students in these classes were guinea pigs for a lot of the ideas set forth in these chapters. To those students, I give heartfelt thanks. Lehigh University provided funds for me to work on Crete, developing many aspects of my argument on "The Cretan Difference." I also owe tremendous gratitude to the Fulbright Association, having won a Fulbright core scholarship to teach at the University of Crete, Rethymnon, in the winter and spring of 2015. And to the students whom I taught at the university, I owe a debt of gratitude, for they were test pilots for the first run of much of the theoretical framing of this book.

There are many individuals I wish to thank, all of whom were helpful in listening to my often wacky ideas and giving me extremely helpful feedback. A very special thanks to Pavlina Karanastasi, professor of Classical Archaeology at the University of Crete, who heard many of my arguments and gave me encouraging support. While working at the INSTAP center on Crete I was able to discuss many of my ideas with fellow researchers who, again, provided very useful feedback: thanks to Flint Dibble, David Blome, and Kevin Glowacki. Some of my INSTAP friends were subjected to many more of my ideas, and for being attentive listeners and providing helpful suggestions I thank John McEnroe, Matt (David) Buell, Melissa Eaby, and Rodney Fitzsimons.

I am very grateful as well to Carla Antonaccio, Donald Haggis, and Antonis Kotsonas, who read various parts of my thesis and provided extremely useful feedback. Lisa Nevett and Anthony Snodgrass read various arguments from this book and provided useful critiques. I would also like to thank the two anonymous reviewers for Cambridge University Press, who read the whole manuscript very closely and helped me avoid some egregious errors.

Very special thanks to Rita Wright for her incredible patience and belief in me while I labored so long over my manuscript. A special salute to my son, Colin Small, an author is his own right, who read the entire manuscript and helped with flow and issues of clarity and grammar. And finally, a heartfelt thanks to my wife Susan, who endured what must have seemed like an endless time over which I struggled with the writing of this book. She was always there to support me.

1   My Analytical Frame

This is a book about the ancient Greeks. But it is not a history of the ancient Greeks. It does not treat issues such as the lives of great people, military campaigns, and battles – the common themes of books on Greek history. It is also not a traditional cultural overview of the ancient Greeks, which often provides a broad outline of the world of the ancient Greeks and focuses on some of the more well-known and high-profile issues, such as the development of participatory democracy in some of its city-states. This is also not a book, like many on ancient Greece, which highlights some of the more well-known ancient Greek communities, such as Athens or Sparta. Rather, this is a case study of the ancient Greeks which seeks to dig deep, to expose the underlying timbers that made up the social structure of a society which could manifest itself in the Bronze Age in varying centers such as Knossos or Mycenae, and later on in polities with internal constitutions running from democracy to tyranny (unconstitutional one-man rule) to monarchies.

This book looks at civilization in Greece from the Neolithic to the second century CE when the Greeks were embedded into the Roman Empire, and outlines the tremendous spread of the ancient Greeks from the Iberian Peninsula to the mountains of Afghanistan. As such, this book has a very wide temporal and spatial scope. To deal with this situation I am employing the concept of social structure to identify what the underlying armatures of ancient Greek culture were, and I am using evolutionary theory, here complexity theory, as an analytical frame for interpreting its development. Let me turn to the issue of social structure first.

Social Structure as an Analytical Frame

My concept of social structure is somewhat unique but close to Giddens's (1986) idea of structuration, in which culture is defined as made up of units of shared repeated behaviors and associated meanings that direct the actions of individuals. For me, these units equate with our concept of institutions, recurring sets of behavior which are recognized as valued in society. As an archaeologist, my units equate with the remains of identifiable contexts of interaction, spaces marked by specific features and landscape where actors negotiated for identity and social position. As we shall see, these contexts could be linked together in larger social strategies that drove evolutionary change in ancient Greece. I use the total number of these identifiable contexts of interaction, their internal dynamics, and how they link up with other contexts in the Greek past, as an index of social complexity.

In arriving at my concept of social structure I have been very much influenced by Humphreys's (1978) application of concepts of developing social articulation in ancient Greece. She described the development of ancient Greek culture by charting the birth and development of different social interaction contexts. These contexts were spatially and temporally separated, and had their own rules and norms. A measure of increasing structural complexity for ancient Greece was the birth of new social interaction contexts as the culture in general became more structurally articulated. I plan to follow that analytical view in this book.

Following Humphreys's analysis, I see these contexts of interaction as those of cultural performance, similar to Goffman's (1967) contexts of dramaturgy, a concept which still resonates in studies of performance in past cultures (Hodder 2006; Inomata and Coben 2006). That is, people create their contexts and, in turn, are shaped by them.

I have an open definition of performance within these contexts. I would not restrict performance to only formal activities within an interaction context, but would include any repeated, therefore institutionalized behavior taking place between two or more people (see Houston 2006 for excellent overview of definitions of performance contexts).

I seek to analyze social structure through a strong focus on these distinct social units of interaction, which are amenable to archaeological investigation because they were spatially distinct in their social settings. Therefore, a great deal of my approach deals with the spatial units visible in the archaeological record. The distribution of these spatial units through time and space allows me to identify the various cultures which occupied the territories which the Greeks inhabited throughout time. Yet there are caveats to this approach, as with any. Sometimes the archaeological record supplies only a limited set of identifiable contexts. But for most periods in ancient Greece the sample we do have is robust enough to allow us to use it as an indication of social structural complexity.

I utilize this analytical window in both a spatial and a temporal analysis of the Greeks. Using social structure as an analytical frame allows me to effectively compare different spatial dimensions of ancient Greek culture, be they similarities or differences. A case in point is the eighth century BCE and after, when the Greeks spread throughout the lands of the Mediterranean and the Black Sea. A social structural frame highlights the amazing similarities that many of the Greek poleis (city-states) exhibited among themselves in this tremendous cultural exodus, as it also allows us to document cultural differences. Looking at cultural change over time, the use of this analytical frame provides a unit of comparison between different developmental periods in the Greek past. It focuses our attention on what was newly created in the culture as time progressed. Therefore, throughout this book, I will take time to measure aspects of social complexity through this structural frame to give us both a chronological and spatial bearing in our treatment of the ancient Greeks.

Complexity Theory

To study the dynamics of structural change I am applying the concept of complexity theory. This theory is enjoying a dramatically increasing popularity in the fields of science, economics, management, and the social sciences (Cleveland 2009; Garnsey and McGlade 2006; Manson 2001; Reitsma 2003). My interest here is its application to archaeology (Beekman and Baden 2005; Bentley and Mascher 2003, 2007; Kohler 2012; Levy 2005), because it is well suited to the study of social change and concepts of cultural evolution. An enormously widespread interest in complexity theory has produced numerous definitions of what it actually is, often dissimilar and sometimes at odds with one another. Yet it is possible to chart some common characteristics and apply them to archaeological investigation.

Complexity theory defines societies as open systems, where the relationship between different units is nonlinear; that is, the result of their connections produces a set which is greater than one would expect from the sum alone. In a temporal sense, complexity theory sees society moving through periods of identified structure, then a chaotic rapid transition to an identified new social structure. When moving from a chaotic phase, societies self-organize and are affected internally by attractors, repeated behaviors which produce internal structure, seen in the presence of new social units, new organization, new forms of social control, or new social boundaries. The transition is labeled a "phase transition" and is quick and totalizing, not limited to a piecemeal creation of new social structure.

As in the employment of any theory, I am using complexity theory as an analytical frame which can suggest important links between various bits of data in the historical record. At best, it can suggest important linkages between disparate information we have on the past and can help us frame meaningful questions to be applied to our record of the past. I do not believe in applying theory with a sledgehammer, however. I have witnessed far too often the application of theory in archaeology where the data do not quite fit the complete features of the theoretical perspective, and the value of the application of that theory is damaged by a focus on where the theory does not fully apply. Theory should be applied with care, as a useful analytical frame. It is a tool, not an outcome.

To see how complexity theory has been used in a very useful sense, I turn to Yoffee (2005: 198–232), who gives a good description of evolution in Mesopotamia seen through this analytical frame. He describes a situation in which a gradual increase in the number of new social institutions reached a tipping point, then produced chaos and a quick phase transition to a new level of social organization:

> Mesopotamia, and I believe elsewhere, persisted as modest villages for thousands of years, while social roles and identities changed in significant ways. From the environment of village life, the circulation of goods and marital partners led to institutionalized interconnections among unrelated people and to the formation of interaction spheres. Codes of communication and symbols of shared beliefs allowed and expressed new aspects of cultural identity among the villagers. Certain individuals, nascent elites, began to restrict access to the technology of symbol manufacture and also the means of communication and the venues of communication such as feasts and ceremonies. Control over these symbols and esoteric knowledge became a domain of power in these early villages ... In Mesopotamia, the formation of larger spheres of interaction over time and the growth of a belief system that connected both northern and southern Mesopotamia resulted not only in regularized exchanges of goods but also reasons to shift production goals from local consumption to production for exchange ... Within interaction spheres, cities crystallize, at some point, rapidly ... as phase transitions. (Yoffee 2005: 229–30)

In Mesopotamia the phase transition from the stage of villages to large polities included the invention of written language and the associated bureaucracy (food rations, military regulation, etc.) that utilized it. There were also new temple precincts with new religious and political institutions, rulers, slaves, tribute-bearing associations with foreign cultures, etc.

A review of Yoffee's description highlights two important points about complexity theory. The first is the question of what produced the rapid change. Somehow the old social structure was not able to meet the needs of new social entities. For Yoffee these were new social roles, new connections between people, and – reading between his lines – new wealth. These new features in Mesopotamian society had built up until the old social structure could not adequately meet the new demands they created, and there was a rapid transformation to a new social structure which did. It is highly important to ask the question, what produced the structural crisis which triggered the phase transition? It will be asked in our analysis of structural change for ancient Greek culture.

The second point is just as important. Yoffee correctly mentions "certain individuals, nascent elites" who began to change the ways in which society was structured and triggered the actual phase transition. The search for these individuals and the period in which they were operating is a key focus in my analysis of the ancient Greeks. In my search for periods of phase transitions and those actors who were behind the creation of new social structure, I am going to focus on evidence of feasting. Recent work has made headway into an understanding of how ancient feasting can supply a context for the mitigation of social scalar stress, the creation and solidification of social roles, and the integration of communities. These functions would have been supplied not only through the very context of the feast itself but also through the effect that creating a feast would have had on the social and economic spheres of a community. In its transformational character, a feast would have filled the needs of a society in rapid transition.

To isolate feasting in the archaeological record I define this institution as an occasion different from daily meals. A feast includes a larger number of people participating; consequently, there would be more food and drink. There might also be specialized foods or foods which require unusual methods of preparation. Feasts are often held in special temporal or physical settings, which might include the use of specialized dining arrangements, distinct serving materials, and particular seating configurations. Within the archaeological record of ancient Greek culture, we shall see that there are several examples of commensality that meet this definition.

The role of feasting in cultures in transition has been crucial, in the Paleolithic/Neolithic transition (Munro and Grosman 2010), in the European Mesolithic (Hayden 2004), the Levantine Neolithic (Benz 2000; Twiss 2008), sixth to fourth millennium Syria and Anatolia, and early Bronze Age Ban Non Wat in Thailand (Higham 2014). In prehistoric Europe, Dietler (1996) has argued for the power of feasting in developing political economies. In the Classical world, the same author (Dietler 2007) has also demonstrated the important role that feasting can play in mitigating the social chaos engendered by colonialism, by constructing and validating new social norms. In studies of the Greek past specifically, Halstead (2004) has noted the potential social transformative power of feasts in the Neolithic.

Some of the best ethnographic information we have on the power of feasting within cultures in transition has come from work with transegalitarian societies (Blake and Clark 1999; Clark and Blake 1994; Hayden 1995). Transegalitarian societies are societies that moved away from an egalitarian structure to a hierarchical one. In these societies power and prestige have moved beyond the level of the individual households, but they are not yet guaranteed by inherited wealth or title. In a close way a transegalitarian society matches the description of a chaotic period of a phase transition. New wealth, new positions, and new prestige exist, but they are not secured by the then current social structure. In these societies, Yoffee's nascent elites, or as they are often referred in egalitarian societies, aggrandizers, create new institutions that will eventually secure their positions.

Hayden (2009; see also LeCount and Blitz 2010) demonstrates that within transegalitarian societies elaborate funeral feasting, and I would add other feasting venues as well, provides an institutionalized context in which these nascent elites can act like aggrandizers and work to secure the positions which they hold outside the structure of the family. They often use these funeral contexts to create alliances with others. These alliances could provide social assistance in endemic warfare, offer affiliations with others who can help with the high cost of bride prices and dowries, offer access to investment in wealth, create alliances for regional trade, and protect the interests of the deceased family from the exploitive schemes of others. All these alliances operate above the level of the family and create new contexts of interaction or institutions, which become permanent as the society moves to a more hierarchical social structure. A focus on this type of feasting isolates the actors or aggrandizers who were instrumental in directing the self-organization of societies, as seen through the frame of complexity theory.

Structure and Scope of This Book

Book titles can be difficult. Although "Ancient Greece" is in the title, this book has temporal boundaries which are larger than those the reader might be accustomed to associating with ancient Greece. It begins with the Neolithic and continues until the middle of the second century CE of the Roman Empire. There are therefore several cultures which are analyzed here, rather than just those of the period from 1000 BCE to the Roman Empire, which are most often identified as "ancient Greek." While these earlier cultures differed in many ways from that of the Greeks in the first millennium, they are important structural antecedents to the creation of those later cultures and are crucial to our understanding of the full context of their evolution.

In what may be seen as unusual, I do not follow established chronological units for Greece. The periods used by scholars of ancient Greece
can be arbitrary, not matching those of significant cultural development.
My chapters often divide or lump together these units. Readers who wish
to know the accepted chronologies may turn to Whitley (2001: 60–74)
and Mee (2011: 3–7).

Because this is a case study, I have chosen to analyze this period
from the Neolithic to the Roman Empire with foci on social structure
and evolutionary change as seen through the application of complexity
theory. A focus on complexity theory produces a pace for this book
which is somewhat different from other treatments of ancient Greece.
More attention is paid to some periods than others, especially those
periods when we can study elements of evolutionary change. In an
unusual deviation from other treatments of Greece, I have interrupted
the story of Crete with an analysis of the development of social structure outside the island (Chapters 7 and 8). The social structure of Crete
after 1000 BCE was unique and is best analyzed in the light of developments in the rest of the Greek world. And some nontraditional
periods are included, such as the history of Greek communities in the
Roman Empire, which rounds out the developments seen in the evolutionary changes of the eighth through sixth centuries BCE. In cases
where the scope is more narrow than usual, such as the Classical era of
the fifth and fourth centuries, the reader who wishes to explore these
periods in greater depth is directed to the sections on further readings,
which, in the case of the Classical era, supply reference to issues which
do not receive the attention that they might have in more traditional
treatments on the ancient Greeks. I have also included several topical
boxes, which highlight some interesting topics, such as the Greek
statue-erecting.

The scope of the book is large in time and large in geographical extent.
Each chapter therefore includes a section which summarizes its developments with an index of complexity. This allows the reader to compare the
nature of social complexity between different periods and between different parts of the Greek world. Differences between Crete and the mainland after 1000 BCE are highlighted, for example. The complexity index,
focusing on the issue of social structure, also allows for a comparison
between the ancient Greeks and other past cultures, here, the Classic
period Maya.

Readings

Those who would like to read further on the various internal subcultures
and the historical development of the ancient Greeks are encouraged to

turn to excellent historical treatments such as that of Cartledge (2011), Hall (2013), Martin (2013), Ober (2015), Osborne (2009), and Pomeroy et al. (2011).[1] My focus in this book is on social structural complexity and evolutionary change, and I therefore do not focus on some important social issues. Those interested in women in ancient Greece are encouraged to read Blundell (1995) and MacLachlan (2012). For slavery, Finley and Shaw (1998) is a must as well as Bradley and Cartledge (2011) and Wrenhaven (2012). I shall refer to more specific cultural studies as the chapters develop.

The application of theory is vital to the development of observations in this book. For additional readings on the use of theory in Greek archaeology, see Kotsakis (1991), papers in Papadopoulos and Leventhal (2003), in Haggis and Antonaccio (2015), and in Nevett (2017a). In the latter, Nevett's introduction and the contribution by Stone, "A Theoretical or Atheoretical Greek Archaeology? The Last Twenty-Five Years," are extremely insightful.

For excellent additional introductions to the power of feasting within cultures, see Dietler and Hayden (2010), Hayden (2014), and Hayden and Villeneuve (2011). Although I am using feasting in a new way to look at the Greek past, I make no claim to be the first person to focus on feasting or even funeral feasting in ancient Greece. The study of feasting in general has been of recent interest. Wright's edited section in *Hesperia* (2004) was one of the first publications to focus on feasting itself. Another is the edited work by Hitchcock et al. on Aegean feasting (2008). An important additional study is Haggis's treatment of diacritical feasting at Middle Minoan II Petras (2007).

The majority of these studies, however, have not been concerned with funeral feasting. Although studies such as that of Wright (2004) did treat material from the shaft graves at Mycenae to isolate some artifacts that may have been used for feasting, the issue of funeral feasting was not pursued. Perhaps the only person to treat funeral feasting so far has been Hamilakis (1998), who gathered much information for funeral feasting at Bronze Age Agia Kyriaki. Hamilakis, however, was not interested in how funeral feasting changed over time.

---

[1] The Readings sections not only recommend works not mentioned in the chapters, but also include a few important works already referred to in the chapters.

2   The Ancient Greek Landscape

Ancient Greece was not the Greece we are accustomed to seeing today. In antiquity the Greeks spread out along many of the coastal regions of the Mediterranean and the Black Sea. In this chapter I will introduce the extent of Greek occupation as well as treat issues of economy and landscape.

People, Land, Environment

Just as we cannot begin to discuss the evolution of the Greeks without an understanding of time, we must also review the environment within which the Greeks lived. When Herodotos, the Greek historian and ethnographer of the fifth century BCE, defined the Greeks he referred to "the kinship of all Greeks in blood and speech, and the shrines of gods and the sacrifices that we have in common, and the likeness of our way of life" (Herodotos 8.144.2–3). He did not, as we would do today, identify the Greeks by a certain region or land which they occupied. This would have been difficult for him, because in his time, the Greeks had moved to settle a large part of the Mediterranean. They lived not only in what today constitutes Greece, but on the western coast of Asia Minor, the Black Sea, North Africa, Sicily, Southern Italy, Southern France, and the eastern coast of Iberia (Figure 2.1).

The Greek philosopher, Plato, writing in the fourth century BCE, described the dispersion of Greeks in the Mediterranean world with the famous simile, "we who dwell between the pillars of Hercules (the straits of Gibraltar) and the river Phasis live in a small part of it about the sea, like ants or frogs about a pond, and that many other people live in many other such regions" (*Phaedo* 109a–b). Sometime later in the first century BCE, the famous Roman orator and author Cicero painted a similar description of Greece: "The shores of Greece are like hems stitched onto the lands of barbarian peoples" (Cicero *de Rep.* 2.9, from Malkin 2011: 15). The imagery of both authors is compelling. Greece was more than what we call Greece today, an invention of the last two centuries. It

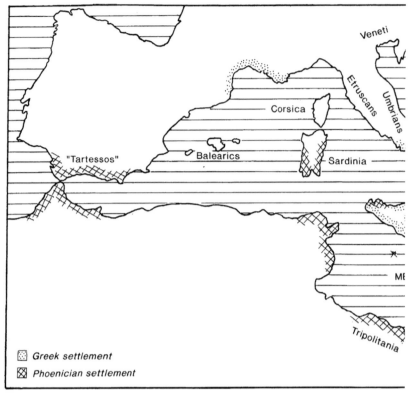

Figure 2.1 Spread of Greek and Phoenician settlements in antiquity.

surrounded the Mediterranean. Greece was defined, rather, by the sea. One got to Greece and one traveled around Greece not by land but by the sea. As I will argue, this point is very important to our understanding of how many of the principal characteristics of ancient Greece evolved.

The territory occupied by Greeks was not constant. As we shall see, Greeks in the Bronze Age, ca. 3000–1000 BCE, lived in more circumscribed territories, much like how we think of Greece today. It was not until the eighth century and even somewhat earlier that Greeks began this diaspora to other shores. It is thus difficult to detail the environments they inhabited in total. An attempt to describe the geographical and climatic features for all of the regions where they settled would require a book unto itself. I am eschewing that onerous task, and for the purposes of this study, I will describe only the general characteristics of the world inhabited by the ancient Greeks, highlighting issues which

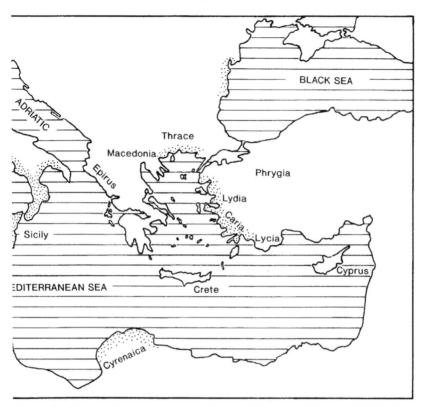

BLACK SEA

ADRIATIC

Thrace

Macedonia

Epirus

Phrygia

Lydia

Caria

Lycia

Sicily

Cyprus

MEDITERRANEAN SEA

Crete

Cyrenaica

(Drawn by Howard Mason, courtesy of Howard Mason and James Whitley.)

are important for understanding the nature of their culture and the dynamics of their social change.

The Topography

Mainland Greece is a southern peninsular extension of Balkan Europe (Figure 2.2). Eighty percent of the its land mass is mountainous, with Mount Olympus, at 2919 m above sea level, the famed home of the Greek gods, standing as its highest peak. The Pindus mountain chain runs across most of the country in a northeast to southwesterly direction, continuing on to form islands further out in the sea to the south. Understandably, there are few plains. Thessaly is perhaps the largest of all, followed by nonmountainous areas around Athens and Thebes, and the littoral area of the Peloponnesos. The region just to the north, ancient

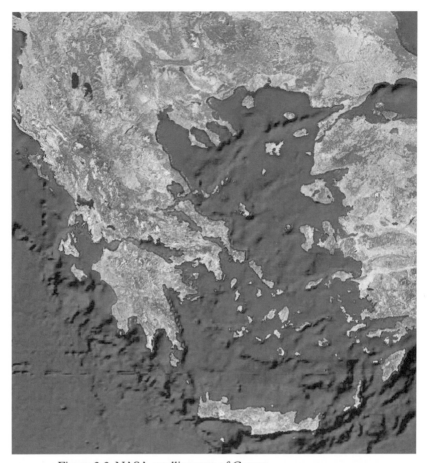

Figure 2.2 NASA satellite map of Greece.

Thrace, was mountainous as well, with plains following three major
rivers. Western Turkey, which the Greeks were to occupy as early as
the end of the second millennium BCE, is composed of multiple mountain chains leading into the Mediterranean. The spaces between the
mountains are taken up by various fertile river valleys. Along its northern
coast the Black Sea is dominated by flat plains which extend further
north. Its southern and western shores are more mountainous with
limited, small lowlands near the sea itself. The islands in between Greece
and Turkey and those between Crete and the mainland to the north can
best be described as the tips of the Pindus mountain range. They are in

general steep, with a few valleys and limited flat topography. Crete itself is very much the same, with a large mountain range that runs from east to west along the spine of the island. What level land it owns is limited to the coastal areas, as well as some identified plains, such as the Messara in the south and the Lasthithi plain, isolated within the eastern half of the mountain range itself. Further to the south, on the coast of Libya, the areas around the Greek city of Kyrene (Cyrene) were fairly flat, broken only by a few small mountainous outcrops. Sicily, especially the eastern half where the Greeks settled, was not as mountainous as the Greek mainland, but did have mountains along its eastern coast, where Etna, its still active volcano, continues to threaten. There is also a mountainous area on the southeast part of the island and in the west. There are two large plains, that of Catania on the eastern half of the island, and to the west of Mount Iblei on the south. The southern part of the Italian peninsula, which was settled by the Greeks, is dominated by the Apennine mountain range, but contains low-lying plains in the heel of the peninsula and others on the coast. These coastal plains run up on the western side of Italy as well. The Provence region of France, where the Greeks also settled, is characterized by coastal plains. The same is true for the eastern coastal area of Spain, which also saw immigration from Greece.

The Seas

The Greeks were to settle on the coasts of the Mediterranean and the Black Sea. Both bodies of water served as the principal means of connection between Greek communities. The Mediterranean also contains a major counterclockwise system of currents, which aids navigation. Sections of this sea break down further into smaller circuits. The Adriatic, for example, contains its own system which flows north along the Dalmatian coast and south against the eastern coast of Italy. The eastern Mediterranean has a similar system of currents, moving north along the Levant and western Turkish coast, then west through the Aegean, and finally south toward the northern shores of Libya. A similar counterclockwise current flows along the coasts of the Black Sea.

Rather than standing as a barrier to communication, the seas in ancient Greece thus fostered connections between different communities. Not only was the sea open for navigation, but the rugged terrain of most of Greece made overland travel difficult and expensive. Studies point to the connecting power of the sea (see Horden and Purcell 2000; Abulafia 2011, for an even larger picture). Broodbank (2002), in an important study of the cultures in the Cycladic islands, showed forcefully that the sea connected different coastal communities on different islands and provided a means by which various settlements combined to create unified identities. Malkin (2003, 2011) has also rightly observed that seaborne connections in the ancient Greek world provided important avenues for ethnic identity even between such far-distant communities as the Greek communities in the western Mediterranean and those on the west coast of Asia Minor.

Climate

Most of the areas that the ancient Greeks inhabited have a Mediterranean climate, wet winters from October to March, and hot, dry summers, excepting the northwestern part of Greece and the coastal areas of the Black Sea. The Black Sea's coastal regions are predominately of a continental climate. Only the southern tip of the Crimean Peninsula and the northwestern coast of the Caucasus have a Mediterranean one.

A very important point about the ancient Greek climate is that many areas within mainland Greece and Crete contain microenvironments. A microenvironment is a small area with its own particular climate. Of great concern to farmers, different microenvironments, even if they are somewhat close to one another, can exhibit varied reactions to interannual climate variation, especially rainfall. This means that parts of Greece were quite often a mosaic of differing microenvironments with very different degrees of rainfall. The impact of this becomes clear when we discuss the various forms of subsistence in the Greek world.

Subsistence

The Greeks lived on a mix of wild and domesticated plants and animals. Wild game included red and roe deer, wild boar, rabbit, bear, pigeon, partridge, and duck. Domesticated animals included pig, goat, sheep, cow, and by the second millennium, chicken. Communities on the coast also had access to fish. Dried and salted, it was also available to people living farther from the sea. There was a variety of domesticated plants. We find emmer and einkorn wheat and barley as early as ca. 3000 BCE, along with lentils, peas, bitter vetch, chick peas, and horse beans. There is also some evidence to suggest that the Greeks had domesticated the grape as early as this time as well. The domestication of the olive is less well understood. We have some evidence of olive stones in communities as early as ca. 3000 BCE, but it is not certain whether or not these stones came from wild or domestic trees. In the later second millennium Mycenaean palaces were producing perfumed olive oil for export, but here too, it is not certain that they were utilizing domestic olives, since wild olive oil, with its lower fat content, was preferred for making perfume. It appears certain, at least, that the domesticated olive was becoming more utilized by ca. 1100 BCE.

Subsistence and the Environment

A large part of the world inhabited by the Greeks was subject to subsistence risk (Gallant 1989, 1991). It was not certain that crops would do well during the dry, hot summers. Farmers of course would have to take this risk into close account, and they had some means by which they could minimize the risk. One of the strategies was intercropping. By planting a variety of crops on the same land, many farmers bet that one or two of the crops would provide a sufficient harvest, even if the summer rains were low. Another method was the fragmentation of land holdings. Farmers would often own small parcels of land, which were not connected and sometimes at a significant distance from one another. Since microenvironments would often react differently to a summer's climate, there was a good chance that a crop that would not do well that summer on one parcel of land might very well do better on another. Another strategy was food storage. Any surplus from a good summer's harvest would be stored as long as possible, hopefully serving as insurance in a year of poor returns. Another strategy was alliance. Through social ties some families could call on their kin in years of bad harvest to help them out. This was a social reciprocal arrangement. One was obligated to help a family member in the event of a surplus, so that one would be able to ask for assistance further on.

Demographics

The Greek peoples were living not only on the Greek mainland but on Crete, Western Asia Minor, coastal areas of the Black Sea, North Africa, Sicily, South Italy, Southern France, and Spain by the fifth century BCE. These Greeks were united by a common language, art, philosophy, and political structure. The native Sicil in Sicily or Celt in France might well have wondered who these people were and where they had come from. If we had asked this question fifty years ago, the answer would have been quick and simple. Although there were competing arguments (Drews 1988 gives a good overview), most agreed that Greek-speaking people migrated from the east into Greece around 2000 BCE and took over mainland Greece from a people who were not Greek speakers. This argument was supported by the appearance of a new pottery type, commonly known as Minyan ware (Haley and Blegen 1928) in Greece at this time and the observation that some place names in Greece appear to have been pre-Greek and linked somehow to similar names in Anatolia. The appearance of Greek speakers in Greece has also been keyed to the appearance of shaft graves around 1600 BCE in several parts of the peninsula (Drews 1988).

But the quest for the arrival of the "Greeks" suffers from an a priori assumption that the Greek people did not inhabit the land before 2000 BCE and that they must trace their ancestry to some sort of migration. The assumption is debatable. Minyan ware appears to have precursors in the archaeological record before 2000 BCE, and Renfrew has even argued (1987) that the introduction of Greek speakers into Greece could well have come with the introduction of farming, as early as the Neolithic. In the end, just when the first Greek-speaking people were living in Greece is still not known, and will probably never be settled.

Similarly, Greek ethnic identity becomes a problem when Greeks come into contact with non-Greek peoples. This cultural contact occurred a number of times, when they started to live in eastern Anatolia, when they began a vibrant period of colonization in the Mediterranean, when they settled into the Black Sea, and when they began to live in polities in places as far away as Afghanistan after the conquests of Alexander the Great. It was once generally accepted that we could recognize the presence of these migrating Greeks by the appearance of their material culture. But analysis of this situation has become more nuanced, strongly arguing that there was a hybridization of cultures in these contact zones, that what we would quickly call Greek is actually a mixture of Greek and local cultures (see Waldbaum 1997, for early arguments on this issue, and Demetriou 2012; Stockhammer 2012 for more complete accounts of the general problems).

Readings

Several years ago Lionel Casson (1951) gathered together what we know of sailing times between principal ports in the ancient Mediterranean. The impact of winds and seasons on ancient sailing is just beginning to be understood. See Tammuz (2005), on the issue of sailing in winter, and Leidwanger (2013).

There have been several good treatments of agriculture and ancient Greek society, at least on the mainland and western Anatolia. Some of the best are Gallant (1989, 1991), Isager and Skydsgaard (2013), and Sallares (1991). Halstead and Jones (1989) supplies an excellent review of decisions which have to be made by agriculturalists in these environments. Marston (2011) is a good overview of current research and an application of the theory of risk management to a diachronic study of agriculture and society at Gordion in central Turkey. There is little out there on what the ancient Greeks actually ate. But a fun book about this is Dalby (1996).

3   The Neolithic in Greece

In this chapter I will treat the Neolithic period in the land occupied by the Modern Greek state.[1] The Neolithic period represents the era from the introduction of agriculture and sedentism into Greece up to the appearance of the first use of bronze (ca. 6800–3200 BCE).[2] Its earliest phase in Greece is referred to as aceramic or prepottery (ca. 6800–6500 BCE) because agriculture and sedentism was evident before the invention of pottery. The introduction of these two features of the Neolithic into Greece is not well understood and contentious, with some arguments for its origins in the Near East (Ammerman and Cavali-Sforza 1984; Childe 1983; Perles 2001) and others for a more indigenous development (Reingruber 2011; Séfériadès 2007). In my presentation of the Neolithic I focus on households and turn to the issue of possible social structure between households.

Yet even though there is uncertainty as to the origin of Neolithic culture in Greece, there are some general characteristics of the period as a whole which stand out. The two most salient are that of agriculture, that is, domesticated plants and animals, and sedentary lifestyles. The plants which were domesticated included beans, peas, bitter vetch, lentils, emmer wheat, einkorn wheat, and barley. Domesticated animals were sheep, goats, pigs, and some cattle. We have good examples of Neolithic

---

[1] I am not treating the Neolithic in the Cyclades in any way, but to mention connections between the Cyclades and the mainland in the Mesolithic and Neolithic (Melos especially). It is often hard to separate the Neolithic from the early Bronze Age in Cyclades, and I will pick up Cycladic cultures in the next chapter. Those interested in the Cycladic Neolithic are advised to read the first few chapters in Broodbank (2002).

[2] The Neolithic is divided into Early, Middle, Late, and Final Neolithic periods. Information on the Final Neolithic is spotty, and I am choosing to concentrate on the first three Neolithic phases, rather than include the Final Neolithic into the discussion. I am also restricting my treatment of the Neolithic to the mainland, with minor references to Crete. I am not treating the Neolithic of the Cyclades, preferring to begin discussion of settlement there in the Early Bronze Age.

settlements on rich agricultural lands, such as those in Thessaly. But Neolithic peoples also settled in more marginal territory. Indeed, except for parts of Thessaly, a great deal of Greece is made up of hard soils with low water tables. The introduction of the agricultural practices of scratch or ard plowing with draft animals, and raising sheep for wool, rather than meat, allowed Neolithic Greeks to occupy these marginal territories. The settlement density in these areas was not great, however, and the most common type of settlement was isolated farms or small hamlets.

Box 1   Caves Can Be Important: Franchthi Cave

Franchthi cave (Figure 3.1) is an important archaeological site which provides a continuous record of occupation in Greece from ca. 22,000 to 5000 BP (Before Present: 1950 CE). The cave offered analyzable stratigraphy up to 11 m deep. Located on the Argolid Gulf, the cave was excavated continuously from 1967 to 1976, by teams led by Thomas Jacobsen from the University of Indiana (Jacobsen 1976, 1981). Although now the mouth of the cave almost touches the Mediterranean, it was once at least 12 km from the coast.

The cave tells us something about the connection between the Neolithic and earlier cultures in Greece. The Mesolithic period (10,300–8000 BP), right before the Neolithic, contains evidence that the cave was a base camp for hunter and gatherers. There were several burials, one was of a twenty-five-year-old male, who apparently died of blows to his forehead, although

Figure 3.1 Franchthi cave. (From https://en.wikipedia.org/wiki/Franchthi_Cave, WP:CC BY-SA; accessed 7/20/2018.)

Box 1   (*cont.*)

there is additional evidence that he suffered from malaria. The appearance of fish bones and some obsidian from the island of Melos shows that they were utilizing marine resources. This is also the period when we first see ground stone tools, millstones from the Saronic Gulf. This indicates the probable processing of wild grains.

In the Early Neolithic (8000–7000 BP) the cave holds clear evidence of the advent of agriculture. We now have bones from domesticated sheep and goats; evidence of barley, wheat, and lentils; grinding stones; and sickle pieces. This is also the first appearance of pottery, but its rather fragile nature and shape may well indicate that it was used more for display than any utilitarian function (Vitelli 1993). This is also the period when we have our first example of architecture. In front of the mouth of the cave several walls and associated rooms have been excavated (Wilkinson and Duhon 1990). The architecture probably represents the house and associated buildings, and the cave is now just adjunct space to the community. There is some evidence that the cave had actually become a pen for animals.

The middle Neolithic (7000–6500 BP) saw continued development of the new elements which appeared at Franchthi in the Early Neolithic. The range of pottery increases, with strong evidence that it was used for purposes such as feasting and storage. There are also some pots which best fit our description of coarse ware cooking pots, indicating an important change the way in which food was prepared.

After this period the occupation of the cave basically comes to a halt.

For a more detailed overview, see Vitelli (1993, 1995).

Tell Sites

In more productive regions, such as Thessaly and Greek Macedonia, the settlement system was different, with several tell, or archaeological mound, sites (Figure 3.2). Three stand out: Nea Nikomedeia (Pyke 1993, 1996; Rodden 1962, 1965, 1996; Wardle 1996) in Greek Macedonia, and Dhimini (Figure 3.3) (Chourmouziadis 1979) and Sesklo (Figure 3.4) (Tsountas 1908) in Thessaly. Although a great deal of the data from their excavations has yet to be published, what we possess can help us gain an idea of what life was like in communities in the Greek Neolithic. Their architecture and artifacts give us a window into their social structure.

One of the most important observations is that social institutions, religious, crafts producing, burial, etc. in these communities were strongly embedded in the household, which was the basic unit of social organization (the best treatment of the household is Souvatzi 2008). It is important to realize that the term "household" does not equate with that of family. Households were composed of individuals who ate and slept in the same house and who were economically tied to one another. It does not mean that all members of the household were related by kinship. Various individuals such as slaves, independent retainers, economic partners, and others could and probably did occupy positions within the household. The concept of the house probably held some special significance in some communities at least, as witnessed by what appear to be ancient house models (examples are numerous; see references in Boggard and Halstead 2015). Household units varied in size from those which would occupy one or two rooms to larger, multiroomed structures which were set apart from the rest of the community's housing (Kotsakis 2006; Kotsos and Urem-Kotsou 2006). There was little spatial differentiation within the houses, however, which indicates that the household was not strongly articulated by gender, age, or various functions. That is, all activities took place in the same or closely adjacent areas of the house.

There were various institutions contained within the household. Some were associated with crafts production. Evidence for craft production is found within the space of the household, but there is also some evidence that craft production was shared by different households as well. Various artifacts associated with craft production were located in space which was shared by different households.

The household was apparently the center for institutions which incorporated ritual practice as well. These ritual contexts must have included some sort of feasting activity. Recent arguments (Halstead and Isaakidou 2011), which build on an innovative analysis of serving ware and social position (Haggis 2007), point to the fact that some of these feasts could have accommodated a large number of participants and that the serving ware, which lacks special vessels such as pitchers, indicates that there was little elaborated distinction between those involved in the feasts themselves. The presence of pitchers, which would have specifically pointed to a distinction between host and guest, was missing in Neolithic communities. Neolithic feasting appears to have taken place without pre-established asymmetrical relationships. These ritual feasting contexts appear in various sites and forms. There is some evidence for a possible altar at the sites of Achilleon (Gimbutas 1974) and Prodromos (Chourmouziadis 1971).

The household also incorporated funeral rituals as there are several examples of intramural burial at settlements such as Dhimini. We lack strong evidence of extra-household funeral behavior, which suggests that funerals, because they were contained within the household, might not have been an important means of social integration outside the

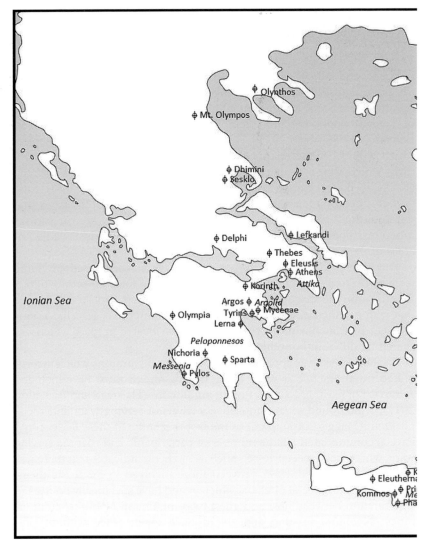

Figure 3.2 Map of Greece with major sites mentioned in the text.

household itself. In general, there was little elaboration of the funeral institutional context. Four different types of funeral are seen in the archaeological record: intramural, pit, disarticulated and scattered, and some sort of funerary complex (Souvatzi 2008: 186–93). Grave goods were few, and absent as in the case of disarticulated burial, where the body was put into a ditch with other bodies.

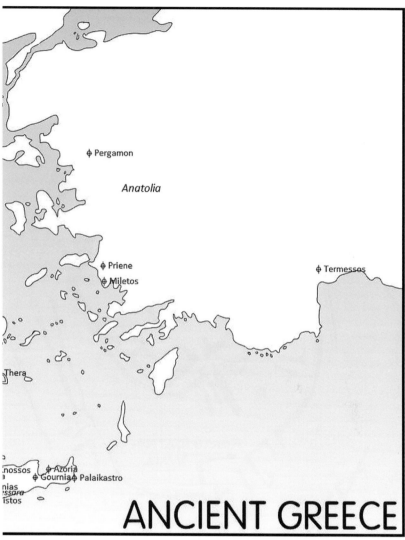

Pergamon

Anatolia

Priene

Termessos

Miletos

Thera

nossos   Azoria
         Gournia Palaikastro
nias
ssara
istos

ANCIENT GREECE

(Drawn by author.)

The only sense we have of elaborate funeral behaviour is in the "funerary complex." In these cases we have found examples of the collection of bodies and of body modification such as in the case of the archaeological record from Prodromos in the Early Neolithic (Chourmouziadis 1971, 1973). Here we have evidence of secondary burial, with eleven skulls and some thigh and rib bones deposited carefully in three levels beneath a

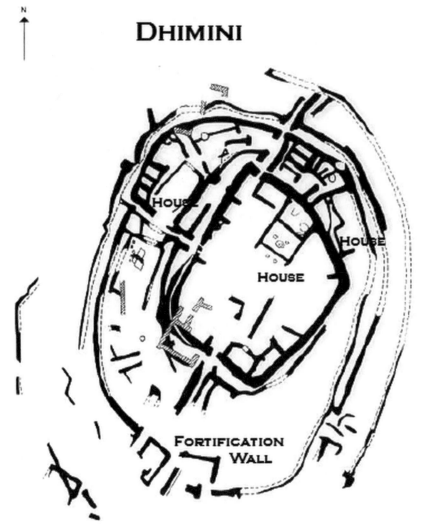

Figure 3.3 Plan of Neolithic Dhimini. (Redrawn from Souvatki 2008: figure 5.31.)

house floor. While we do not fully understand the reasons for this secondary burial, it does represent some sort of ritualized attempt to remember parts of the past.

We lack strong evidence for religious ritual existing outside the household. Neither Sesklo nor Dhimini contained an independent building

SESKLO
PLAN OF NEOLITHIC ACROPOLIS
SOLID WALLS - MIDDLE NEOLITHIC (5800-
    5300 BCE)
HATCHED WALLS - FINAL NEOLITHIC
    (4500- 3200 BCE)

0   30
                                          M

Figure 3.4 Plan of Neolithic Sesklo. (Redrawn from www.arxeion-poli tismou.gr/2017/06/Sesklo.html.)

which was unambiguously religious, representing an ideological institution not attached to a household, and I remain unconvinced by
attempts to identify such a building at Neo Nikomedeia because the
argument is based on very slim evidence (Marangou 2001). We are left
to conclude that what religious practice there might have been in the
Neolithic was embedded in domestic life.

Just what the ideology of these domestic religious rituals was is only
incompletely understood. Bucrania, or plastered over bulls' skulls, have
been found in some Greek Neolithic domestic contexts. This shows
that the ideological attention paid to the bull in later Greek history has
a deep local history, as well as connections to similar Neolithic art in
well-excavated sites such as Çatal Hüyük in Turkey. There was a flourishing use of figurines, animal and human, with the female figurine predominant. But here we are not much closer to any concept of Neolithic

ideology, since the female figurines have been identified as goddesses, ancestors, fertility symbols, and even toys. Considerations of archaeological association may in the future help to a limited extent. For example, figurines that have been found associated with food storage areas might allow us to at least suggest that one of their roles was to protect the fecundity of the food supply (Preziosi and Hitchcock 1999). Talalay (2004) has also noted that several figurines are headless, which might allow us to suggest that they may well have had a function similar to that of head veneration in Neolithic communities further to the east, such as Çatal Hüyük in Turkey.

There is good evidence that some of these institutions, e.g. those embedded in trade and craft production, were associated with intercommunity networking. Both Dhimini and Sesklo, as well as several other sites, supply us with evidence of obsidian sourced from the Aegean island of Melos, which points to some sort of intersite commerce, perhaps even the presence of itinerant stone tool makers. Spondylus shells have been found in abundance in several Neolithic houses, a noteworthy example being the more than 5000 pieces recovered from Dhimini. Workshops, located within households and shared by more than one household, were making spondylus beads and bracelets which were traded between various settlements throughout Greece. Talalay (1987) has argued that split figurines found at some Neolithic sites were products of formal agreements between families in different communities – a point to which I will return shortly. Numerous ethnographic studies of communities with similar social structure indicate that the contexts for this type of association were feasting ceremonies within which there was an exchange of intercommunity goods, by either redistribution or formal exchange.

A similar situation of household production and exchange can be seen outside Sesklo and Dhimini, and indications of intercommunity networking can be seen at other sites in the later Neolithic. There is a change from ceramics of rather plain design to those of more elaborate forms and decoration, which indicates that pottery manufacture would have tied into larger exchange networks. A salient example is Urfinis ware (Jacobsen 1984). More prevalent in communities of the southern mainland, this ceramic type was extremely uniform in style from settlement to settlement, which indicates it was the product of distinct types of social bonding, represented by the use of similarly styled vessels in feasting, or, at the least, shared concepts between potters of different communities. A ceramics trade network at least 70 km in length was operating in Neolithic Knossos (Tomkins 2004). Given our overview of agricultural risk in Greece, pots like these may well represent participation in feasting activities, used as contexts for the creation of bonds of connection and possible assistance, to be tapped in times of subsistence shortfall (Halstead 2004).

While we have been talking about positive aspects of connection and cooperation between settlements, there is another, somewhat more sinister form of connection, raiding, which probably played an important role. Settlements such as Sesklo and Dhimini had defensive features such as stone walls with baffle gates, and ditches with V-shaped slopes. There is additional good evidence for a concentration on defense in settlement distribution in Thessaly which goes back to the early years of the Neolithic (Runnels et al. 2009). Here survey indicates that there were no man's lands in between the settlements. In respect to stealing animals and food, raiding could easily have met the need to avoid subsistence shortfall. Again, these raids must have been organized and carried out within the households themselves, either alone or in conjunction with other households.

Were Communities Hierarchical?

We have seen that the institutions of Neolithic communities were embedded in the household. But was there an asymmetrical relationship between households in communities like Nea Nikomedeia, Dhimini, and Sesklo? Were there institutions between different households where one could negotiate asymmetrical differences in relationships between the households? These questions have been central to much thinking about Neolithic society in Greece. Earlier analyses by archaeologists such as Halstead (1984, 1993, 1995, 1999) concluded that there was significant inequality between households in settlements like Dhimini. The argument ran that the difference in sizes between houses and concentrations of prestige goods such as spondylus arm bands by possible elite pot latching behavior (House 23 at Dhimini) represented the first phases of the trajectory of elites, termed "megaron elites," who were to appear in the Bronze Age (Halstead 1984, 1995, 1999). Halstead (1995) also notes that in the early and middle periods of the Neolithic the location of many cooking facilities was in open spaces between houses in communities. These spaces would have represented major feasting areas, which would have tied together different families within the community, producing social ties and obligations between them. In the late Neolithic, however, he sees a shift to cooking facilities being controlled by single families. This would mean that individual families were becoming competitive within their own communities, rather than cooperative. Rather than sharing food and the ideology of feasting, they were probably hoarding their supplies instead. As Halstead sees it, this may well have been the beginning of the rise of powerful families who were to surface in the later Bronze Ages (3rd to 2nd millennium BCE), and whose social power was vested in the control and redistribution of materials.

While Halstead has focused on aspects of feasting and house size, subsequent sensitive analysis (Souvatzi 2007, 2008, 2013) has demonstrated that size differences between households is a function not of hierarchy but of differences in household activities, which were not linked to asymmetrical relationships between households. That is, different households were engaged in different types of production specializations which affected their size. Furthermore, Greek Neolithic communities demonstrate a rather homogeneous distribution of various classes of artifacts (figurines, pottery, lithic tools, imported obsidian, etc.) and subsistence evidence from household to household with some clustering of specific artifacts tied to production specializations, either within one household or, as seen in area S8 at Dhimini, tied to shared functions between households. But the central problem with these analyses is that they center only on the material from the acropoleis (that is, the actual tell areas) and not the totality of the entire town. Any conclusions therefore would apply only to a minor percentage of the entire population of these communities.

What existed on this large, whole community scale? If we cannot directly outline a hierarchy between households because of a lack of large-scale data, is there any method which might allow us to understand the relationships between different households indirectly? There might be one. Bintliff (2012: 54–59)[3] argues that the size of the settlements indicates that there was some sort of supra household institution or institutions which would have provided mechanisms for such a large community to function. He notes that communities with fewer than 250 people can often be called "face-to-face" societies where all the important decisions pertaining to the community as a whole are worked out in meetings of equals. But this means of cohesion does not extend to larger communities where face-to-face communication could not include the entire community. Therefore there must have been some sort of centralizing, decision-making institution which would function to hold the community together. This could have been the case for large communities in the Greek Neolithic. Dhimini, for example, is estimated to have held up to 5000 people. So its size would require some sort of hierarchical

---

[3] Bintliff is drawing on some early and important work by Johnson (1982), who looked at the issue of scalar stress in effective communication in small communities. The issue of community fissioning is not particular to Greece; see Bandy's (2004) excellent work with community fissioning in South America.

organization. But just what this type of institution might have been remains in the dark, because the lower towns have either not been investigated or, if they have, the results of the research have yet to be published.

While we cannot identify a hierarchical relationship between households at settlements like Dhimini, there is one view of the community as a whole which suggests some sort of disparity between different areas in the settlement, based not on any notion of wealth inequity but on the subtle differences which might exist between older, more established neighborhoods of a community and newer ones. As mentioned, Sesklo and Dhimini were often associated with lower towns, which made them the high grounds or acropoleis of their larger communities. The architecture of these tells differs from that of the lower towns, in that houses in the lower towns appear to have been less permanent, with growth over time witnessing abandonment and the construction of new houses. The tells were different in that the construction of their successive houses remained in place. This rigidity of successive house construction might have produced a sense of ancestral authority for those occupying the tells, a sense which was probably missing in the lower settlements. This might well have produced a strong sense of inequality between occupants of both the acropoleis and the lower towns.

Measures of Social Complexity

Neolithic communities, especially the tell sites, have enough archaeological evidence to allow us to say something about their social structure and hence their complexity. As noted, the hallmark of these communities was the observation that the household was the basic social unit. And the household incorporated important social institutions, such as those of religion, craft production, burial, trade, and even raiding. The full articulation of these institutions into independent social entities was not to occur for some time to come. Although embedded in the households, it was likely that it was these social institutions which helped to hold the communities together, but the glue must have been weak. Our knowledge of extra-household institutions is slight, and there is little to indicate that there was a pronounced hierarchy among the households themselves. Tradition might have signaled that the households of the acropoleis were in some respect seen as more privileged, but we cannot speak beyond that.

Readings

An expansive overview of the Neolithic can be found in Perlès (2001). Various important sites have also been published. For Knossos, see

Evans (1964, 1971), Efstratiou et al. (2004), and chapters in Efstratiou et al. (2013). Important sites, such as Sesklo and Dhimini in Thessaly, were excavated around the turn of the last century. Further studies have been limited, but see Adrimi-Sismani (2008), Chourmouziadis (1993) (mentioned above, in Greek) for Dhimini, and Wijnen (1981) for more recent overviews.

4   Developments ca. 3200–2200 BCE

The introduction of bronze working signaled the start of the Early Bronze Age in Greece around 3200 BCE. In this chapter I am going to cover a thousand-year period, up to dramatic developments which were to take place ca. 2200 BCE. During this period, different forms of cultural development on the mainland, the Cyclades, and on the island of Crete are seen. There is a general increase in evidence for greater social complexity throughout these areas, with attention being paid to feasting, defense, intercommunity communication, and exchange. At the period's end one thousand years later, important cultural changes occurred, which were to carry these cultures into new configurations of social structure for the next several centuries.

This period is regionally divided, with archaeologists accustomed to treating the regions of the mainland, the Cycladic islands, and Crete separately. This era is normally broken down into three temporal subphases: Early, Middle, and Late. But since the 1970s archaeologists have begun to use the term "cultures" when referring to the Early Helladic (mainland) and Early Cycladic (Cyclades) phases rather than the terms Early Helladic and Early Cycladic with their subphases I, II, III, etc. While it is perhaps preferable to use such labeling, because it contains a sense of time and space, the use of the term "culture" has its own problems, because what is being referred to is an "archaeological" culture. An archaeological culture is the recognized temporal and geographical spread of a set of artifacts. This is often a useful thumbnail view of the past, but there is no guarantee that the spread of a recognized set of artifacts shares the same borders as a past living culture. Hodder (1982: 58–73) argued this point well when he described the spread of calabashes or decorative gourds in contemporary Africa. Archaeologists would have equated a single culture with the geographical spread of very similar calabashes, but the reality is that two very distinct cultures were using the same material in the area covered by the distribution of these calabashes, in quite different ways. So, even though the use of "culture" is preferable to the rather nondescript term Early Helladic, etc., we must keep in mind that we might be lumping together groups of quite different internal structures in our use of a single cultural label.

Developments on the Mainland

Two early cultures have been identified, the Eutresis and Korakou. Each culture takes its name from the site from which it was first identified. The Eutresis Culture dates from ca. 3100 to 2650 BCE. Survey has shown that this culture differs somewhat from its temporal predecessor, the Final Neolithic (4500–3200 BCE) because many of its sites are located on fertile coastal plains, rather than inland, as in the Final Neolithic. This could represent a shift from an earlier way of life in the Final Neolithic, based on pastoralism, to one which focused on farming. The coastal location of many settlements could also indicate that this culture was actively connected to contemporary settlements in the Cyclades. The presence of some trade items in the archaeological record supports this point.

Material evidence for the Eutresis Culture is mainly ceramics. The pottery in general has a limited repertoire, focusing on commensal convex-sided (wide) bowls, with or without a stem, storage jars with collar necks, and wide-mouthed deep pots for cooking, a style with roots in the Final Neolithic. We can see a variant in this assemblage in the Talioti phase of this culture, most recognizable by the appearance of a "fruit stand," a deep-sided bowl, sometimes attached to a stem. This pottery was recently discovered in sites of the Argolid: Makrovouni, Kephalari, and Talioti.

The presence of "frying pans" (Figure 4.1) in some ceramic assemblages indicates that this culture was in contact with the Cyclades. Frying pans are ceramic vessels which look like modern frying pans, with short handles, a flat bottom, and a significant rim (Coleman 1985). Frying pans are common at contemporary sites in the Cyclades, but rare in mainland settlements. Those found at Tsoungiza have a noticeable star decoration which also appears on Cycladic ware. I will discuss their social function in the Cyclades later.

With so little by way of material from this culture, it is difficult to determine its degree of social complexity. The distribution of similar cooking, storage, and dining ware would indicate that there might well have been a common feasting institution between different communities. But we have little to take our analysis further. For example, we do not know how many different domestic and possible community institutions existed, and what their contexts were.

The Korakou culture appeared from ca. 2650 to 2200/2150 BCE. This culture is seen widely in the Peloponnesos, Attika, Euboia, Boiotia,

Figure 4.1 Cycladic "frying pan." (From https://en.wikipedia.org/wiki/
Frying_pans, WP:CC BY-SA; accessed 7/8/2018.)

Phokis, Lokris, and west up to Lefkas. The material record from this
culture is richer than that for the Eutresis and gives us a better analytical
window. The ceramic inventory includes fine pottery with saucers, bowls
with T-shaped rims, large dippers, small spoons, and sauceboats.

Box 2   The Emblematic Sauceboat

Shaped somewhat like our modern gravy boat (Figure 4.2), this vessel is found on sites in the southern mainland, the Cyclades, western Asia Minor, and Crete. We have no idea of its function, but its ubiquity must indicate that its unusual shape was considered appropriate to function in some sort of context where the act of pouring was highlighted. Many examples do not have handles, and those that do have one at the rim of the vessel just opposite the spout. It was probably held with two hands, one holding the base of the boat in the palm, while the other raised the back of the boat. Its shape was unique, with its spout sometimes decorated with ram's heads, as seen at the site of Zygouries on the mainland. Some ceremonies in which it was used must have been important, since we do have some examples of this sauceboat in gold. Its ubiquity does not mean that it was used or held the same

Figure 4.2 Sauceboat. (From Metropolitan Museum of Art, Accession Number: 27.120.4, CC0 1.0; Public Domain Dedication.)

Box 2   *(cont.)*

ideological meaning in all communities, however. The boat could have been
used in different ways by different groups. Most of the boats were of similar
size, however, which does indicate that it was meant to fit into some sort of
standardized pouring ceremony. The boat disappears from the archaeological record around 2000 BCE.

Unlike the case with the Eutresis culture, we have a better opportunity
to look at feasting institutions here, probably in the domestic, communal
(that is, more than one household), and funeral spheres.

Different settlements present us with different views of domestic architecture, which tells us that there was no common plan in domestic
layout. We have information from excavations at Zygouries and other
communities (Blegen 1928a) which appear to show small houses. Several of the rooms in these houses have only one door and are small by
any standards. This leads one to be cautious in equating a room within
one of these houses with a household. Its function may well have been
otherwise. However, if identified with a household, the agglomerative
(gathering in a clustered mass) appearance of several of these rooms
would argue for some sort of matri- or patrilocal residence system, with
children being married off, but, depending on the sex of the offspring,
either remaining with the family or joining a different one. The houses at
Manika (Sampson 1985, 1988) show, through the artifactual record of
their central rooms, that the household was engaged in several institutions: eating, sleeping, and preparing food within the houses, probably
in the central room itself, as we already saw in Neolithic communities.

Large buildings can be seen at several sites. They appear to follow a
common design, which has been labeled the "corridor house" (Shaw
1987, 1990). The most famous example is the House of the Tiles at
Lerna, but the design has been attested as well at Akovitika in Messenia,
Kolonna on Aigina, Thebes, and Zygouries.[1] There is a strong similarity
between these buildings. They are rectangular and large, with large
interior spaces and a hearth edged by two-story-high walls and interior
staircases (Figure 4.3).

The mortuary record of this archaeological culture is more complete
than that of the Eutresis culture and provides us with a better window
into its cultural complexity. There were several different types of burial,

---

[1] Mention should also be made of a large round building which was identified in the
Korakou levels at Tiryns. See Haider (1980) and Kilian (1986).

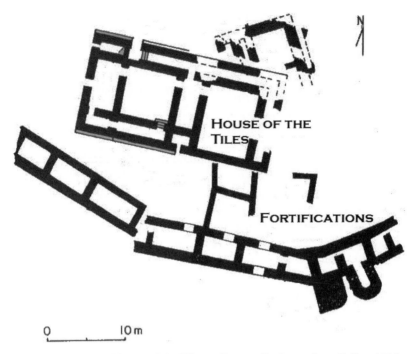

Figure 4.3 House of the Tiles at Lerna. (Redrawn from Pullen 1985: figure 36.)

which must have correlated with different funeral institutions. In several cases, infants and young children were buried under the house or very near to it. In some instances, adults were buried outside the limits of the community, often in cemeteries. Some burials were cremations, which were probably carried out in the cemetery itself. There are good indications that some funerals housed institutions which linked the burial to previous interments, and therefore to close memories of the past. Some tombs housed only single burials, but other tombs held multiple, which would correlate to a funeral which was actively engaged in removing or displacing the bones of previous buried individuals in the tomb. Some tombs were ossuaries, which indicate that the funeral institution was a string of various processes and celebrations, where the dead were first treated to some sort of "burial," but later, after the flesh had left the bones, there was some sort of secondary burial of the bones in a tomb.

Unlike the Eutresis culture, the Korakou culture contains evidence for craft specialization. Objects, such as ornate gold bowls, reveal a high level of craftsmanship, not achievable by part-time application. Serving ware, such as sauceboats and other high-end ceramics, indicate a substantial level of craft specialization as well.

There is ample evidence that settlements of the Korakou culture were in contact with one another and generally trading throughout the eastern Mediterranean. As in the Neolithic, Melian obsidian has been found at almost every site. We also have copper, lead, and silver, which indicates that places, such as Manika on the island of Euboia, were in contact with the islands of Siphnos, Seriphos, and Syros, which had mines producing these ores. Several graves on the mainland contained marble statuettes, which came from the Cyclades. Some also contained stone vases and seals which came from the island of Crete. The sauceboat is typical of ceramic assemblages in this culture and is also seen in contemporary contexts in the Cyclades.

Measures of Social Complexity

This period does appear more complex than that of the Neolithic. The mortuary record shows that there were probably different new distinct institutions and contexts bound into funerals. In domestic contexts families were involved in several different productive institutions, as well as communal eating. The useful record of craft specialization also shows that there must have been crafting institutions which were more than simply another sphere of household activity. The high level of quality of some of the ceramics indicates that they were most likely the products of skilled independent crafts producers. All in all, the record shows that the Korakou culture was probably more complex than the Eutresis, although the slimmer archaeological record on the Eutresis side might be biasing the observation to a degree.

An important consideration when we compare the social structure of this period with the previous Neolithic is whether or not there were institutions now outside the confines of the household. In most cases of increasing social complexity we would expect to see some sort of extra-household institutions appearing as a society such as the Greek Neolithic becomes more complex. We do have some indication that these institutions did now exist, but our evidence is limited.

One way we may witness the presence of such institutions is indirectly through documented hierarchical relationships between households, where institutions outside the households would have served as contexts for the creation of this type of social asymmetry. One window into this issue is through feasting. An important observation by Halstead and Isaakidou (2011) is that the Early Bronze Age differs markedly from the Neolithic in its feasting activities. Unlike feasting in the Neolithic, people in the Early Bronze Age were using a different set of feasting ware, specifically pitchers. These pitchers, which do not appear in the Neolithic cultures, signal an asymmetry between those serving and those being served. Feasting now, as seen in contexts such as the House of the Tiles (Pullen 2011a) and in contexts which must have been associated with the more elaborate ware of the Eutresis culture, was an occasion where the inequalities between different groups of participants were now marked.

Corridor houses, such as the House of the Tiles at Lerna, have been cited as examples of extra-household institutions (Pullen 1986, 1994, 2008, 2011b). The House of the Tiles has been seen as an early stage of a political economy. A political economy is an extra-household economic system which ties together law, politics, and economics and is seen as a hallmark of cultures which have social institutions active above that of the household. One of the primary arguments for the presence of a political economy in the early years of this era is that the numerous seals found in the House of the Tiles indicate that there was some type of top-down means of collecting and storing goods as a form of tax from other households. The "taxes" in the form of storage containers filled with agricultural products would have been housed in the House of the Tiles (Heath 1958). The seals are often thought to represent an overarching interest in and control over the storage and probable distribution of these agricultural products which came from other households, a hallmark of early political economies, especially chiefdoms (most recently, but less emphatically, Pullen 2011b; see Pauketat 2007 for an opposite view).

But there are some serious problems with this identification. The most salient is that the seals themselves are too divergent. More than seventy different seals were collected from the House of the Tiles (Peperaki 2004, 2010). This might indicate that rather than a top-down tracking of goods, seals were used by the owners or producers of the various goods which were stored in the building itself to identify their own goods (Weiberg 2007). A secondary point is that we do not know if the seals represent a system of records contained *within* the same household or kin group or were used to control goods *between* households, which would indicate the beginning of a real political economy.

Stronger evidence for an extra-household community institution can perhaps be seen in the frequent fortifications around many Early Helladic sites. That around Lerna is early, but represents what these fortifications could have looked like elsewhere. Lerna has a casemate fortification wall with interior rooms. At points on the wall there were also horseshoe-shaped bastions, which would have made approaching the wall difficult for an enemy. The coordination and the expense of such wall constructions speaks indirectly but strongly for some sort of economy which operated outside the confines of a single household, not just because the expense of the fortifications might well have been more than one household could support, but because such fortifications would have required some sort of hierarchical organization to be constructed.

In addition to the question of a political economy, it has been argued that the Korakou culture was a chiefdom (Pullen 2008, 2011b).[2] The argument often relies on data from surveys which show differences in size between settlements within a region, such as the Argolid (Jameson et al. 1994). A two- to three-stepped hierarchical relationship in settlement size is thought to correspond with a chiefdom-level polity, marking a regional institutional framework where the size of the settlement is a factor of stepped relationships in politics, economics, religion, etc. But like the situation with identifying a political economy in the storage system in the House of the Tiles, there are problems with these data as evidence for a chiefdom polity. In truth, we know too little at the moment to clearly demarcate differences in settlement size which would indicate a distinct settlement hierarchy. Currently there are really no discriminate size differences between the surveyed sites, which would allow us to isolate a distinct hierarchy in size or rank categories.

The Cyclades

Perhaps more so than in research on the mainland, it was in the study of the Cyclades that strong attempts were made to replace old chronological terms with cultural labels. The Early Cycladic period, whose approximate dates are 3200–2000 BCE, is thus divided into various cultures. But it is difficult to follow the Early Cycladic period closely, due to the very uneven nature of the evidence for occupation, which comes largely from graves and settlements which have little chronological depth. The situation is alleviated somewhat by the fact that the site of Phylakopi on the island of Melos, and Ayia Irini on the island of Kea, both have a rather well-studied stratigraphy (see Readings section later), but it is further hampered by the unfortunate fact that much of the material we have from cemeteries has been looted and sold illegally on the antiquities market.

---

[2] Recent presentations by Pullen show that he might be reconsidering the chiefdom identification.

Box 3   The Problem with Cycladic Figurines

Popular in today's art market, Cycladic figurines (Figure 4.4) were produced
in the Early Cycladic period by Cycladic peoples. Carved from local
marble, a majority of the figurines represent women, in an abstracted form,

Figure 4.4 Cycladic figurine. (From Metropolitan Museum of Art,
Accession Number: 34.11.3, CC0 1.0; Public Domain Dedication.)

Box 3   *(cont.)*

with arms across the chest, possible breasts, and a pubic triangle. Other figurines show people in the act of playing musical instruments, often either a sitting harp or flutes. Most figurines are not large, with dimensions close to those we would associate with dolls, although some are close to full human height. In most cases the human form has been abstracted to focus on features such as the nose, arms, legs, and hips. Most female figurines are flattened with the body in a backward-bending stance. Many were apparently painted as well (for a good overview, see Getz-Preziosi 1994).

What were these figurines used for? Their context, which was often within graves, leads us to believe that they had some sort of association with funeral institutions (Hendrix 2003). Perhaps they represented ancestors, servants, or concubines for the interred. The fact that many show the female with obvious representations of female sexual attributes has led some to suggest that they were some sort of mother goddesses. We will probably never know their original function. The fact that they have been found at Keros in an obvious religious context does show strongly that one of their functions was religious.

These figurines were popular in the Early Cycladic, appearing in contexts as far from the Cyclades as communities on the mainland, on western Turkey, and on Crete. They remain popular today and have unfortunately been actively sought by looters, who have sold them to private collectors (Gerstenblith 2007; Gill and Chippendale 1993). As a consequence, many are without provenance and much of their original cultural meaning has been lost. Because of their modern popularity, it is also suspected, probably quite rightly, that many in various collections are fakes.

The first culture to be identified from this period is the Grotta-Pelos culture, dating from ca. 3200 to 2650 BCE.[3] Its archaeological material ranged over most of the islands, with an emphasis on islands in the south. Unlike the large villages of the Final Neolithic in the Cyclades, this culture is one of small settlements, probably small farms. This new type of settlement is seen in uninhabited areas of the Cyclades and is probably best understood as a "filling in" movement. Survey shows that the settlements were small, most probably representing two to five households at most. Their associated cemeteries indicate that members of the farmsteads

---

[3] This terminology was first offered by Renfrew in the 1970s (Renfrew and Cherry 2001). The Greek archaeologist Alexander Doumas (1988) has accepted Renfrew's designation of the Grotta-Pelos culture. He has further subdivided Renfrew's culture into four subgroups, labeled after artifact assemblage variations on the Grotta-Pelos culture in different Cycladic cemeteries. His subdivisions are Lakkoudes, Pelos, Plastiras, and Kampos. He viewed the Kampos culture as a transitional subdivision which linked the Grotta-Pelos culture to Renfrew's next Cycladic culture, the Keros-Syros.

received burial, with single inhumations being common. Most of our pottery and marble objects from this culture were recovered from tombs, although the provenance of each is often unknown because of tomb looting. Most represented vessels are ceramic pyxides (small cylindrical jars), collared jars, and marble figurines.

The materials from the tombs indicate that most trade appears to have been limited to the island settlements themselves, rather than between island settlements and those on the mainland. This might reflect a more immediate need to tap into risk-aversive networks in this time period, because the settlements were smaller than in the Neolithic.

The Keros-Syros culture extended from ca. 2650 to 2400 BCE. In general the settlements remained the same size as those of the Grotta-Pelos, with some exceptions such as Chalandriani on the island of Syros. The spread of this culture can be seen in similar artifact assemblages on most islands. Although there is some difference in tomb construction, most tomb assemblages are similar to those from the Grotta-Pelos culture, indicating no real change in funeral institutions.

But what separates this culture from the preceding are its new forms of intersettlement contact, both within and outside the islands. This culture utilized a type of stone vessel that we call, for want of a better term, the frying pan, which we saw briefly in excavations on the mainland. The frying pan began as a shape in the Grotta-Pelos culture, but its use exploded with the Keros Syros. We have absolutely no idea what the frying pan was used for. Because we find it in tombs, it must have had some sort of significance in funeral institutions, at least.

The bottom of the pan was often decorated with geometric shapes, such as stars, circles, and triangles. The Keros-Syros culture introduced a new artistic depiction on the bottom of the pan. In several examples (Figure 4.1) the bottom of the pan was incised with the depiction of a long, narrow boat, without sails, but equipped with oars. The depictions of these boats indicate that they would have required a minimum of twenty-five men to row them. Given the small settlements which identify the cultures of the Cyclades at this time, outfitting such a boat would have been beyond the ability of a single settlement and suggests that the staffing of such a craft could have required a concerted effort from more than one settlement. What is more likely, however, is that the boats themselves are associated with one of the unusually large settlements like Chalandriani. A majority of the frying pans appear to have been from the area around that settlement.

The use of longboats was probably a unique phenomenon in the Cyclades. What makes this even more interesting is the fact that long-boats are not well suited to carry cargo. What materials were traded in the

Cyclades at this time were probably traded on small, wide-bottomed boats. This means that a principal function of these boats was not trade. But whatever it was remains a mystery. One is tempted to suggest that they were used by raiding parties, who would have attacked island settlements. But this suggestion is challenged by the fact that they could not hold much cargo, and stealing goods was the most common reason to conduct a raid.

One of their uses was probably to travel between islands, in order to participate in ritual at intercommunity assemblies. Recent excavations (Renfrew et al. 2007a, 2007b, 2009, 2013, 2015) on the island of Keros have uncovered evidence of an early maritime sanctuary. Dating to the years 2750–2300 BCE, the sanctuary sits squarely within the most active period of the Keros-Syros culture. The presence of such a sanctuary in the Cyclades is truly remarkable. Renfrew has rightly compared the significance of this sanctuary to the importance of the center at Gobekli Tepe in eastern Turkey and to other sanctuaries as far afield as Caral in coastal Peru.

The sanctuary was unfortunately looted as recently as the 1960s, but excavation has uncovered a deposit which was not disturbed. The undisturbed deposit, Special Deposit South, is filled with broken pieces of Cycladic figurines and marble bowls. The figurines themselves were of a common type found in numerous contemporary contexts in the Cyclades (see Box 2). They were often representations of humans carved in a flat, not heavily incised fashion. Analysis of the pieces at Keros shows that the figurines and bowls were broken before they were deposited. This indicates that there must have been some ritual symbolic importance to the figurines and the bowls, which necessitated their burial specifically on Keros.

The distribution of Cycladic figurines extends beyond the Cyclades into Crete and the Greek mainland. Thus the importance of Keros as a site which would have functioned as a center of pilgrimage and assembly for these various locations in the early years of the Aegean Bronze Age cannot be overemphasized. It must have been a site for the exchange of ideas between people coming from the islands, mainland, and Crete and an assembly point for the creation of a common identity among these early people.

Importantly, the Keros-Syros culture, unlike the previous culture, was in contact with settlements on the mainland and possibly Anatolia. For example, an important material seen now in the Cyclades as well as on the mainland was the sauceboat. Yet whether or not this means that the institutions within which the sauceboat was used on the mainland were now at play as well in the Cyclades is uncertain. It could well have been used in a fashion by the people in the Cyclades which was quite different from its original intent.

Measures of Social Complexity

There are many important institutions in Cycladic culture which are invisible to us, yet we can say something about Cycladic culture in this period from what evidence we have. Our knowledge of domestic activities is very slim, so we cannot reconstruct what some of the domestic institutions might have been. The fact that a large percentage of our archaeological information does come from burials allows us to at least reconstruct a possible funeral context, probably limited in participation, where Cycladic figurines were used within the funeral celebration, as well as pyxides and collared jars. The importation of feasting vessels, such as the sauceboat, from the mainland shows us that there were some commensal institutions which probably highlighted connections that various groups held with settlements other than their own. This moves us to the observation that the longboat was probably employed to a greater extent by larger communities, which would probably have hosted feasts using imported ware more than smaller communities. Renfrew's recent work with the sanctuary at Keros shows strongly that some people and therefore their households were participating in offsite institutional contexts in which various people from the Cycladic islands were gathering for distinct religious purposes. No doubt these intercommunity contexts also functioned to facilitate communication, alliances, and possible exchange between different groups in the Cyclades.

Crete

The island of Crete housed several different cultures during this era. These can be found in pockets of habitation throughout the island. Crete is internally divided into several geographical zones by its own topography. Unlike the mainland and the Cyclades, archaeologists on Crete have eschewed the call to develop cultural labels for the settlements in these various parts of the island. The custom is to continue to use the chronological sequence originally set out, with modifications, by Evans in his excavations at Knossos.

The early history of the island (ca. 3000–2000 BCE) shows that it was divided into distinct regions, each of which apparently contained a distinct culture. The first 400 years (ca. 3000–2600 BCE), known as the Early Minoan I period, presents us with a limited amount of cultural material. What we have from this period are basically burials, which exhibit regional characteristics. A particularly dramatic example of this regionalism is the culture which inhabited the area around Ayia Photia on the northwest coast (Betancourt and Davaras 2012; Davaras and Betancourt 2004; for nearby Petras, see Tsipopoulou 2012a, 2012b). Seen mainly through their remaining cemeteries, groups in this part of Crete were strongly connected to contemporary groups in the Cyclades. One might even argue that the northern plain of Crete should be considered a Cycladic rather than a Cretan culture. These cemeteries shared many burial goods with those in the Cyclades: frying pans, chalices, copper tools, and ceramics not only with Cycladic shapes, but made with Cycladic clays. But I would argue that this situation should be seen not as a mark of cultural intrusion but as the product of an integrated culture which occupied various coastal communities, not only in the Cyclades, but on the north coast of Crete as well.

In addition, it has been observed that the use of this Cycladic ware within the funeral institutions of the culture at Ayia Photia was probably embedded in strategies of competition within the local communities themselves (Legarra Herrero 2009, 2012). A similar situation can be observed in the southwest and the Messara plain. In the Asterousia region of the southwest, people were burying in tholoi (round tombs). Unlike on the north coast, these tombs could fit several burials, and it appears that the funerals associated with these tombs were used to link settlements in this region. Further to the east, in the Messara plain, tholoi were also used, presumably for the same purpose. We can see just how isolated the Messara was by the fact that it also had its own ceramic tradition.

While the burial materials aid us in understanding that Crete was not a unified culture during this period, we have little further information about what the communities themselves in these different regions of Crete would have looked like. The best-known community is Myrtos, located on the south end of the isthmus of Ierapetra. Excavated in the 1970s, the material from this community reveals a small settlement of perhaps five to six households. Fortunately, the state of preservation at Myrtos was good enough to see what domestic activity was like in the household. At least one kitchen has been excavated, which housed storage, grinding, and probably cooking functions. This small community also supplies us with evidence for agricultural storage within the house, and possible cult activity in an enigmatic female figurine found in one of the storerooms and the burial of a skull in a room adjacent to that storage area. The finds from the excavation at Myrtos also contained a seal and sealings, which were probably used in food storage. Tombs in the Messara, Lebena, Archanes, Mochlos, and Palaikastro also contained seals, which indicates that funeral institutions at that time also included the use of sealed containers, either in the celebration or in the burial itself (Weingarten 2012).

Already by the end of the early Minoan period, some settlements appear to have been developing additional communal institutions. We have examples of large open courts at Knossos and Phaistos, and a possible one at Malia. The effort expended to create these courts and their function should be correlated with communal feasting institutions (as early as Final Neolithic at Phaistos; see Todaro and Di Tonto 2006). This development might be correlated with a noticed change in feasting, from a focus on small groups, such as a family, to larger congregations (Wilson 2007). We will return to the importance of these courts when we turn to the development of these centers in the next chapter.

Measures of Social Complexity

It is hard to get a true measure of social complexity on Crete for this period. The mortuary evidence shows that funeral institutions were becoming elaborate and probably spinning off institutions of collective intersettlement gatherings, as seen probably in the presence of tholoi in the south-central region of Crete. The situation on the northeast coast also indicates that the funeral institution there might have been active in competition between households. Seal use begins during this time. But the correlation between seal use and some sort of social administration is thin, since, except for their association with food storage at Myrtos, most seals are found in burials and could well have been a method of personal identification rather than oversight of production and distribution (Schoep 2004, 2006). We have only Myrtos to tell us what a community might have looked like, and while Myrtos shows no hierarchy between its composite households, a kind of hierarchy might well have been playing out in other settlements. Likely areas for this type of relationship between households might well have been not only at Knossos and other later palatial centers but at communities on the north coast as well. Here we have burial goods which appear to be part of a larger strategy of household competition and community status aspirations. Some have claimed a settlement hierarchy between sites, but again differences in size do not necessarily transfer over into a hierarchy of function (Haggis 2002).

Readings

The best overview of developments on the mainland is Pullen (2008); see also Forsen (2010), Rutter (1993), and Wiencke (1989). Additional data on Lerna can be found in Wiencke (2000). The issue of the role of seals in Early Helladic society extends beyond the evidence at Lerna. For further examples, see Weingarten (1997) and Weingarten et al. (2011). Additional views on the corridor house can be found in Overbeck (1969). For good general overviews of the Cyclades, see Barber (1987), Broodbank (2002, 2008), Davis (1992), MacGillivray and Barber (1984), Renfrew (2010), and papers in Davis and Cherry (1979). Phylakopi and Ayia Irini have had a long history of excavation. There are many individual volumes, especially for Ayia Irini, to recommend. But for an introduction to each, see Atkinson et al. (1904), Dawkins and Droop (1910), Evans and Renfrew (1984), and Renfrew et al. (2007). Renfrew and Wagstaff (1982) give a more totalizing picture of Phylakopi and the island of Melos. For Ayia Irini, see Wilson (1999, 2013) and Wilson and Eliot (1984). Good additional thoughts on the longboat can be found in Papadatos and Tomkins (2013). The looting of Cycladic burials has had a truly devastating effect on our ability to understand Cycladic culture. Additional reading on this troubling topic can be found in Marthari (2001) and the papers in Brodie et al. (2001). Good overviews for early Crete are Tomkins and Schoep (2010) and Wilson (2008).

5   The Beginning of Change and the Evolution of a Koine

Shortly before the turn of the third to second millennium we can detect some significant changes in Crete, the Cyclades, and the mainland. The changes were not the same in each region. In Crete we see a dramatic evolution of cultural complexity in the appearance of palace centers, towns, and rural peak sanctuaries. New modes of feasting appear in the Cyclades as they become more interconnected by the introduction of sail-equipped ships that bring the Cycladic cultures into closer connection with the Near East and Asia Minor. The mainland experiences similar commensal innovation as it provides a foundation for the later rise of the Mycenaean polities in the second half of the second millennium. These three regions are becoming more and more interconnected, producing a "cultural koine" of shared customs by the early years of the second millennium, if not somewhat earlier. It is in this chapter that I first employ complexity theory as a frame to better understand important periods of social change.

Crete

We will start with a look at Crete. The early second millennium was a period in which Crete witnessed profound social structural transformation, a transformation which would eventually produce the social structure of what are referred to as the Middle Minoan or palace periods (ca. 1900–1500 BCE). To better understand what was happening at this time on Crete I am going to apply concepts from complexity theory to provide an analytical frame, within which I can situate their development. This does not mean that complexity theory will supply us with definite answers to the question of why such change occurred. But it can help us situate these developments within a larger picture of social complexity and help us focus on important questions which need to be addressed in order to supply a greater understanding of these social changes. I am going to focus on three aspects of complexity theory for this period: chaos, attractors, and the resultant new structural order. My window into this analysis is feasting, which provided a context for aggrandizers whose behaviors became attractors for the creation of new social structure. I shall focus on changes on the community or village level as well as the elite centers or palaces and peak sanctuaries.

Evolution on the Community Level

Unfortunately, we have only meager information on what the communities of Crete toward the close of the third millennium were like, with Myrtos being the exception. Most of our information comes from burials, but the burials themselves, when seen through the frame of complexity theory, signal that some important changes were occurring. There is strong evidence for increasing elaboration in funeral feasting starting in the Early Minoan (EM) III period (ca. 2100 BCE) and continues into the Middle Minoan (MM) IA (ca. 1900 BCE) (Legarra Herrero 2012). This phenomenon is widespread, seen in tombs in the Messara, the coastal region to its south, Malia, Gournia, and elsewhere. Along with an increase in the construction of buildings and special areas alongside the tombs, which would have been used for ritual and cult activities, archaeologists have found large deposits of feasting ware outside the tombs themselves. For example, at Platanos, the rooms outside the burial chamber contained more than 300 stone vessels. Storage of such stocks of feasting ware strongly indicates that the associated funerals were large, probably multistaged, and lasted over a period of several days, which would have allowed for the participation of attendees from other communities.

The Complexity Theory Frame

Using the frame of complexity, we would locate this period of elaborate funerals in a period of chaos, after the original social structure of the communities in this area had broken down. The old social structure was not able to meet new social demands, brought on by some sort of stimulus. People were using funeral feasting as a context within which individuals or groups could ameliorate social tensions. Funeral feasting was a context where aggrandizers were creating new institutions and new connections with those inside and outside their own communities. The elaboration of funeral feasting also had a more immediate impact on change, as the demands for increased foods and goods for the feasting would also have engendered institutions related to the increased production of agricultural goods, the need for storage, the need for oversight of the goods themselves, etc.

What remains to be asked is what stimulus brought about a change to chaos in this period. The archaeological record may not yet be up to this challenge, because of its serious gaps in material. As we shall see, there were significant changes occurring in the Cyclades at this time, with the introduction of sail-fitted ships, new contacts with the Near East and Anatolia, and striking nucleation. But to what extent this was affecting life on Crete is debatable. One possible stimulus might be sought in possible social ramifications (political or economic stimuli) of changes which had taken place at centers such as Knossos, Phaistos, and Malia. At these centers transformations in community social structure were beginning shortly before we see the emphasis on funeral feasting at tombs. It is to this change at these centers that I now turn.

Evolution on a Different Scale: The Palace Polities and Peak Sanctuaries

Somewhat contemporaneous with the rise in funeral feasting at tombs on Crete was the ascent of the political and economic centers at Knossos, Phaistos, and Malia. These early centers were later joined by those at Galatas, Petras, Archanes, Gournia, Palaikastro, and Kato Zakro.[1] The palaces of Knossos, Phaistos, and Malia are roughly from the same time period, with initial work on the construction of the palaces commencing around 1900 BCE (see McEnroe 2010 for guidance and references to the hundreds of publications on the palaces at Knossos, Phaistos, and Malia). Knossos swamps the other two of this trio in size, with a size of approximately 14,000 square meters, 8000 square meters for Phaistos and 7500 square meters for Malia. Of the three, the palace at Malia appears to be the earliest.

Later centers included Kato Zakro, located on the easternmost tip of the island. Kato Zakro (although dated, the best introduction remains Platon 1971), has its earliest phases close to the dates of the first three. This palace is not as large as Knossos, but spans an area of approximately 4500 square meters. Petras (Tsipopoulou 2012a, 2012b) is another palatial site. Built around the same time as the others or slightly later (ca. 1800 BCE), the palace covers 2500 square meters. Galatas (see Buell 2014), built close to 1700 BCE, appears to be about the same size as

---

[1] It has long been held that there was a palace on the western part on the island at Khania. There are problems with this, the major being that we still lack good information about this part of Crete in the Bronze Age. But see Andreadaki-Vlasaki (2002) for an overview of the situation.

Petras, but actual figures have not been given. The palace at Archanes, for which we have little information, might be contemporary with the construction at Galatas.

The roles that these palaces played in the culture of Bronze Age Crete must have been varied, and archaeologists have yet to arrive at a consensus as to their true character. Some conclusions are obvious, however. They must have been the residences of powerful families. Mythological tales, such as that of Theseus and the Minotaur, refer to the palace of Minos (that at Knossos) at least, as the home of the legendary king Minos, which gives credibility to arguments that many of these powerful families were political rulers on the island. The great size of the palaces would indicate that they played some sort of centralizing function within Crete. The variety of spaces for gathering and feasting, plus the evidence of large storage facilities in many of them, is strong evidence for one role being that of community gathering, perhaps for political ends. The great corpus of religious material found in the palaces would also indicate that one of the reasons for community gathering was to conduct religious ritual as well. Finds of early forms of writing for administration purposes in the palaces argue strongly for an important role for the palaces in political and economic oversight. Prestige items, turned up in palatial excavations, point to the integration of the palaces in the trade of luxury goods, as both consumers and possibly as producers.

These centers have most often been identified as small states in most literature on Bronze Age Crete (Parkinson and Galaty 2007; Hamilakis 2002 for an opposing view). I find this neoevolutionary paradigm limiting, in that it often covers over important inherent features of past polities in its need to classify them. I am going to use the term "polity" in respect to my discussion of Crete. The term refers to a government or organization, which can include a state, but does not limit itself to a state definition. I use the term loosely, on purpose, hoping to elucidate the characteristics of the settlement I am discussing, because of the very open definition of the term.

The Complexity Theory Window into the Palaces

The appearance of these palace centers represents the adoption of a new social structure for much of Crete. I am again applying concepts from complexity theory to provide an analytical frame, and I am focusing on the concepts of a system in chaos, aggrandizers, attractors, and resultant institutions in a period stretching from the EM II to the MM IB/II A, ca. 2300–1800 BCE, thus overlapping with the elaboration in funeral feasting in communities and villages, which we saw earlier.

There was increased activity associated with large-scale feasting at two of the palatial centers, Knossos and Phaistos. In fact, feasting is associated with these centers at a very early date. The area of the palace at Knossos was terraced and leveled as early as the Final Neolithic, almost 1000 years before the period we are currently discussing (Tomkins 2012). My attention is directed to a later major reorganization of residential and ceremonial space which occurred at Knossos in the late EM I or early EM IIA (ca. 2700–2600 BCE). The end product of this reorganization was an early emphasis on courtyard space, suggesting a focus on gathering, most likely ritualized feasting. Along with this courtyard there were buildings around its periphery, maybe early predecessors of later administrative and religious sections of the later palace at Knossos itself. Further data from ceramic analysis (Day and Wilson 1998, 2002, 2004; Wilson and Day 2000) shows that feasting began in earnest as early as EM II B (ca. 2500–2300 BCE) when people at Knossos were feasting with fine decorated pottery. This array of feasting ware included a large goblet, which would indicate its function for a large crowd. This focus on large-scale feasting continued into the introduction of Kamares ware, often highly decorated, ca. 2100 BCE.

Investigations at Phaistos show a similar history (Todaro 2005; Todaro and Di Tonto 2006), with similar attention paid to the construction of courtyards. The same is true for Malia. The earliest example of a palace on Crete (Pelon 1992), the site contains an architectural arrangement under the plan of the first palace, which indicates strongly the presence of an earlier courtyard, which could have been a venue for large-scale feasting.

Complexity theory would indicate that the elaboration of these feasts around 2200–2100 BCE stems from rising social chaos within communities connected to these centers. Like the situation described by Yoffee for Mesopotamia, the old social structure was not meeting new social demands brought on by some sort of stimulus. More people were probably affected by this chaos than we saw earlier with the rise of funeral feasting in community tombs in the Messara to the south. The areas which would have supplied participants for feasting at the palace centers must have been larger. As we saw with feasting at the tombs, these feasts would have provided opportunities for aggrandizers to create new social connections and institutions. I will discuss what these connections and institutions were, but before I turn to that description, I must point out the importance of another context for feasting which was active at this time and probably associated with developments at the palace, the Minoan peak sanctuary.

Hard to access even today, Minoan peak sanctuaries were sacred places located on mountain peaks. Many of these sanctuaries first appeared at the time that we witness large-scale feasting at the palace sites. Archaeological investigation shows that they were sanctuaries which were essentially open to the air. Activities associated with these sanctuaries were gathering, ritual, and feasting either at the sanctuary or off-site, as part of a pilgrimage (Haggis 1999; Kyriakidis 2006; Nowicki 1994; Peatfield 1987; Peatfield and Morris 2012; Rutkowski 1988). Like the palaces, the social catchment areas for these peak sanctuaries were most likely larger than those for community funerals. It also may well be that the social catchment area for the sanctuaries was somewhat different from that of the palaces themselves. Both contexts, however, must have been operating to create a new social structure for Crete at this time.[2]

According to complexity theory the old structural order must have been breaking down, and feasting, at the palace sites and at the peak sanctuaries, was producing contexts where aggrandizers, whose actions, heavily entangled in ritualized feasting, were acting as attractors, creating new social links and institutions. These aggrandizers were realigning the old pre-chaos system into a new social structure. The early elements of this social structure at the palace sites are currently only vaguely understood, because the earlier levels at the major palace sites are only partly understood, if at all.

I am therefore going to turn to the palace plans which have been excavated to outline the institutions of the new social structure, noting where possible a suggested timeline for the creation of these new institutions. These plans, however, are from the last phases of each building and at best contain elements of palatial construction which date to a rebuilding of the palaces around 1700 BCE. While we cannot be sure that the social structure which these palaces outline can be retrojected to this earlier period, several of the institutions contained in these palaces must have an ancestry which is older than 1700 BCE. Not all palaces were the same, but similarities between most establishments allow us to make some general observations on the institutions which social negotiations in feasting must have produced (for more comprehensive analysis than I am attempting here, see McEnroe 2010: chapter 8). In referring to various parts of the palaces and their contained institutions I shall restrict myself to identifying what would have been the most salient institutions they contained.

Some parts of the palace have an early history and represent institutions which are older than others. They are thus closer to the period of chaos and give us a glimpse of what the original attractors of the resulting new social order were. I suggest the following "order of creation" for the

---

[2] See Haggis (2007) for observations on the importance of feasting close to the actual construction date of the palace at Petras.

institutions housed in the palace. But I must caution the reader that there is probably no clear temporal division between the dates for the creation of several institutions, since they appear to have been so closely intertwined in their functions. The earliest institutions were those of the west court, possibly those housed on the eastern side of the central court. Either at the same time or shortly after came those associated with the large storerooms and those of the central court. The institutions represented in other parts of the palace appear to have been tightly associated with the institution of rulership, which probably was the last outcome of the processes involved in the elaborate feasting on site. They would be the institutions associated with formal reception, formal banqueting, the residential section of the palace, and various other cult institutions throughout the palace.

The West Court

The west court contained the institutions of formalized gathering, spectating, performance, and religious ritual. There appears to have been considerable architectural attention paid to the area to the west of the main palace building. At Knossos (Figure 5.1, which serves as reference for all palatial descriptions) and Phaistos, this area is paved, and the west wall of the main complex has received special treatment in its construction (Marinatos 1987). There was a shrine in this area at Phaistos. We probably should think of the west court as supplying a special gathering point for some sort of designated ritual. The early development of Knossos and Phaistos, their plans growing from various connected courts, and the fact that the west court at Knossos is a later version of one of these earlier courts all point to a deep historical significance for ritual here. At both Knossos and Phaistos the northern end of this area is occupied by what for want of a better description is called a "theatral area" (Cucuzza 2011). The theatral areas, because of their steps/seats, must have been ritualized gathering areas, possibly signaling that the cultural institutions housed in these western courts were carried out with some participating as actors and some as spectators. The institutions which were housed in the theatral areas indicate the presence of a hierarchy between participant and spectator.

Large Storage Rooms

The large storage rooms of the palace contained the institutions of oversight of agricultural production and oversight of storage and its attendant requirements, such as the production of storage jars and the processing of agricultural goods. Often referred to with the archaic term "magazines," large storerooms were located within the palaces at Knossos, Malia, and Phaistos, with a possible off-palace storage area at Kato Zakro. Remains in these areas indicate that they contained very large pithoi, that is, storage jars which probably contained agricultural goods, such as olives, olive oil, nuts, grains, etc. The storage rooms at Knossos were very large, as were those at Malia (when one considers the size of the storage facility in relation to the size of the palace). The need to gather and oversee large amounts of agricultural produce must have been associated with the very early presence of feasting at these centers. The presence of these storerooms was also once held to explain the economic power of the palaces. It had been argued that the palaces controlled agricultural redistribution, storing large quantities of agricultural goods, so that elites in the palaces could use that storage to disburse food in strategic contexts which would have created or maintained unequal relationships between the palace and others (Halstead 1981; Renfrew and Cherry 2011). However, that thought has been modified (Christakis 2011; Strasser 1997). It has been assumed that the agricultural products in the storeroom were the result of some kind of taxation, goods having been requisitioned by the palace from lands which they do not own. But it is equally possible that the storerooms housed products only from the private estates of those occupying the palace, thereby weakening an argument that their presence was integral to a political economy. These storage facilities probably did not provide the palace with the opportunity to direct agricultural redistribution back into any landowners, but rather to fund elaborate feasting ceremonies and to support crafts specialists who would have worked not only to build and maintain the palaces but to produce status items, such as elaborate ceramics or stone ware for the elites of the palaces.

Central Courtyards

The central courtyards housed the institutions of ritualized performance, congregation, and religious performance. Perhaps the most recognizable feature of the Minoan palaces was their large internal courtyard. To date, all buildings identified as "palaces" possess this feature. In at least three cases (Knossos, Malia, Phaistos) the courtyards are older than the palaces themselves, and the rise of elites at these centers must represent the capture or cooption of the institutions, that is, the rituals and activities which took place in these pre-palatial courtyards. That said, it is difficult to see a single or a particular function for the courtyards themselves. Spatially, they did not serve as foci for activities in the palaces. The rooms around the courtyards were to a great degree self-contained, without the need for courtyard access to make them fully functional.

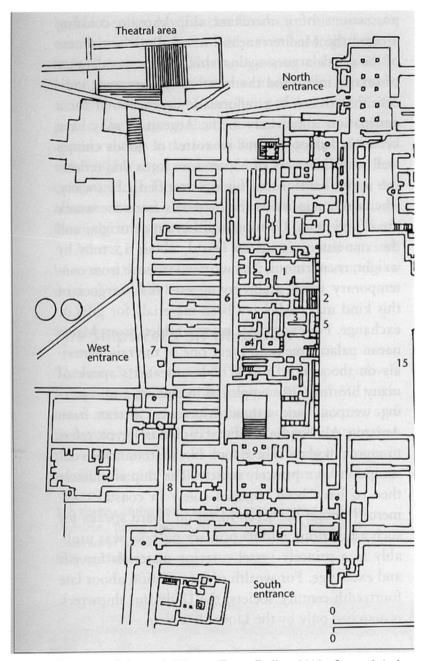

Figure 5.1 Palace of Minos. (From Pedley 2012: figure 3.4, by

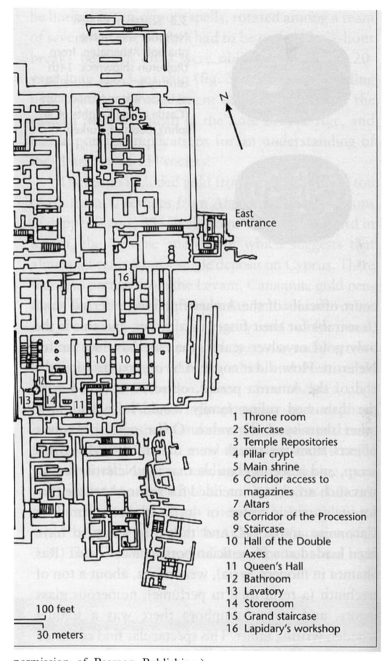

East
entrance

1 Throne room
2 Staircase
3 Temple Repositories
4 Pillar crypt
5 Main shrine
6 Corridor access to
   magazines
7 Altars
8 Corridor of the Procession
9 Staircase
10 Hall of the Double
   Axes
11 Queen's Hall
12 Bathroom
13 Lavatory
14 Storeroom
15 Grand staircase
16 Lapidary's workshop

100 feet

30 meters

permission of Pearson Publishing.)

There are various interpretations of the institutions that these court-yards might have held, and I can focus only on some of the more salient. It is possible that the courtyards provided a space for religious insti-tutions because they offered an open space for congregation in front of obvious religious rooms on the west side of the courtyard (but there are some caveats; see McEnroe 2010: 73–74). This is seen best at Knossos, and might reflect a pre-palace functional relationship between courtyards and religious ritual. Their orientation can also be religiously interpreted, because they are all aligned along a north/south axis, and the courtyard at Knossos even visually connects with the sacred Mount Juktas, perhaps the most important peak sanctuary on the island.

An interesting bull-leaping game might have been housed in the court-yards of Cretan palaces as well. Frescoes indicate that this was probably played by elite men and women, who would leap over a bull as it was in full charge toward them. It could well have been the case that elite power was negotiated over the control of such sporting activities, which took place in specialized court areas, much the same as our rodeo or bull-fighting arenas. Graham (1957) first proposed this function, arguing that the court at Phaistos even had a specialized platform in one corner for use in the game itself. Although the idea has only received rather lukewarm support, the ability of the courts themselves to have supplied an arena for this type of sport has been carefully examined by Thompson (1986, 1989, 1992), who has demonstrated that the palaces have architectural features such as spaces for holding cattle, that actually fit with this proposed function.[3]

Recent thought has turned to identifying the courts as gathering places for rituals of corporate rather than exclusionary power (Driessen 2002, 2003, 2004; Nakassis et al. 2010; Parkinson and Galaty 2007; Tartaron 2008). These observations build on work by Blanton et al. (1996), who argued that polities with large open plazas, such as the Ciudadela at Teotihuacan, would have reinforced political power through the use of corporate, rather than individualizing ideologies (see also Beekman 2008; Urban and Shortman 2004). But problems plague this type of analysis. The archaeological record does not usually have enough data to confirm or to deny whether or not an open space was a focus of corporate power rituals (Small forthcoming). Where we do have some written documentation for behavior in open spaces in the past, such as the Greek theater, we know that, even though these spaces today lack

---

[3] The issue is not settled, however; see Buell (2017).

features which would signal hierarchical distinctions, they were filled by different individuals and groups who were using timing, entrance, costume, and verbal clues to indicate and claim a high-status position in that arena. Furthermore, the argument for the corporate nature of Minoan palaces is tenuous, because it demands that we completely discount the possibility of reception rooms, as argued by Graham. The architectural characteristics of the court at Knossos could correlate with corporate *and* individualizing ideologies of inequality. The elaborate staircase on the western side of the court would have brought attention to the presence and the performance of individuals as they entered or exited the court in order to pass up to the reception rooms on the upper floor of the west wing of the palace.

Reception Rooms

Reception rooms in the palaces housed institutions of formalized hierarchical interface. The presence of reception rooms is indicated by indirect evidence in the architecture of the palaces, and comparisons with formal reception rooms in other examples of palatial architecture (Graham 1956, 1960, 1979). Graham noted that palaces, like those in Renaissance Italy, often had their major reception rooms on the upper floor. With that in mind, he studied closely the lower floor configuration of the western block of the palaces. What he noticed was that the walls of these floors were designed to carry extra weight at critical points. Understanding the nature of these critical points allowed him to reconstruct the possible upper floors in the palaces. Graham also pointed to evidence for elaborate frescoes and architectural elements, such as columns and door jambs, which had fallen into the storerooms under this area at Knossos. The reconstructions show that large rooms were supported. With the presence of elaborate access stairways, such as that at Knossos and Malia, he argued that this upper area of the palaces was the location of the principal reception areas. All this is based on secondary evidence, but the presence of an upper floor is well attested by the configuration of the lower floor, and its importance is definitely indicated by monumental access. The only exception to this observation may be the palace at Kato Zakro, which apparently had it reception room on the ground floor.

Banquet Halls

Banquet halls contained the institutions of formalized feasting. At four of the palaces (Knossos, Malia, Phaistos, and Kato Zakro), there are upper floor rooms which have been identified as banquet halls (Graham 1961). There is much to indicate that one of the chief gathering venues for the palaces was these rooms (Borgna 2004; Letesson and Driessen 2008) located in various forms throughout the structures. Their special architectural layout, often in the northern wings of the palaces, spatially segregated on the upper floors, and with views into the court, argues that the feasting here probably received special emphasis and was probably restricted to a select group from the community.

Residential Areas

The palaces' residential areas contained institutions associated with various undetermined domestic contexts, and controlled contexts for family/ outsider interfacing. Certain parts of each palace were given over to residential functions (Graham 1959). Those at Knossos, although they do not appear until later in the history of the palace, were more than likely based on an earlier similar design, and will serve as an example of what their configurations were like. Here the domestic rooms were built on the concept of the Minoan Hall, with its interior room and antechamber where the amount of air and light that filtered into the inner room was regulated.

Box 4   The Minoan Hall

A standard feature of much Minoan elite architecture was the Minoan Hall (Figure 5.2). The Minoan Hall was a tripartite arrangement of spaces. Although there was some variation on this arrangement, it most often was composed of an open space (often a light well), a vestibule, and a main hall. These spaces were often axially arranged, but in some buildings they may have had slightly different configurations.

The arrangement of the spaces was meant to facilitate the entry of light and air into an inner room or hall. A special door arrangement, called a pier and door system, was used to control the access of light and air into the main hall. Depending on the need to open or close the main hall, the doors could be folded back into I-shaped piers.

The Minoan Hall is found in numerous elite houses and the palaces themselves. It appears to have been used for various purposes, but an underlying function must have been to function as an institutional context(s) where interaction between individuals or groups needed to be controlled. There have been some suggestions that one of functions of this arrangement was to control access to a reception room, that is, the main hall. Perhaps the most elaborate use of this spatial arrangement is in the domestic quarter of the palace at Knossos.

Box 4   (*cont.*)

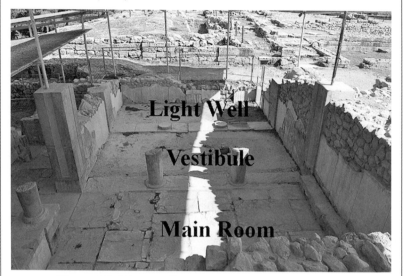

Figure 5.2 Minoan Hall system from the palace at Phaistos. (Photograph by the author.)

We have very little information on what the institutions of family life were like within the palaces. Evans's (1900–1901, 1901–1902) early identification of smaller residential rooms as spaces for women reflects concepts of late Victorian England and cannot be supported by any archaeological evidence. It would appear, however, that the method of controlling the amount of light and air might also have been employed to control access to the actual living chamber itself and thereby control contact between members of the household and outsiders. The apartments at Knossos could be elaborate, even with connections to toilets. The frequent appearance of similar architectural configurations in several Cretan houses from this period indicates the strong domestic nature of this configuration, which was not altered by the fact that it was now being used by a ruling family.

Various Cult Facilities

The palaces housed various places which contained institutions of private and public religious cult. All of the palaces had architectural arrangements which strongly indicate the presence of cult (Marinatos 1993). One of the most common is the pillar crypt. This was a room with a central depression and a pillar rising at the midpoint of the sunken area itself. While we do not know the exact nature of the cult or ritual that was tied to the pillar crypt (but see Hallager 1987), we do have several examples of the pillars themselves being carved with symbols which have been identified as connected with religion. Several of these symbols are the double axe, trident, star, etc. Another probable religious installation is the lustral basin (Campbell 2013). Lustral basins are often associated with other architectural configurations which housed religious institutions. A good example is that next to the "throne room" at Knossos (see below). We do not know exactly what function the lustral basins served. Early ideas that they could have been used for washing are weakened by the fact that they do not have any drains.

Another religious installation is the tripartite shrine (Shaw 1978). With a triple-divided façade, using pillars and horns of consecration (stylized bull horns), this shrine appears not only within palaces (at Phaistos at least), but outside in natural settings as well. Representations of it appear on the so-called grandstand fresco from Knossos, where it appears to have served as a theatrical background, supplying important imagery to what would have been some manner of performance played out in front of spectators. Evans restored a tripartite shrine on the west façade of the central court at Knossos, but this restoration is based on very weak evidence. Shaw has demonstrated from an analysis of the scenes on a specialized rhyton, or drinking cup, that such shrines also appeared outside palaces and were probably associated with religious ritual which included animal sacrifice, as I described in my treatment of peak sanctuaries.

Perhaps one of the most widely known cult rooms is the "throne room" at Knossos. This is a room which lies along the west façade of the court at Knossos. In layout the room contains a large lustral basin, a throne-like chair against one of its walls, and wall benches along three walls. Frescoes on either side of the chair highlight its significance with griffins. The current arrangement and decoration of this area may well reveal more about the last phases of the palace in the thirteenth century, but there is reason to think that the area itself was sacred from at least the end of the Neolithic at Knossos (Manteli and Evely 1995). While this was obviously some sort of room which housed sacred ritual, we do not know what that ritual was. Early on it was believed to have housed a presentation room for the king of the palace (Marinatos 2010). Another reconstruction has it centered on some sort of female deity and priestess (Reusch 1958), although there has been a recent recasting of the room as a venue for the worship of a male deity (Hitchcock 2010).

Other Results of Feasting: Houses, "Villas," and a Return to the Community-Level Scale

Houses and Villas

The results of feasting at the palace centers probably had a direct effect on the development of elite lifestyles outside the palaces. Elites would have imitated the behaviors of the ruling families.

Like the palaces, houses and villas contained institutions related to controlled household/outsider interfacing, cults, and oversight of stored agricultural products. We have quite a bit of evidence for the construction of large houses, and some elaborate houses which have been referred to as "villas." The houses themselves, especially after 1700 BCE, incorporate several features which we have already seen in the palaces. Most notable are the Minoan Hall system and the presence of lustral basins or pillar crypts. The institutions of the palaces and the houses of the well-to-do were also similar in the way that they interfaced with people outside the family, incorporating aspects of the Minoan Hall system. Some of these houses are quite elaborate (Betancourt and Marinatos 1997; Walberg 1994). Perhaps the best known is the villa at Hagia Triadha very near to the palace at Phaistos (La Rosa 1997). Here, we have the Minoan Hall system, and Watrous (1984) suggests that the presence of pithoi, fragments of Linear A, and seals indicates that one of the functions of this villa was administrative.

Box 5   Mysterious Linear A

Linear A is one of three ancient Bronze Age scripts of the Aegean (Figure 5.3). It dates from the later third millennium to the middle of the second millennium BCE. Found not only on the island of Crete but also on islands in the Cyclades and in the Bronze Age occupation strata of the city of Miletos on the west coast of Asia Minor, it is a script which defies ethnic identification. We are accustomed to calling it a Minoan script, but its far-flung dispersal indicates strongly that it was larger than Crete, a real Aegean script.

The script has a large number of characters with probable ideographic, syllabic, and semantic functions. We do not know what language it represents. There have been numerous suggestions, ranging from Luwian (an ancient language of Anatolia) to Phoenician to Etruscan and finally to ancient Greek. Decipherment seems a long way off, because of the paucity of Linear A inscriptions. If Greek, however, its use outside Crete, as far away as western Anatolia and possibly even the Levant, bears witness to an early ancient Greek koine in the Aegean world.

Box 5 (*cont.*)

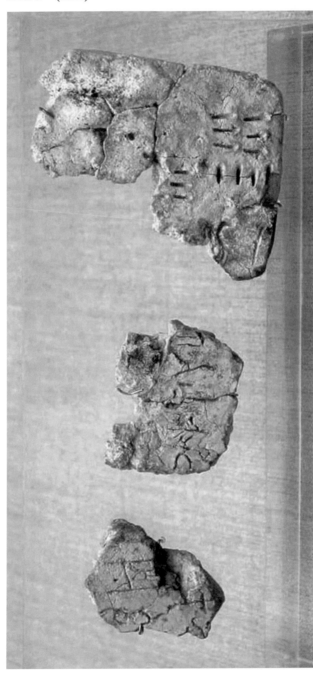

Figure 5.3 Linear A tablet. (Courtesy of L. Sheppard Baird.)

Box 5 *(cont.)*

The script shows that it had a number of uses. It was used for record keeping, since some characters of the script are evidently depictions of stored items such as cattle. It was used to identify the dedicator and the deity dedicated to on various votive objects. This use sets it apart from the later Aegean script, Linear B, which was used primarily for record keeping.

Yet we are left with the same quandary as we saw in the palace at Knossos. We do not know whether these stored agricultural products (those in the pithoi) were used in a system of redistribution which would match a political economy or whether they were for more restricted purposes, limited to the holding of a single household.

Communities

On a large scale, the social structure of communities from this time period would also have reflected the structure of the palaces themselves. We have two types of communities we can analyze: those which were an extension of the palaces themselves and those which were independent.

Communities contained institutions such as that of household/outsider interface, cults in the house and in the community, and those connected with town planning, formalized trade, and crafts production. The archaeological record of Minoan communities indicates that there was a range of different types. Two distinctions are those which were attached to palaces and those which were independent. For the first type we have evidence for communities around principal palaces, such as Knossos, Malia, and Phaistos. But they have not been heavily excavated (but see Poursat 1996). The attached community at Kato Zakro appears to have been complicated and elaborate, but, although excavated, the research has never been published, so its information is lost. For independent communities, we do have some better-researched settlements which supply us with a spectrum of what urbanized life was like. On the eastern end of the island, Palaikastro, a large town of approximately 30 hectares with a suggested population of 5000 people, is somewhat unique in that it has an identified area of blocks of elite houses (Cunningham 2007). These houses were large and quite elaborately constructed, with use of Minoan Halls and lustral basins. Access to the central room of the house was often through at least two vestibules, setting family institutions apart from those of the town itself. If we turn to Kato Zakro, we see a different pattern. The houses are closely associated with the palace in the settlement. Unlike those at Palaikastro, they have an easier access from the street to their inner room. The plan of the residential area shows little attention paid to elaborate streets, as at Palaikastro. Gournia, a large town of up to 1400 people, which covered at least 1400 hectares, was excavated around the turn of the last century. Unfortunately, the research on that excavation was never fully published, which means that a great deal of important information has been lost to us. What we can say of this community is that it had a harbor and possible ship sheds, a possible palace, a public shrine, and a great number of houses. There is also evidence for craft specialization in different parts of the town. The houses themselves, because of the loss of archaeological information, supply us only with their spatial layouts. From these plans, we can discern that the average house appears to have had several interior rooms, probably for storage or for some sort of specialized activity. Most also had a vestibule. This spatial context would have housed institutions which would have tied the family to the larger community.

Polity Size and Measures of Territorial Control

The polities which incorporated the palaces and towns must have controlled various amounts of territory. Understanding the nature of that control has been problematic, however. Most reconstructions are based on unsupported suppositions, such as the dominance of Knossos (Younger and Rehak 2008) on the island or the second-order center characteristics of such places as Galatas (Whitelaw forthcoming). Attempts to understand territorial configuration and extent, such as the use of Theison polygons (Cherry 1986) or walking distances to distinguish territorial extent (Bevan 2010), have been based on inapplicable or inappropriate analyses. The same can be said of attempts to identify territorial control through the distribution of ceramic styles (Betancourt 2004).

Measures of Social Complexity

By 1700 BCE there is much to show that we are looking at complex polities, with a variety of operating social institutions. For the palaces themselves, there is evidence that institutions were in place that incorporated elite participation and possible control of food production, storage, redistribution, manufacture and distribution of prestige items, participation in religious rituals, etc. These institutions must have fit into an evolving social hierarchy. The institutions linked to religion, feasting, and oversight of stored agricultural produce would have had a beginning in the feasting stages of evolution at the palaces, and in their early forms must represent what we know of the effect of aggrandizers and their resultant attractor behaviors. For the towns themselves, we have less of an idea of hierarchical control (but see Buell 2014) than of a range of diversity manifesting itself in political and economic ways. Towns such as Gournia and Palaikastro show that the composition of Cretan towns was not the same from town to town. Palaikastro shows a definite elite presence, with different ways in which the elite would interface with the community. Gournia was somewhat more egalitarian, with similar-sized domiciles and a similar way in which the family interacted with the community. Communities like Gournia do show economic specialization and a communal ritual. Both Gournia and Palaikastro also exhibit evidence of town planning, with various areas of different functions marked out in the community as well as attention paid to the construction and the care of streets.

The Cyclades

Our understanding of the turn of the third millennium in the Cyclades is made difficult by the possibility of a cultural gap in the period from 2200 to 1900 BCE (Brogan 2013; Broodbank 2013; Rutter 1983a, 1984), identified by a lapse in the ceramic record during that span of time. Such a lapse could, of course, mean that there was a definite decrease in population and resettlement later. But such scenarios are not common, and it is more likely that the gap itself reflects problems with our understanding of the ceramic sequences of this period in the Cyclades and elsewhere (Kouka 2013).

Despite the paucity of evidence, we can see that there was significant cultural change in the Cyclades at this time. Between 2400 and 2200 BCE new cultural materials – such as cups with affinities to those used in Anatolia, the use of the fast wheel in pottery manufacture, and the construction of some small fortified sites at places like Kastri on Syros – indicate that there were some new institutions, probably based on feasting, perhaps associated with Anatolian cultures, which were now popular in the Cyclades as well as on the mainland.

Box 6   A New Feasting Assemblage

Often referred to as the Kastri/Lefkandi assemblage, this feasting ware appeared in the Cyclades and on parts of the Greek mainland toward the end of the third millennium BCE (see Figure 5.4). The shapes are similar to shapes known to exist in Anatolia at this time. Thus its appearance in the islands and Greece was more than likely the result of contacts between these regions and Anatolia.

Box 6 (*cont.*)

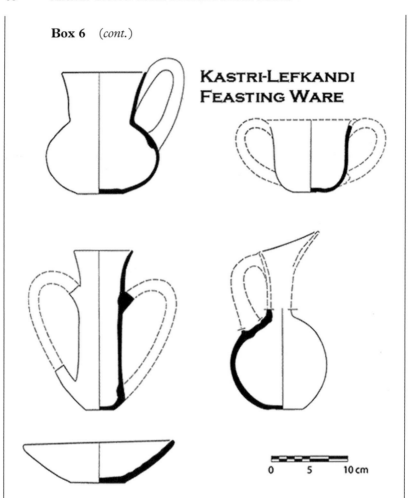

Figure 5.4 Kastri/Lefkandi feasting assemblage. (Redrawn from Pullen 2013: figure 1.)

What is striking about this feasting assemblage is the two-handled tall drinking vessel, often called the "depas" cup. The cup itself is extremely unstable with a small flat or rounded bottom. It was thus not meant to be drunk from and then set down. It was probably meant to be drunk until its contents were finished. The large ear-shaped handles mark it as a cup which was held by both hands. Cups of this character in many cultures are meant to be passed between individuals while the contents were being consumed. Its shape is new in the islands and on the mainland, and it indicates that there was a new and quite different style in feasting, with a new focus on shared drinking.

Box 6 (*cont.*)

The number of these new ceramics at any site in Greece or the Cyclades was small. This meant that this new feasting institution was not ubiquitous within communities, but probably limited to a more select group.

As we approach the Cyclades in the second millennium and move toward the middle of that millennium, we see some dramatic changes in the way of life on the islands (Sotirakopoulou 2010). While there is evidence for a continued infilling of the landscape on some islands, such as Syros and Mykonos, on other islands there was a sharp decrease in the small farm settlements which characterized the islands in the previous millennium. This can be seen very dramatically in the progression of settlement pattern at Melos (Renfrew and Wagstaff 1982; Whitelaw 2004). This movement was also joined by the general disappearance of hamlets and some large sites such as Chalandriani-Kastri on Syros.

What replaces these settlements is a settlement pattern which is totally new. We are again using the "culture" terminology, aware of all its pitfalls, but for the early millennial changeover, the culture which is first singled out is the Phylakopi I. By this I mean the cultural assemblages which appear in the first phase of the town of Phylakopi on the island of Melos, and similar assemblages which appear on other islands. This culture saw a dramatic shift toward greater nucleation and an almost complete abandonment of earlier farmsteads. The settlement data for this culture are spotty, so we cannot speak well to the issue of community social structure, but we do know that burials were now different, signaling new funeral institutions. The predominant burial was a tomb with multiple inhumations. There was also a cessation in burying people with marble figurines. This change could well be tied into the end of Daskaleio-Kavos's use as some type of maritime sanctuary for the disposal of such figurines, as we saw in the previous chapter. This culture is also noted for the spread of a new ceramic vessel, the duck vase. Ceramics like the duck vase appear to have been transport containers. The appearance of this vase in the Cycladic archaeological record at this time is probably signaling the ever-increasing importance of trade in the Cyclades.

What could have produced such a drastic change in the Cyclades? Several explanations have been put forward. One of the most salient has been that of climatic change (Dalfes et al. 1997). This was a period of very low rainfall, which could have had some effect on the islands. But given the great fluctuations in microenvironments in this part of Greece, low rainfall needs to be shown to have affected many of these islands in a similar fashion.

The most cogent explanation appears to be the introduction of sail-powered boats into the Cyclades and the effect that they had on Cycladic cultures (Broodbank 2002). Minoan seals from the EMIII to MMIA periods (ca. 2300–1900 BCE) show what appear to be the first examples of deep-hulled sailing ships in this part of the Mediterranean. Such ships were probably sailing the Levantine coast already for several centuries before becoming part of the transportation system of the Cyclades.

The Phylakopi I culture can therefore probably be seen as a change-over in the islands to a culture participating heavily in an active trading system. Larger and faster ships would have been carrying not only products in liquid containers, but other items such as textiles, metals, and exotica from the Levant and Egypt.

Three principal trading zones have been identified by their shared trade items. One lies in the northern Aegean, one occupied the central Aegean, and one lies on the western edge of the islands, incorporating Crete, the island of Kythera, and the Argolid. The last of these divisions represents the underpinnings for a specific koine, which will manifest itself more fully in the later half of the second millennium BCE. Shortly before the turn of the millennium Cretans settled on Kythera (Broodbank 1999; Broodbank and Kiriatzi 2007). From this island we have recognizable Cretan pottery and even evidence for a peak sanctuary. However, we should not refer to the spread of Cretans to Kythera as "colonization," because that implies some sort of strategic, planned establishment of a Cretan presence on the island, when the migration of Cretans to Kythera probably did not follow this paradigm. But we do need to recognize that from this period until the end of the second millennium, Kythera housed a culture which we could refer to as Cretan. In fact, one could say that Kythera had actually become an extension of Crete.

Measures of Social Complexity

It is difficult to determine what exactly the various institutions in Cycladic society in this period were. We can say that the presence of towns would probably indicate institutional contexts above the household level, although their exact nature remains unknown. There is probably good indication of overall town planning; seen in the later phases (2000–1550 BCE) of Phylakopi on Melos, which were constructed after the destruction of the sixteenth century. Phylakopi probably also now had defensive walls, as did other Cycladic towns such as Ayia Irini, Vrokastro on Tinos, and Rizokastellia on Naxos. New features in burial ritual support an increase in the importance of that institution with new ways of feasting.

The development of the sailing ship indirectly shows that institutional contexts of trade were achieving increased social importance.

The Mainland

The early second millennium BCE is best understood as a formative stage for the appearance of the Mycenaean polities in the later second millennium. Our knowledge of this period is spotty but it becomes richer to a degree as we approach 1500 BCE. As in the Cyclades, there were some new cultural elements, such as new feasting ware associated with Anatolia, appearing on the mainland around 2300–2200 BCE. Well-explored mainland sites such as Lefkandi in Euboia have yielded good examples of Anatolian-style feasting ware, indicating that parts of the mainland were in active communication not only with Anatolia but also with the Cyclades, where this style of feasting was also found (Pullen 2013). The introduction of this new feasting institution occurred before the Middle Helladic period (2000–1500 BCE).

Change on the mainland actually began in the Early Helladic (EH) III period (ca. 2200–2000 BCE), or about the time of the introduction of the new feasting arrangement. During this time there was a decrease in settlements. Places such as Lerna were destroyed and a new settlement pattern was taking hold, which saw settlements more often on elevated hills than more evenly dispersed as in EH II. There seems to have been some decrease in population after 2000 BCE. But this conclusion must be tempered by an understanding of the archaeological record. Most Middle Helladic (ca. 2000–1500 BCE) sites were built over earlier ones, and while survey has shown that there was a reduction in the number of sites in the Middle Helladic period, inconsistencies in identifying the sizes of sites make conclusions based on absolute population figures hazardous (Osborne 2004). What material we are able to identify as Middle Helladic comes basically from southern and central Greece. Western Greece and Thessaly do show some Middle Helladic settlement, but in general the material does not extend into the north. Our best material for understanding towns comes from Lerna and Asine. Offshore, on the islands of Kythera, Aigina, and Kea, there were large settlements with noticeable connections to cultures on Crete and the Cyclades.

It used to be thought that the appearance of two relatively new ceramic types, Minyan and matt-painted cups, around 2000 BCE, heralded the arrival of a new people, perhaps even the first Greek speakers (Blegen 1928b; Haley and Blegen 1928). But the pottery has local antecedents (Rutter 1983b), which makes the migration reconstruction no longer viable. Yet the appearance of these "new" types of ceramics might signal significant social change. The types themselves, especially the Minyan and matt-painted two-handled goblets, probably signal a new attention paid to feasting, possibly funerary.

Most treatments of this period on the mainland describe the Middle Helladic as a foundation for the rise of the Mycenaean polities in the latter half of the second millennium. Following what we know of mainland communities before 2000 BCE, we can probably assume that the social structure of Middle Helladic communities included institutions beyond those of the household, which might have been military or linked to some sort of political economy, as seen earlier at Lerna. But what we know of the social structure of the Middle Helladic period exactly is somewhat limited. Our best information comes from domestic and burial contexts. Only a few sites, such as Malthi (Valmin 1938), Asine (Dietz 1980, 1982), and Kolonna (Felten 2007) on the island of Aigina, offer us a community picture, but even here the information is limited. We are thus restricted to an understanding of this formative period based largely on analysis of domestic and mortuary contexts.

Looking at the household, the archaeological record indicates that several Middle Helladic houses were laid out axially, with up to three areas for the development of social institutions. An example of this house from Eutresis (Goldman 1931) shows a building with three distinct areas: a porch, a middle room, and an apsidal back room (Figure 5.5). Such a house provides several spatial institutional contexts for the household and its visitors. The porch would have been a principal context for the interaction of members of the household with others; the middle room, which was often fitted out with a hearth, probably served as the locus of several intrahousehold or even household–visitor institutions. The back room, which sometimes had its own door, could have served as an area for storage or perhaps a locus for more private household institutions. This house type appears in several communities of the period. Communities such as Asine show us that this tripartite arrangement was used for homes which were incorporated into neighborhoods. But here the apsidal back room has changed to a rectangular one. House E at Asine has two parallel tripartite divided spaces, which might indicate that the tripartite division would correlate with a single household unit; that is, the parallel unit could indicate the presence of another related group living within the larger domestic compound.

Our understanding of any larger plan for a community is not as secure as that of the house. Our best information comes from Asine where a small section of the original settlement has been excavated (Dietz 1991). Work to date indicates that there was very little recognizable difference in domestic construction. The buildings were roughly similar, and none contained evidence of any specialized industry.

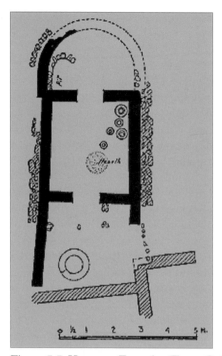

Figure 5.5 House at Eutresis. (From Goldman 1931: figure 37, by permission of the American School of Classical Studies at Athens.)

The major portion of our knowledge of the Middle Helladic period comes from burials (Milka 2010). We can recognize two types: one within settlements and one in separate extramural cemeteries. The intramural burials were located in between houses, with some actually excavated in the remains of earlier domiciles. The burials themselves were not elaborate, usually single inhumations, a majority of which were children and infants, with little enclosed grave goods. These types of burials were the only types in the MH I (2000–1900 BCE) and MH II (1900–1700 BCE). But by MH III we begin to see the start of extramural cemeteries, which were to predominate into the following centuries, or Mycenaean period.

The extramural burials were more elaborate than those within the communities. With space marked off for burial outside the community, burials were now more visible and open to elaboration. Several of these cemeteries had tumuli; marked-off circles; more elaborate grave goods, with many imported from the islands; evidence of multiple and secondary burials; and evidence of funeral feasting.

The material from the burials indicates that these societies were experiencing a social process where different kinship groups were using the context of the funeral as a means for accruing some sort of social hierarchy or distinction. In fact, it is the funeral context which gives us the most dynamic view of changes in the later middle Helladic period, changes which led to the appearance of Mycenaean institutions.

The period after 1500 BCE is marked by greatly increased interchange with a larger Aegean koine (see Chapter 6), which provided a stimulus for structural change. As described by Wright (2010), the mainland was probably divided into different regions, each with a high degree of internal intercommunity interaction. One region was the Saronic Golf, which was probably dominated by the powerful and heavily fortified city of Kolonna on Aigina. Regions such as the Argolid and Messenia represented areas which were internally interactive, but also with long-distance relationships with the Cyclades and Minoan Crete. As I will describe in the next chapter, it was at this time that aggrandizers were beginning to use elaborate funeral feasting to create new lines of power, connecting with families in other communities in the Argolid and Messenia, but also connecting with the Cyclades and Minoan Crete. This activity would produce significant change in specific locations in Greece: the Argolid, Messenia, and Boiotia. Notable graves, such as those from this period at Mycenae, attest to this dynamic (Wright 2010). As we shall see, elaborate funeral feasting would become one of the principal contexts where aggrandizers would create Mycenaean polities.

Measures of Social Complexity

There was apparently little new elaboration of the household and household/community institutions over what we witnessed in the third millennium BCE on the mainland. Fortifications, such as those at Kolonna, show that some institutions were above the household level. A very active institution was that of the funeral, with new attention paid to its social context. New feasting ware, often found in burial contexts, supports this development.

Later Developments and the Creation of an Aegean Koine

The period 2000–1500 BCE in Greece is noted for two things (for an overview, see Younger and Rehak 2008). The first was the destruction and the rebuilding of the palaces on Crete. Around 1700 BCE the palaces at Knossos, Malia, Phaistos, and probably Kato Zakro suffered some sort of damage. New palaces were constructed, which gave the descriptor "neopalatial" to this period. In many ways this activity on Crete represents a further confirmation of the social structure which we saw in the pre-destruction period. Some of the palaces, such as that at Galatas, which we have already looked at, were actually built at the start of the neopalatial period. Putting a chronological cap on the neopalatial period is not easy. For our purposes, we will consider the neopalatial to be undergoing significant changes in the sixteenth century, when several sites were destroyed, an event which is somehow tied to the explosion of the island of Thera ca. 1625 BCE, an event we will turn to in the next chapter.

The second feature of this time period is the evolution of a cultural koine which stretched from Crete to the Cyclades, possibly into Western Asia Minor,[4] and into southern Greece. This region shared many similar institutions, borrowed from various cultures. A common term for this cultural phenomenon is "Minoanization" (Broodbank 2004; Davis 2008). This attribution is due to our habit of either seeing the first examples of these cultural features on Minoan Crete or assuming that the power of Minoan civilization aided the spread of their cultural traits beyond Crete. But in reality the parentage of many of these institutions was probably lost in the lively interchange of this koine. The use of a pier and door system outside Crete, for example, either could be a very conscious act of aping Cretan culture or could just as easily be an attempt by people to use architectural forms which were considered attractive, rather than solely Minoan.

We can establish some basic points for understanding this koine. Work at major Cycladic sites, such as Phylakopi, Akrotiri on Thera, Ayia Irini, Trianda on Rhodes, and even Miletos on the western coast of Asia Minor has shown some important shared cultural features, which we should label as representations of the common features of an Aegean koine. Linear A is seen in Akrotiri, Ayia Irini, Phylakopi, and Miletos. This must represent a shared ability to read the script. Other common features are seals found on Crete, Ayia Irini, and Akrotiri. Similar looking frescoes were also common, seen in Minoan Crete, Phylakopi, Akrotiri, and Ayia Irini. Archaeologists have long recognized common pottery types seen on Crete but also on every major site in the Cyclades, as well as Miletos. The same can be said of ideological symbols. Images of the bull and bull-leaping, of horns of consecration, and of possible goddesses

---

[4] I am not treating the topic here, but there is growing evidence of interaction between some contemporary sites on the western coast of Asia Minor, such as Miletos and the rest of the Aegean world. This issue is treated in Broodbank (2004).

are found all over the Aegean (for an argument for a religious koine based on the mother goddess, see Marinatos 2010).

I would like to extend this argument even further. The longtime interaction between Crete, the east Cyclades, and part of the mainland, such as the Argolid, created its own smaller koine as well. The language of that koine was probably Greek, spoken and used here and on parts of Crete, from at least ca. 2200 BCE, if not earlier. Contact within this koine was so active that shared features became quite specific. One of the most salient was an approach to economic oversight of lands owned by ruling elites. I will turn to this issue specifically in the next chapter.

Readings

For the Minoan palaces I highly recommend a thorough reading of Tomkins (2012), who gives a very detailed overview of the early periods of construction at Knossos. He also postulates that the rather segmental layout of the buildings might indicate that the court complex was a gathering venue for different corporate groups, each with its own area for storage of equipment, corporate ritual, etc. For further thoughts on the role of various sections of the palaces within larger strategies of social competition, see also Schoep (2010) where she argues for the rise of new power relationships and institutions within a scale which focuses on household competition. As argued here, I see a parallel context of negotiation for social positions at the palace centers and within the communities themselves. For a similar argument, see Schoep (2006). Although already mentioned in the text, McEnroe (2010) presents the most perceptive and most recent take on Minoan architecture. See also Preziosi (1983) for an interesting and very useful spatial analysis of the Minoan built environment. Some scholars have recently argued that we should jettison the term "palace" for Minoan Crete, and instead see them as ceremonial centers. This is a debate over definitions, which I prefer to avoid. What remains important is the presence of various functions of the "centers/palaces," which are more often than not shared by both terms. For insight into this issue, see Driessen (2003). The issue of redistribution, which was an early argument for how the Minoan polities developed, has recently been reviewed. See "Forum: Redistribution in Aegean Palatial Societies" in volume 115 of *American Journal of Archaeology* (2011). A good overview of the art of the period is Preziosi and Hitchcock (1999).

The exact role that peak sanctuaries played in the development of Minoan culture remains difficult to determine. See Haggis (1999) for an argument for their role in a staple finance model. Minoan villas come in all shapes and sizes, but for a good overview of their characteristics, see papers in Hägg (1997). A reasonable overview of Minoan towns is Branigan (2001), yet one needs to be careful of his use of site hierarchy, which as we saw, is difficult to apply to polities in Bronze Age Crete.

For the Cyclades, an excellent study of the use of pottery in creating identity in the Cyclades is Berg (2007). A good consideration of interisland migration can also be found in Abell (2014).

Turning to the mainland, a good overview of Middle Helladic burials, although now somewhat dated, is Boyd (2002). A great deal of recent research has focused on human faunal analysis of the burials themselves. For a representative study, see Ingvarsson-Sundström et al. (2009).

6   Changes in the Latter Part of the Second Millennium BCE

Significant changes and events occurred in the latter half of the second millennium: the island of Thera exploded; Crete witnessed dramatic changes in the loss of several centers and the possible extension of the role of Knossos on the island; and on the mainland, various households rose to prominence.

The most catastrophic of these three changes was the eruption of the island of Thera (Figure 6.1). Occurring ca. 1625 BCE, the explosion devastated the island. Settlements were completely destroyed. We know most about ancient Akrotiri (Doumas 1978, 1981, 1983), which by the time of the explosion was probably half a century old. Further from the island we can see evidence of the extent of the tsunamis (Minoura et al. 2000). They traveled as far away as the coast of the Levant. Their impact on the island of Crete, however, is difficult to understand. For example, we have evidence for a tsunami at Palaikastro (Bruins et al. 2008), which was at least 9 meters in height and inundated the entire town. Similar catastrophic evidence exists for Malia. But the archaeological record shows that parts of Crete, such as Knossos, continued to flourish. Despite this unevenness, there have been recent attempts to link the effect of the explosion on Thera to a noticed decline on Crete (Driessen and MacDonald 1997). Indeed, there are some arguments that the seismic activity from the explosion made it difficult to access fresh water on Crete, since a common effect of strong seismic activity is the rerouting of underground springs. Others (Knappett et al. 2011) argue that the loss of Thera in a larger trading network was to eventually have devastating effects on Crete as well.

Whatever the cause, and they might well be multiple, there were major changes on the island of Crete in the latter half of the millennium. In this period we have evidence of destructions at Khania, Phaistos, Ayia Triadha, Gournia, Malia, Petras, Kato Zakro, and many other sites. It is difficult to coordinate closely the ceramic dating between these different sites, but it does look like they were suffering from this disaster, while Knossos was still thriving (Preston 2004; Rehak and Younger 1998).

Charting Social Evolution on the Mainland: Complexity Theory's Frame

The rise of new centers on the mainland parallels what we know of the rise of the Cretan centers of Knossos, Phaistos, and Malia, in the importance of elaborate feasting. I am therefore using the complexity theory frame to help us understand the dynamics of this change. There are several features in the evolution of these polities which fit into the complexity theory model. The later part of the Middle Helladic period (ca. 1550–1350 BCE) is known for the presence of increased elaborate funeral feasting, seen at Mycenae and later at Pylos. This would accordingly signal a period of structural chaos, as new social demands were not being met by older social structure. We do not have enough material to pinpoint what stimulated this change. But it would be reasonable to suggest that a good suspect would have been the effect of intercommunity trade within the larger Aegean koine. New households were gaining wealth but were not served by the current power structure. This period of chaos and subsequent change was short, lasting no more than two centuries. This was a period of feasting elaboration when aggrandizers were creating new institutions of hierarchy and power. The attractors were those behaviors which were operational within the households of rising families. The result was the evolution of new institutions often embedded in households, which made a few households dominant within the Argolid, Messenia, and sections of Boiotia.

Our evidence from Mycenae is quite striking. The rise of the dominant house there was actively tied to the funeral context. The palace at Mycenae, which housed the family which had made it to the top of the hierarchy, was actually built on the edge of a cemetery. In a later alteration of the palace, one of the actual elite burial circles was incorporated into the design of the palace, in a possible attempt to legitimate the rise of power of a new ruling group (Alden 2002; Small 2002). The cemetery was quite large. Among its numerous burials, two grave circles give us excellent evidence of elaborate funeral feasting, before the creation of the palace.

The earliest of these circles was grave circle B (ca. 1675/1650–1550 BCE). Excavated in the 1960s, this was a stone-lined circle within which

Figure 6.1 Santorini (Thera) after explosion. (Copyright 7reasons.net/

there were numerous ostentatious burials (Mylonas 1973). Human faunal analysis has shown that some of those buried were kin (Bouwman et al. 2008). The rich interments indicate strongly that there was great attention paid to their funerals. The early tombs were simple, often cist graves. As time went on the burials became more elaborate, not only in their construction but in their grave goods. The grave goods of these later tombs were part of the material which made up the Aegean koine. Several

LBI ArchPro, Michael Klein.)

of the male graves from the later phases of the burials contained drinking ware, pointing strongly to the fact that elaborate funeral feasting played an important role in the creation of position and power at Mycenae.

Grave circle A is the newer of the two. It dates from the sixteenth century and may well have been a circle which became *the* burial circle at Mycenae, since a good case can be made for overlap and transfer of elaborate funeral feasting from circle B to circle A after A was constructed (Graziadio 1988, 1991). As Mycenae moved into the six-teenth century, the graves became even more elaborate, as the funerals must have as well. Objects interred with the dead in this grave circle display a strong connection between these people and the larger Aegean koine, with art emphasizing bulls, Aegean deities, Aegean-made material-ials using Egyptian themes, etc.[1]

After the burials in grave circle A, funerals at Mycenae continued to be elaborate, even more so than in the circles. This can be seen in the construction of the tholos tombs on the site. Nine tombs were built between the sixteenth and fourteenth centuries (Fitzsimons 2011; Wace 1921–23). One of the last of this series, the tomb of Atreus, remains the best preserved and known. Unfortunately, unlike the grave circles, the tholoi were subject to grave robbing, but the size and elaboration of the tholoi themselves probably reflected the elaborateness of the funerals.

Institutions of the Palaces: What the Architecture Tells Us

In the end, the social maneuvering in elaborate funeral feasting led to the development of a constellation of institutions related to the hierarchical position of a single house at various Mycenaean centers: (for a good overview, see Fields 2004), Pylos (Blegen and Rawson 1966), Mycenae (no definite excavation report, but start with Schliemann 1878), Tiryns (start with Schliemann et al. 1885), Midea (Walberg 2007), and Thebes (Symeonoglou 1973).[2] My description of this constellation of institu-tions will use two chief pieces of evidence: the architecture of the palaces themselves, and textual information. The construction of elite palaces at each of these centers was not contemporary (for late Pylos, see

---

[1] Graziadio's analysis is excellent and sensitive to the minute details of burial change. My only disagreement with his final analysis is that he argues that the inclusions in the grave represent the social standing of the buried. They represent, instead, the aspirations and attempts of those burying to build social positions and to use those social positions to reproduce hierarchy.

[2] Although often mentioned as having a Mycenaean palace (Hurwit 1999; Iakovidis 1962, 2006; Mountjoy 1995), Athens does not meet any criteria for membership into the club of Mycenaean palace centers. There is no evidence for any palace on the akropolis. The thinking is that Athens "should have been a palatial center," so evidence for its palace is often sought. The akropolis was fortified in the Mycenaean period, however, with a tower design, which is similar to that used in the palaces at Mycenae and Tiryns. See Wright (1994).

Voutsaki 1998). Not all areas produced the same constellation at the same time. Mycenae and Tiryns built palaces in the early to mid-fourteenth century. Pylos did not see its palace until close to the end of that century.

The best understood palace is that at Pylos (Blegen and Rawson 1966) (Figure 6.2). The interior of all three palaces was extremely similar, so explanations for life at Pylos can be applied in general to life at the other palaces. The palace at Pylos is divided into several different spaces. Several sections of the palace housed various functions, from elite ceramic manufacture (Figure 6.2, northeast building) to storage (Figure 6.2, wine magazine) to domestic functions. A wing at this palace (Figure 6.2, rooms 7, 8, and adjacent spaces) includes a series of domestic rooms, with one containing a bathtub, the first known in Europe. The most important part of the palace, however, from a political and economic viewpoint was the series of rooms which included the megaron complex (Figure 6.2, rooms 1–6). This suite of spaces began with a monumental entrance which led into a large forecourt. From the forecourt one preceded into the megaron, which was divided into an entrance way, a room behind that, and then a large room with a hearth, which was open to the sky.

There is much to signal that the megaron, in its tripartite spatial division, found its ancestor in Middle Helladic houses. The fact that the megaron became the center of the Mycenaean palaces hammers home the fact that the core of the Mycenaean polity was composed of transformed domestic institutions rather than brand new political ones (Kilian 1988; Wright 2006). The megaron is even a repeated element in the palaces and has been attributed to different levels of political rank between political leaders, perhaps in the same household (Kilian 1987a, 1987b, 1988; Younger 2005).

A functional analysis of the spatial configuration of the megaron and its relationship to other areas in the palace gives us insight into these new institutions. With its giant hearth the megaron appears to have been the most important of these spaces, and the other areas were lined up to give access to it, providing what might well have been a processional way. Each space could be sealed, enabling the residents of the palace to control access to the megaron.

The arrangement of these spaces, leading up to the megaron, and the fact that each could be sealed off from the other indicates that each had a unique importance relative to the others, with that of the megaron being the most important. It was here that feasting was probably conducted. The walls of the inner room of the megaron at Pylos have frescoes which depict aspects of feasting, such as a lyre player who would have sung at these feasts.

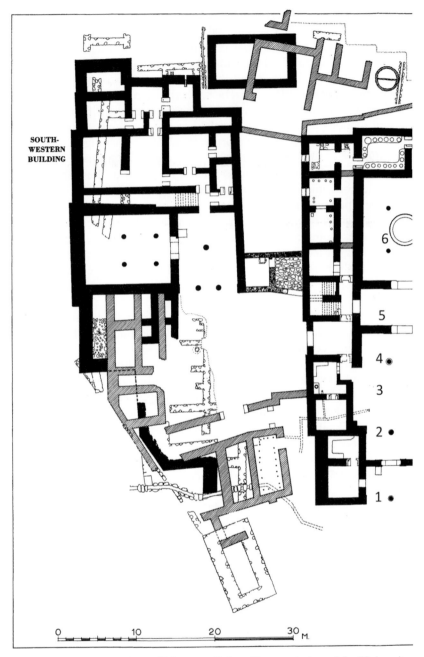

Figure 6.2 Palace of Nestor at Pylos. (By permission of the University

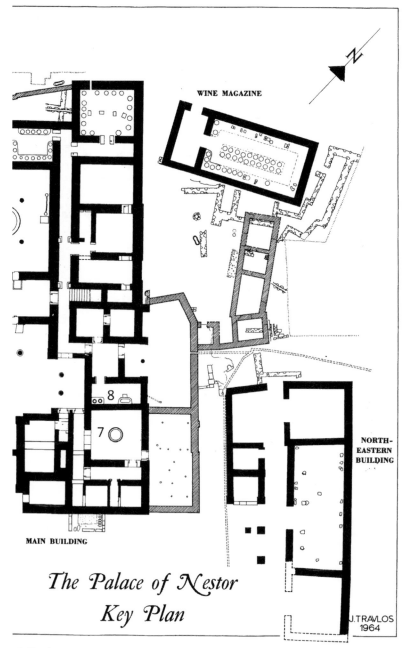

WINE MAGAZINE

NORTH-
EASTERN
BUILDING

MAIN BUILDING

The Palace of Nestor
Key Plan

J.TRAVLOS
1964

of Cincinnati.)

Box 7   The Mycenaean Kylix Cup

By far the most ubiquitous drinking cup of the Mycenaean period was the kylix cup (Figure 6.3). This tall-stemmed cup was too small to be held with both hands and must have been held in a fashion similar to today's champagne glasses. Frescoes show people in the Mycenaean palaces drinking from these cups in formalized feasts. The association of these cups with feasting in the Mycenaean palace is made clear by the fact that the storerooms at Pylos housed more than 2800 of these vessels. While many were decorated, often with marine creatures, as seen in the figure, a large quantity of cups in the storerooms at Pylos were not. This suggests that the feasting in the palace was diacritical; that is, some members of the feast were signaled as more important than others. In this case it would have been the elites who were drinking from decorated cups. It was this cup which disappeared with the fall of the palaces, showing that its purpose was heavily embedded in the political feasting of the palaces themselves.

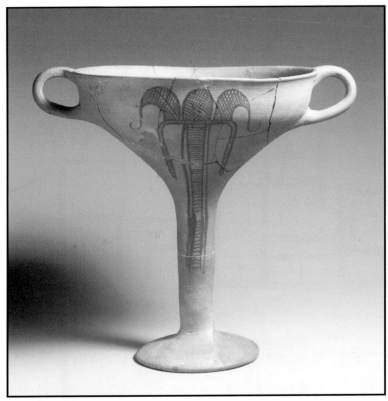

Figure 6.3 Mycenaean kylix cup. (From Metropolitan Museum of Art, Accession Number 27.120.8, CC0 1.0; Public Domain Dedication.)

There was also a possible offering table in the inner room of the megaron at Pylos. Installations of a large hearth at Mycenae, Tiryns, and Pylos, plus "thrones" at Pylos and Tiryns, also indicate that there was a probable other function for these inner rooms. The megaron probably also served as some sort of reception area. But this function is far from clear. The "throne" in these rooms is set to the side, and not on a focal axis with any entrance (Farmer 2011), and could well be of greater significance to other rituals than to interfacing with those who would be presenting themselves to any kind of ruler.

Anteroom/vestibules within the megaron design itself could signal areas where those being received would wait for entrance. Unfortunately, the outer courts which connected to the megaron have little archaeological material within them to indicate their functions. An altar in the court at Tiryns and a possible altar at Pylos point to a religious function. Their large size could accommodate a number of people and they might have served as foci for feasting as well. There is evidence for feasting, probably in the forecourt at Pylos (Stocker and Davis 2004).

Record Keeping

At Pylos there are two rooms near the gate to the megaron's forecourt. These rooms housed numerous Linear B tablets, records which oversaw transactions between those within the palace and others. It is tempting here to conclude that this gate was the locus for reviewing and checking obligations between those within the house and those outside. If so, the position of this archive would indicate that transactions were reviewed at the gate, face to face with those coming to the palace and not further within the building.

The archives were written in Linear B, which was the last Bronze Age script we have from Greece. Written on tablets and on jars, this script was a partial syllabary. It used 87 different signs for syllables and 100 signs which were ideograms, that is, signs which represent a specific thing or concept (Figure 6.4). We have examples of Linear B now from a variety of sites. Several excavations have unearthed jars with Linear B inscriptions: Gla, Orchomenos, and Eleusis on the mainland, Malia on Crete. Inscribed tablets, preserved because they were fired in conflagrations, have been found at Knossos and Cydonia (Khania) on Crete, and Pylos, Mycenae, Thebes, and Iklaina on the Greek mainland.

Just which language Linear B represented was of intense interest to scholars of prehistoric Greece and language in general for many decades after knowledge of its existence became generally known in the late nineteenth century. Important advances to our understanding of the

Figure 6.4 Examples of Linear B. (From www.omniglot.com, by

script were made by Emmett Bennet and Alice Kober, who were able to isolate various syllabic equivalencies for the script. The real breakthrough came in 1954 with the work of Michael Ventris, who established that Linear B was actually an early form of ancient Greek (best described in Chadwick 1967).

The script itself appears to have been used by scribes whose job it was to oversee the flow of goods into and out of the palaces. No evidence exists for the use of Linear B for any type of literature, however. Its use is thus extremely circumscribed.

permission of Simon Ager.)

Institutions of the Palaces: What the Texts Tell Us

Our understanding of the economies of the Mycenaean polities comes from Linear B records from Pylos and Knossos principally, plus archaeological materials found at the palaces and extensions to analogous situations in modern-day Greece. With the cracking of the Linear B code, it was initially thought that the economy of the Mycenaean polities was similar to redistribution patterns which were associated with Near Eastern city-states (Finley 1957; Renfrew and Cherry 2011). This

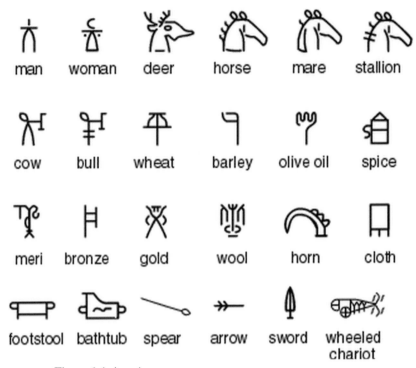

man   woman   deer   horse   mare   stallion

cow   bull   wheat   barley   olive oil   spice

meri   bronze   gold   wool   horn   cloth

footstool   bathtub   spear   arrow   sword   wheeled chariot

Figure 6.4 (*cont.*)

model of redistribution was challenged later by Halstead (1993, 2007), who argued instead that the Mycenaean polities incorporated a wealth-finance economy. What that means is that prestige manufactured items were used to pay off those who were supplying the palaces with staple goods. This was also the argument of Galaty and Parkinson (2007b), who, in an influential work on the Mycenaean palaces, argued that there was a heavy dependency in Mycenaean polities on wealth finance through the distribution of non-fungible status items[3] (Galaty and Parkinson 2007a: 26).

Recent research (Galaty et al. 2011; Halstead 2011; Nakassis 2010; Schon 2011; Shelmerdine 2011), however, is elucidating a somewhat different picture of the Mycenaean economy. Most of what was distributed by the palace was staple goods. But the bulk of these goods appears

---

[3] I am following closely the presentation of Nakassis (2010), who provides the most lucid description of the rather confusing use and history of economic models for ancient Mycenaean polities.

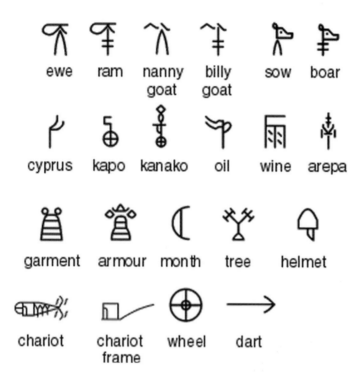

| ewe | ram | nanny goat | billy goat | sow | boar |

| cyprus | kapo | kanako | oil | wine | arepa |

| garment | armour | month | tree | helmet |

| chariot | chariot frame | wheel | dart |

to have been redistributed at feasts. This argues quite clearly that redistribution had not become a codified system, since it was still embedded in feasting institutions, which probably predate the construction of the palaces.

Despite some recent new thinking on the Mycenaean economy, some earlier observations still appear to be valid. The palaces at Pylos and Knossos oversaw the input of raw materials for their workshops. These materials were flax, bronze, wax, hides, honey, and spices. The obligations were bundled in a fixed ratio of 7:7:2:3:1.5:150, respectively. This indicates that these materials were sought directly for production, with specific quotas important, rather than being a general tax. There also appears to have been some sort of exchange of land for obligations. The palaces themselves probably owned land close to the center and grew on that land wheat, olives, figs, and grapes, and raised sheep. It was probably from these lands that the palaces obtained goods to pay laborers, and we have some records of the palaces supplying wine, probably from their own estates, to communities for drinking in festivals.

What I have outlined so far is attested in the Linear B records, but the archaeological record also indicates that the palaces obtained pottery, cereals, and pulses, and young male sheep from their own lands or from non-palatial holdings. Within their territories we also find evidence of jewelry and stirrup jars for perfumed oil, which must have come from palace workshops. Outside their territories the palaces were also involved in additional trade. We have found raw ivory (probably from Africa or the Near East) and semiprecious stones (such as amber from northern Europe) within the palaces, and stirrup jars for perfumed oil at sites outside their territories as well.[4]

Our Linear B documentation sheds some light on different officials who would have been part of these new institutions within the palaces. Because of the amount of documentation at Pylos and Knossos, most titles can be witnessed at both locales. The importance of this is that the Knossosian and Pylian texts are removed by both geography and several generations. These officials apparently were part of the structure of these polities for quite a time. We know little about how these officials functioned, but it is clear that some sort of administration was in operation.

The titles and their possible functions are shown in the following list. Unfortunately, we know little of the actual functions of each of these people. In some few cases these titles match those mentioned by later poets such as Homer and Hesiod in the eighth and seventh centuries. It appears that they were associated with some sort of administrative structure.

Wa-na-ka	(Wanax in Homer) Leader of the polity, seen later in the Iliad as a "lord." Stirrup jars at Thebes, Eleusis, Tiryns, and Khania (containing olive oil) are marked as connected to the wanax, indicating that he was a landholder, who was processing oil. In later Greek (Homer to Hellenistic) the word is used to signify lord or leader, used with gods and kings.
Ra-wa-ke-ta	(Lawagetas in Homer) The term in Greek means "leader of the people." Little is known about this title. At Pylos the person with this title appears to have been the second largest landowner, next to the wanax.
E-qe-ta	Possible representative of the palace or center in the territories. Perhaps also a companion of the wanax.

---

[4] Although we are now reconsidering the role of redistribution in models of the palatial economy, one of the most insightful reconstructions of the palatial economies remains Halstead (1993).

Da-mo-ko-ro	Some kind of territorial functionary
Du-ma-te	Perhaps similar to the da-mo-ko-ro
Po-ro-du-ma-te	Possible territorial functionary
Mo-ro-qa	Possible territorial functionary, possible military commander
Qa-si-re-u	(Basileus in Homer and Hesiod) Possible territorial functionary, possible leader of a small group
Ko-re-te-re	Possible leader in charge of a major administrative unit at Pylos
Po-ro-ko-re-te	Perhaps similar to the ko-re-te-re

Problems in Understanding Mycenaean Greece

This is not the place to dwell at length on difficulties in understanding the Mycenaean world. But two issues need mentioning. The first is that the nature of the political and economic territorial control within Mycenaean polities is misunderstood. The second is that the relationship between the culture of the Mycenaean Argolid and Messenia and the rest of Greece is more assumption than reality.

The first issue refers to the obvious limited nature of its internal political structure. The Mycenaean polity was constructed around the rather rapid rise of one lineage over others in its region, and the transformation of that lineage into a political and economic center of a polity. The palaces themselves illustrate this well. Rather than elaborate political institutions which refer to reception, as we saw in the probable reception rooms at the Cretan palaces, and rather than separated institutions of feasting, as seen in the banqueting installations in those polities as well, we have only a megaron, which represents the internal focus of a family, now transformed to do service in a larger political and economic environment.[5]

Analysis of the settlement pattern around Pylos indicates that its oversight was incomplete and weak. This can best be seen in the application of rank-size analysis to the settlement pattern from Pylos. The rank-size rule, which has been empirically supported (Drennan and Peterson 2004), shows that, when a region is evenly well integrated economically,

---

[5] The issue of the relationship of architecture, which houses institutions, to the identification of an archaic state was brought forth by Flannery (1998). His attempts to understand the nature of power in past polities and relate that to the identification of a state are limited, however, by the fact that he identifies institutional complexity, but does not relate that to any larger issues; the question of whether or not that complexity is embedded in lineages or in a structure which spans lineages is one of the most important.

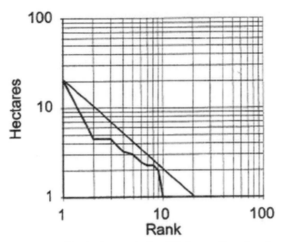

Figure 6.5 Rank-size analysis of Pylian polity. (by the author)

the size and rank of each site will multiply out to 1. When the rank-size ratio multiplies to 1, the graph shows a normal falloff and indicates that the territory and the center are well integrated, which is the hallmark of an evolved polity (see work by Grove 2011; Johnson 1977, 1980; Peterson and Drennan 2005).

Deviations from that equation indicate two things. First, the center is not as large as it should be. This shows that it had little effect on territorial integration, being somewhat equal in size to territorial sites, and that the sites themselves contain a lot of economic activity which would normally be in the center. Second, the center is larger than it should be. It is too centralizing, containing too much economic activity, which should be spread out to the territorial sites.

The application of rank-size analysis to the Pylian polity shows that the relationship is in a primate distribution (Figure 6.5).[6] This indicates that the various sites, including Pylos itself, had not yet interfaced long enough to produce a more thoroughly integrated polity. What we see in the Pylian polity is more of an economic and political overlay of its territory. It had not attained a level where the relationship between the center and the territory were integrated, where the overlay had had an opportunity to sink into the economic and political contexts of its territory more fully (see my earlier arguments in Small 2007). The rather rapid development of the palaces at Tiryns, Mycenae, and probably elsewhere indicates that this

---

[6] See Buell 2013; 328, figure 4.35 for similar analysis.

weak territorial control probably existed in these polities as well. If we put Pylos and the other Mycenaean centers on a larger scale, linking them into a network which includes Knossos and some of the larger centers in the Near East and Egypt, we can see that their disproportionate size in relation to their territories is due to the fact that they were being pulled into this larger network more than they were growing from an integration of their territories (Parkinson and Galaty 2007 make this argument as well).

The second problem has to do with the identification of the Mycenaeans and their relationship to other contemporaneous groups in Greece. The last stages of the developing koine, which we discussed at in the last chapter, and in which those in the Argolid and Messenia participated, has been unfortunately equated with the Mycenaeans themselves. In reality the presence of tholos tombs, megarons, military equipment, Linear B, etc. was part of the koine rather than strictly Mycenaean, as often argued. The presence of these features has been equated with Mycenaeans as far distant as Anatolia (for an overview, see Kelder 2006, who uses a very loose description of Mycenaeans). A classic case of misidentification comes from seeing Mycenaeans inhabiting Dhimini because of the presence of a megaron-looking building (Pantou 2010).

Coupled with this last issue is the relationship of polities like Pylos with contemporaneous Crete. One of the most common arguments is that Crete was now occupied by Mycenaeans and places like Knossos were controlled by Mycenaean leaders. The basis for the argument that Mycenaeans were living on Crete and in control of the palace at Knossos is the fact that Linear B has been found at Knossos and some other Cretan sites, as well as on the mainland. Since Linear B has been shown to be a script which records a Greek language, we can indeed assume that Greek speakers were part of the palatial administration of late Knossos. But does that mean that Crete was therefore conquered by Mycenaeans?

It is questionable. First, if the presence of Greek speakers on Crete represents some sort of migration from the mainland, there is a strong assumption that Greek was not already spoken on Crete. In truth, we know too little about the topic to say that it was or was not. Linear A has not been deciphered, and it could have been a representation of ancient Greek, or it could well have been that it represented just one of the languages on the island. Remember that Linear A was probably not a script limited to parts of Crete alone. We cannot say whether Crete was an island of one or multiple languages. With the noticed differences between various parts of the island as early as the pre-palatial, the possibility that more than one language was spoken on the island remains real. The strong connection between the mainland, Kythera, and Crete argues strongly for some sort of cultural koine, one aspect of which could well be Greek as a "lingua franca."

Unfortunately, the argument for the appearance of Mycenaeans on Crete relies too heavily on the assumption that the presence of Linear B means that they were there. This presents some significant problems, because it would mean that the Mycenaeans, who are then identified at Knossos as early as the first presence of Linear B in the mid-fifteenth century, must have been there already to have established the use of Greek as the language of administration. This means that the Mycenaeans would have to have been able to strategically conquer and govern a large part of Crete, when they were still evolving as competing families in the era of the grave circles.

However, the assumption that there were Mycenaean Greeks on Crete and that they were in charge of political and economic administration is often taken as a given, because of the Linear B material. Research on this period has basically focused on elucidating their presence by analysis of "Mycenaean features" such as warrior or militaristic themes appearing in art, "warrior graves," and megarons on Crete.[7] Unfortunately, this approach suffers from a false sense that we can equate artifacts with specific ethnic groups. Again, these chosen attributes, rather than identifying Mycenaeans, are common, shared attributes of the larger Aegean koine. Militaristic themes were appearing in art in general in the Aegean in the Late Bronze Age. Megara were not exclusively Mycenaean features and appear at various locations outside the Argolid.

In fact, recent research is now challenging the assumption that such features actually indicate a Mycenaean presence on Crete. Nafplioti (2008) has shown that assumed warrior graves at Knossos, which have been linked to invaders from Mycenae (Doxey 1987; Driessen 1990; Driessen and MacDonald 1984) actually contained locals and not Mycenaeans. We need to rethink the issue of Mycenaeans on Crete.

The Palaces Disappear

All was not well in the palaces on the mainland as early as 1250 BCE (for a good overview of the decline, see Deger-Jalkotzy 2008). Elite houses outside the walls at Mycenae were destroyed by fire, and in the next century the Mycenaean palaces were further weakened and finally disappeared. Early on, the citadel at Gla was destroyed by fire and not reoccupied. At the same time, in obvious reaction to some sort of growing danger, the palaces at Mycenae and Tiryns strengthened their fortifications. Both palaces also made attempts to secure access to water while

---

[7] Analysis has not been limited to just these major features. See also Blomberg and Henriksson (2005), Burke (2005), and Driessen (1994).

under siege, by linking springs outside the fortification walls through secret tunnels.[8] Back on Crete, the palace at Knossos faded from view in the thirteenth century (Doxey 1987).

Within 100 years the palaces were gone. Pylos fell, as well as Midea, and probably Thebes. We have some data which show that Mycenae perhaps, but Tiryns for certain, did manage a short comeback during that period, but it was unsuccessful. The danger which the palaces were fortifying themselves against apparently got the upper hand, because by ca. 1100 BCE the palaces ceased to exist.

Why this happened is still subject to speculation, and complicated by the fact that we do not have very tight chronological control for this period, control which would allow us to see trends and relationships between the disappearing palaces themselves. The best that can be said is that the destruction of the palaces took place around 1200 BCE. Explanations for their fall have been numerous: social unrest, disruption of commerce, invasion, drought, new people, or overspecialization.

Yet one of the more interesting explanations has to do with the larger Aegean involvement in social movements in the eastern Mediterranean (Cline 2015). This was a period of insecurity as Egyptian texts refer to seaborne raiders, such as the "Sea Peoples" (Oren 2000; Sandars 1978) who were attacking communities in the eastern Mediterranean. There were increasing interconnections between the Mycenaeans and the people on Cyprus and the Levant (for a good synthesis, see Voskos and Knapp 2008). There were also further connections with the Philistines, a people who were invading Canaan at that time and eventually establishing the cities of Philistia (Killebrew and Lehmann 2013; Yasur-Landau 2010). The exact relationship between the fall of the Mycenaean palaces and these movements in the eastern Mediterranean has not been fully understood. What we do know, however, is that by the time of these social movements in the more eastern part of the Mediterranean, Mycenae had been destroyed, as well as Pylos; Tiryns had been hit hard; Midea was destroyed by fire; and the palace at Thebes appears to have undergone a similar destruction.

The period right after the fall of the palaces, referred to as post-palatial, represents not so much a civilization collapse, but a cultural shift. That

---

[8] There is an additional argument (Broneer 1966, 1968) that remains of a large wall, which might have been planned to span the Isthmus of Korinth, was also a feature of this period of insecurity, but the argument has significant problems, in that it assumes that the Peloponnesos was trying to defend itself from an invasion coming from the east. There is absolutely no reason to assume such a scenario. It also does not make sense in that a wall could easily be circumnavigated by sea travel (see also Tartaron 2010).

shift was away from the palaces with all of their cultural features to a more dispersed cultural identification. What disappeared with the palaces? Linear B for one. The writing system was so enmeshed in the oversight of the palaces that it vanished with them. Ceramics also tell us about changes in other contexts as well. The Mycenaean kylix cup, which had been entrenched in official palace feasting, was also disappearing, to be replaced by the skyphos, a somewhat larger cup in general, which might indicate that feasting after the palaces was a smaller, more communal affair, with men sharing the same drinking vessel (Fox 2012). Likewise, the stirrup jar, which had become so much a part of palatial life in personal behavior and trade, was lost. As we shall see in the next chapter, much of what remained culturally in Greece was an extension of the lifeways of earlier Middle Helladic peoples, who were not so affected by the rise of the households of the palaces.

Measures of Social Complexity

The most important feature of this period, when it comes to understanding cultural complexity, is the fact that less complex cultures in the Argolid and Messenia were strongly affected by developing contact and inclusion into a larger Aegean koine. This inclusion brought about a measure of structural insecurity as various households were scrambling to establish positions for themselves in a quickly changing environment, as seen in the elaboration of funeral feasting. New institutions developed which grew from former domestic institutions, now operating to control the politics and the economies of these new mainland Greek polities. But, as we shall see, these new institutions were so embedded in the operating institutions of a household that they vanished with the disappearance of the palaces themselves.

Readings

An extremely interesting reconstruction of the faces of some of those buried in Grave Circle B was done by Musgrave et al. (1995). These reconstructions have even been able to single out family features. The corbeling system used in the tholos tombs represents a very high degree of architectural craftsmanship. For more on this topic, see Cavanagh and Laxton (1981, 1982). Those interested in further study of Mycenaean architecture should look at the construction at Gla. Not only was a citadel fortified, but an entire lake was drained to make a large agricultural plain. See Iakovidis and Threpsiades (2001) for a good description.

The explosion of Thera is continuing to attract scientific investigation. The best overview is Sigurdsson et al. (2006).

Recent discussion has also focused on the possibility of markets in Mycenaean Greece. Although we should not envision the Mycenaean economy as "market driven," the presence of markets within the Mycenaean world should not be denied. See Nakassis et al. (2011) and associated papers in same volume.

7   The Eleventh to Eighth Centuries
From Collapse to Created Chaos

We pick up our evolutionary thread again after the collapse of the Mycenaean polities in what has often been described as the Greek Iron Age (ca. 1050–800 BCE). By the eighth century much of Greece was adopting an entirely new social structure which was to become dominant for much of the Greek world until the end of the Roman Empire. My goal at this juncture is to frame the evolution of Greek culture during this period through the concept of complexity theory. For the next two chapters I will outline the nature of the social structure of ancient Greece before it was stimulated into chaos, and I will outline how that stimulus brought about a new social structure by the seventh century or shortly later. This chapter treats the period before the chaos, or that from the eleventh to the eighth centuries BCE. It focuses on the issue of the chaos and what might have caused it. The next chapter looks at the new institutions which evolved as the Greek world was moving toward a new form of social structure.

With the beginning of the Iron Age we can see several new developments in society. What follows are short descriptions of the most salient new social features.

Demographics

The old Mycenaean leadership was gone. What appears to have replaced it was a horizontal span of somewhat equally powerful leaders. We know that there was a decline in population in mainland Greece. Numerous surveys (i.e. Alcock et al. 2005) indicate that the amount of population decline from the Mycenaean period might have been as large as 60 percent. Snodgrass (1981) has argued that this represents a move away from settled village life to pastoralism. But support for this model is slim. Foxhall (1995) has built a solid argument for no significant change from sedentism in this period. It is also commonly held that the faunal sample from Nichoria (McDonald, Coulson, and Rosser 2013), one of our few studiable communities from this period, supported this change from sedentism to pastoralism. But there are significant problems. The sample is from only one household, hardly robust enough to be used for an overarching reconstruction of the economy of society in general, and preservation issues have biased the sample (Dibble and Fallu 2015).

While we can chart a population decline right after the disappearance of the palaces, there is evidence – growth of new settlements and a rise in the number of burials – to indicate that there was a rise in population which began in the eighth century and lasted to the fifth and fourth (Scheidel 2003). This population increase was not uniform throughout Greece; the rate in Attika differed from that in Boiotia, for example. But as a whole, Greece fit into a larger global rise in population which stretched from Iberia to Iran. We do not know exactly what produced such a population change, but one possibility is that there was a climatic change, which affected the health and subsistence of the Greeks (Grove and Rackham 2003; Scheidel 2003). From ca. 1000 BCE there was a significant climatic change in Europe and the Mediterranean. It became cooler and wetter. This could have had a positive effect on population growth in the Mediterranean as a cooler climate would ameliorate deaths due to intestinal diseases in hot summers and even out somewhat the interannual fluctuation in rainfall, thereby ensuring more consistent crop yields.

It is not easy to identify the impacts that this population increase had on Greek peoples in the archaeological record. But we could postulate that the opening up of new lands, as seen in the spread of settlement into uninhabited areas, might have produced some sort of change in the relations of production. As new lands were opened, either the elites became richer, with more dependents who would be working the new lands, or there was an increase in independent landholders (see Morris 2009).

Regionalism

We also know that there was a noticed degree of regionalism. Greece in the previous millennium was hardly a unified culture. Great differences existed between the Argolid, the Korinthia, Thessaly, and other locales. The Iron Age was no different in this regard. Several scholars (Coldstream 2003; Snodgrass 2000; Whitley 1991) have highlighted differences in artifacts between regions, which would represent regional preferences for design and the recognition of a shared style between workshops within different parts of Greece.

Close work within the area around Euboia has allowed Mazarakis-Ainian (1987, 1989) to suggest that he might have identified a regional architectural tradition. Here he has singled out a composition of parallel oval buildings (perhaps one for living, one for working), interspersed round structures, and a rectangular peribolos (encircling) wall which surrounds them all.

There could also have been possible differences in social structure between communities (Whitley 1991). Some regions appear to have been less stable than others; e.g. the stability of Athens contrasts to the transience of a settlement like Nichoria, which disappeared in the eighth century. Whitley takes a neoevolutionary view and would see structural differences between such polities as signs of Big Men societies occupying unstable polities. I am not inclined to put much value in the use of this type of analytical frame, but as I will describe it, the overall picture does indicate that leadership was weak, with leaders without formalized institutional ranking (Drews 1983) in the early years of this era.

New Ways of Feasting

Feasting was now no longer embedded in the political and economic institutions of the Mycenaean palaces. We have seen how feasting changed with the collapse of the palaces, when the use of the Mycenaean kylix cup, which was so attached to palace life, ceased. In general what evidence we have for feasting now comes from excavations of houses such as that at Nichoria, and Asine, the large elite tomb at Lefkandi, and perhaps megaron B at Thermon, a building which was probably the house of an elite household. So we are working with evidence of feasting in a few houses and a grand tomb. That said, there exists a general similarity in feasting in all these contexts. The presence of the krater (a wine and water mixing vessel) indicates that attention was paid to the mixing and the serving of the wine. An important difference between feasting associated with the Mycenaean palaces and this one is that drinking in this era appears to have included the practice of passing the drinking cup from person to person, similar to what we saw in the late third millennium BCE. The shape of oinochoai, skyphoi, kotylai, and "mugs" (Figure 7.1), often with two large handles, found in many of these contexts, indicates that drinking vessels were probably passed around from person to person, rather than serving an individual drinker, as is more likely with the smaller kylix cup of the Mycenaean palaces.

Introduction of Iron

One of the chief developments in this period was the introduction of iron working into Greece (the best overview to date remains

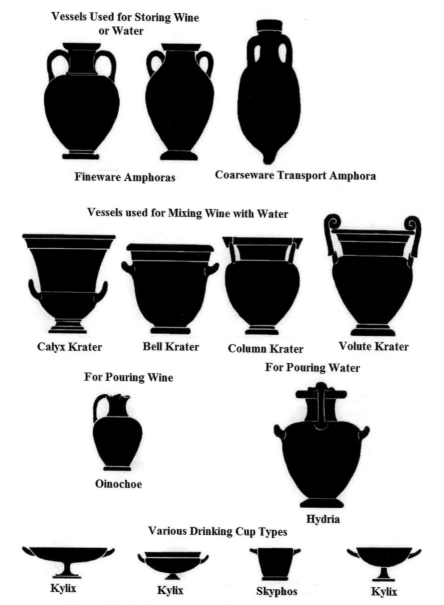

Vessels Used for Storing Wine
or Water

Fineware Amphoras   Coarseware Transport Amphora

Vessels used for Mixing Wine with Water

Calyx Krater   Bell Krater   Column Krater   Volute Krater

For Pouring Wine   For Pouring Water

Oinochoe

Hydria

Various Drinking Cup Types

Kylix   Kylix   Skyphos   Kylix

Figure 7.1 Greek feasting ware for the Iron Age and after. (Redrawn
from Schrieber 1999: appendices.)

Snodgrass 1999, 2000). When it comes to the appearance and use of iron in Greece at this time, Greece was not isolated, but fit into an ancient world which was shifting over to the use of iron generally. In fact, the use of iron was taking off in Greece from a slim beginning in the twelfth century. But the major share of our evidence for the use of iron comes from burials, where we come across an increasing number of iron weapons in the century between 1000 and 900 BCE.

The Return of Literacy

We do not fully understand how writing returned to ancient Greece. Our best evidence tells us that an alphabet was created from the Phoenician alphabet along similar lines in different parts of Greece in this period (Janko 2015). A look at the use of the early alphabet within Greece shows an amazing amount of similarity between the design of its letters among various peoples (Jeffery and Johnston 1990) (Figure 7.2). This suggests strongly that it was the result of a quick adaptation from the Phoenician, with some slight regional differences (Janko 2015), and that it spread quickly throughout ancient Greece.

The dates for the earliest use of the Greek alphabet are debated. It has been commonly held that its first appearance was in the eighth century. But there is some indication that its use can be pushed back to the later part of the ninth. Whatever the more correct date, there are a few different ideas on why the Greeks invented an alphabet at this time. Powell (1989, 1996, 2002, 2012) has argued that the introduction of the alphabet resulted from a push to transcribe the Homeric poems. But there is some debate over this issue. Rather than serving to record epic poetry, the function of the alphabet might have been more personal, often seen in inscriptions on cups (Whitley 2017). Archaeological evidence indicates strongly that different regions within ancient Greece used writing differently. In a careful study Whitley (2017) has distinguished these differences. In Attika we have evidence of writing on pottery with painted images, as well as tombstones and votives. In Euboia the use of writing was similar. Writing appears on drinking cups, kraters, and transport amphorai. The use of writing on Crete was different, however. Here writing was more or less limited to use in community inscriptions, which broadcast different community laws. There were also some inscriptions on Cretan pithoi.

The introduction of the alphabet also affected Greek oral tradition, which produced bards such as Homer and Hesiod. Written composition has often curtailed oral composition when it is introduced into cultures. While the case in Greece might not have been quite that straightforward,

Euboia	Ionia	Athens	Korinth	Modern
A	ΑΑ	ΑΑ	ΑΑ	A
B	B	B	ЏП	B
<C	Γ	Λ	C<	Γ
DD	Δ	Δ	Δ	Δ
ᚨE	ᚨE	ᚨE	ᛒ	E
Ϝ	-	Ϝ	Ϝ	(F)
I	I	I	I	Z
ΘH	ΘH	ΘH	ΘH	H
⊗⊕⊙	⊗⊕⊙	⊗⊕⊙	⊗⊕⊙	Θ
I	I	I	I	I
K	K	K	K	K
L	ΓΛ	L	ΓΛ	Λ
ᛗᛗM	ᛗM	ᛗM	ᛗM	M
ᚾN	ᚾN	ᚾN	ᚾN	N
X	Ŧ	(XϚ)	Ŧ	Ξ
O	O	O	O	O
ΓΓ	Γ	Γ	Γ	Π
M	-	-	M	(M)
Ϙ	Ϙ	Ϙ	Ϙ	(Ϙ)
P	PD	PR	PR	P
Ϛ	Ϛ	Ϛ	-	Σ
T	T	T	T	T
ᚱYV	YV	ᚱYV	ᚱYV	Y
ΦⲒ	Φ	ΦⲒ	ΦⲒ	Φ
ΨV	X	X	X	X
(ΦϚ)	ΨV	(ΦϚ)	ΨV	Ψ
-	Ω	-	-	Ω

Figure 7.2 Various regional forms of the Greek alphabet. (From www.webtopos.gr/eng/languages/greek/gre.anc_alphabets.htm; by permission of Alexandros A. Theodoropoulos.)

the introduction of an alphabet must have resulted in the disappearance of a great part of its oral tradition. When the Greek alphabet was in its initial stages of development, ancient Greece was probably the home of numerous oral bards, and there were numerous sung epics in what was probably a rich tradition (Snodgrass 1998). The advent of the alphabet must have eradicated much of this tradition. The effect of the arrival of the alphabet in Greece was the crystallization of only four major poems: the *Iliad* and the *Odyssey* by Homer and the *Theogony* and *Works and Days* (Athanassakis 2004) by Hesiod. With their preservation in written form, they were available to a wide readership among the Greeks, and in doing so provided a canon for stories of the Trojan War and wanderings around the Mediterranean, as well as one for the creation of the world and the "good life" of a farmer in ancient Greece. This canon was to have a profound effect on developments shortly after the arrival of the alphabet, as we shall see in the next chapter.

Our Analytical Frame

While a review of some major social developments in the Early Iron Age is important, my interest in this chapter and the next lies not so much in identifying these early social features, such as a decrease in population, the introduction of iron, etc., but in understanding the evolutionary development of Greeks in this period. From a rather inauspicious start in the later eleventh century, by the opening of the sixth century BCE Greece had undergone a dramatic evolution. Within its many poleis, that is, Greek city-states (Hansen 2006) and ethne (regional ethnic groups with internal political institutions; Mackil 2013), there were new or transformed institutions – councils, assemblies, funerals, markets, new religious practices, etc. – linked in ways which formed a new social structure. There is little evidence for a gradual evolution of this structure, and the change was rather sudden and total, coming in a period of about two to three centuries (Small 2018). Apparently, by the end of the sixth century there was a consensus as to what would structurally constitute a proper polis or ethnos. This type of evolution, when there is a rapid development of a new social structure, rather than a more piecemeal one, is similar to what we saw earlier in Crete and in the middle of the second millennium in the Argolid, Messenia, and Boiotia, when evolutionary change ran from structure to chaos to a return to structure. It is also what Yoffee described in his analysis of the rise of new social structure in early Mesopotamia. So it is complexity theory then to which I turn again to develop an analytical frame for the period from ca. 1000 to 600 BCE.

As I shall describe it, the start of the Iron Age, or the period right after the collapse of the palaces (ca. eleventh century BCE) was one within which the Greek world had a rather stable social structure which was affected by the stimulus of new wealth, which began to appear as early as the eighth century. This produced a period of structural chaos and associated social conflict. Sometime in the beginning of the seventh century there was a phase transition and we can begin to see the emergence of a structure which was to set the development of communities and their principal institutions for the next several centuries. In Chapter 8 I will outline the institutions which were created as a result of that stimulation and return to structure.

Aspects of Social Structure before Chaos

Since complexity theory allows us to highlight changes in social structure before and after phase transitions, I am going to first focus on what we know of the institutions shared by the Greeks before the change in the eighth century BCE. My sources will be archaeology and Greek poetry, specifically Homer. I will then address the issue of the stimulus. As we might expect, the issue of stimulation and the new institutions it produced is better understood as an effect which is compounding; that is, the results of stimulation are stimulating as well. In the rest of this chapter I will outline the Greek world before any stimulus produced a breakdown in that structure and how particular cultural contexts and dynamics produced the distinctive institutions and social structure of the sixth and following centuries. I start with an examination of social contexts and their institutions before the eighth century.

Institutions within the House

Our material evidence for domestic institutions in the Early Iron Age is thin. We have evidence from just a few sites, and there is no certainty that what these sites tell us can be applied to much of the Iron Age Greek world as a whole. Yet two sites provide us with some material, which, with an obvious caveat, can supply us with an image of what the houses were probably like in some communities, and what institutions they contained. They are Nichoria and Oropos.

Nichoria's Early Iron Age phase is represented by a small number of excavated houses. Perhaps the most famous is house IV-1, an apsidal (with an oval end) construction dating from the tenth century (Figure 7.3). The overall characteristics of its plan show that the house was essentially divided into two areas, with a space in between. One end

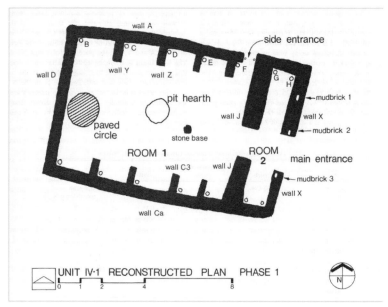

Figure 7.3 House at Nichoria. (From McDonald et al. 1983; figure 2-22;

of the structure is marked off with what could have been a porch, but easily an animal pen as well. If a porch, then those residing in the house would have had an intermediary space between their domestic space and that of the community. This would have provided a context for some sort of institution at the interface between household and town. The other room in the house was much larger and curved on its short end. An interesting feature of house IV-1 is the circular hearth in the main room. Some have labeled this an altar (Mazarakis-Ainian 1992), but there is very little strong evidence to suggest that its function was more than a hearth. It is most likely that this room housed feasting activities, between household members and also between household and outsiders. In general there is a correspondence between the inner room of this house and the hearth rooms of Middle Helladic houses, and the megara of the Mycenaean palaces, which would indicate a continuation of domestic institutions from these earlier periods.

Work at Oropos (Mazarakis-Ainian 1989) in northern Attika has uncovered similar domestic construction. Houses were apsed or oval, but with no clear separated area for community–household interaction. Houses at Oropos appear to have been grouped with other buildings, possibly housing various production activities, such as metalworking.

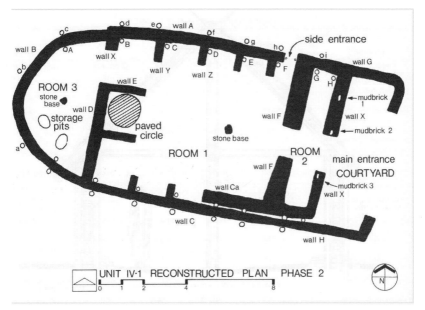

UNIT IV-1 RECONSTRUCTED PLAN PHASE 2

by permission of University of Minnesota Press.)

A peribolos, or wall, surrounded these grouped buildings. The exact function of the peribolos is not known, although it could have been to contain small livestock.

Although our information is still fragmentary, two observations can be made about houses in this early period, at least at Nichoria and Oropos. First, the layout of the houses, with one main room, shows that there was little internal spatial articulation of status, roles, or occupation in the household. Unless we consider the possibility that occupation of this area was allocated to different people at different times of the day, we would have to conclude that there was little attention paid to institutionalized segregation of males, females, children, slaves, visitors, etc. within the house. Second, there appears to have been no separate spatial context for the interface of the household with the rest of the community, although, in the one case of house IV-I, the porch, if a porch, could have housed some institution of this type. What institutional context existed for the purpose of household/outsider contact was mainly in the main room of the house, where the daily activity of the household took place. This would have made the prohibition of various members such as women and children from interacting with outsiders almost impossible. The institutions of household /outsider contact must have included all the household members.

Religious Ceremonies and Sacrifice

Our ability to understand religious institutions from this period is hampered by a lack of archaeological material which would correlate with religious practices. Yet the few religious contexts we have from this time present an extremely interesting picture. We have two locales for religious behavior, the house and the sanctuary. Mazarakis-Ainian (1992, 1997) has put forth an argument that we can witness a transformation of rulers' houses to official temples in many Iron Age communities. This is the type of argument we would find with the application of a chiefdom model to the Iron Age: the religious behaviours of the chief would evolve from his household to an independent community context. This is an interesting argument, but it contains some significant problems. The first is that Mazarakis-Ainian's methods for the identification of a ruler's house would have to be based on strong comparison to other dwellings in a community, and we do not have excavated sites which would give us that information. Second, his evidence for religious activity within the houses rests on evidence for feasting, possible benches for participants to sit on, and controversial and unsupported identification of altars within houses. Third, and very importantly, the argument that household ritual transforms into communal religion is here under-conceptualized. The issue is complex and not at all straightforward, involving considerations of the multiplicity and nature of domestic rituals as well as the nature of any transformation from a domestic or ancestor cult to a community cult (see overviews in McAnany 2002, 2014; Plunket 2002)

Public religious services were held in the open, and not associated with any temple, in this period. Homer, describing customs which must have been familiar to audiences of his time, supplies us with what we know of the services themselves (Kitts 2011). They were primarily sacrifices at a makeshift altar. The sacrifice was the killing of animals, the burning of part of the carcasses as an offering to the deity, the pouring of a libation, and a sprinkling of barley grouts into the flames.

One context in which open religious services were conducted was the sanctuary. There were two types, that within a polis and that which was shared by several poleis. For this early period most of our information comes from intercommunity sanctuaries. Several important sanctuaries can trace their birth to this period, and a few appear to be continuations of sanctuaries from Mycenaean and earlier periods. In two cases we have good evidence for Iron Age cult sites continuing earlier cult practice. That is, the material indicates that there was earlier religious feasting on the site.[1] At the sanctuary of Apollo at Kalapodi in Phokis (Felsch 1996, 2007; McInerney 1999), excavation has uncovered an LH IIIC (twelfth century BCE) cult building under part of the later sixth-century temple. In Arkadia recent excavation has revealed early cult activities at the sanctuary of Zeus at Mount Lykaion (Romano and Voyatzis 2010), a famous sanctuary rumored to have been the birthplace of Zeus and also the locus of human sacrifice in later Greek times. The cult might well date from at least 3000 BCE.

One of Greece's most famous sanctuaries, Olympia, is not so old, and can trace its ancestry only to the ninth century (Morgan 1990).[2] Located in the western Peloponnesos, in the region of Elis, the sanctuary in this early part of the Iron Age offered up terracotta figurines of Zeus and small bronze figurines dating to the ninth century. These appear to have been votive offerings, as were large bronze tripod cauldrons, which might date from this early period as well. The bronze figurines were mainly bovine, suggesting strongly that herding was an important agricultural pursuit, and thereby dedicated by cattle-owning Greeks. The sanctuary had not yet adopted its role as an athletic complex. Its role was most likely focused on the worship of Zeus (and possibly other deities, such as Hera) and elite feasting. Zeus presumably had an altar, traces of which might well have been the famous ash altar, referred to by the second-century CE travel writer Pausanias.

Sanctuaries are critical institutional contexts for the evolution of ancient Greece because one of their additional functions was to provide a neutral space for elites from different communities to gather. This function can be seen in the later athletic contests, held at not only Olympia, but Delphi, Nemea, Isthmia, and elsewhere, which were often dominated by Greek elites, but this role must have been operational in the early years of the Iron Age as well. The ability to leave one's own community and travel to a peripheral center like Olympia must have been a privilege to those who could afford to leave their homesteads. The fact that the dedication of expensive bronze tripods began in the ninth century also supports this conclusion, and also indicates that one of the things elites did when they visited Olympia was engage in feasting. The tripod has a long history of use in formalized feasting among the Greeks (see Gimatzidis 2011 for evidence from other sanctuaries).

---

[1] There is a possible third case, the sanctuary of Poseidon at Isthmia, but the material showing a continuity of cultic practice is problematic. See Morgan (1999).

[2] Mycenaean material has been excavated at the site, but its context is one of mixed debris, and we do not have a good understanding of the relationship of this material to later periods. See Eder (2001).

Who were the elites coming to the early sanctuary of Olympia? Morgan (1990) is probably right in identifying those coming as traveling from communities in Arkadia, Messenia (notably Nichoria), and the Argolid. In her view, those from Arkadia would have been dedicating the early terracotta and bronze figurines, while those from communities more distant would have dedicated more elaborate pieces, such as the bronze cauldrons.

In all of these cases – Kalapodi, Mount Lykaion, and Olympia – it appears that the sanctuary was serving as a focal point for meeting and communication between people in different communities within the regions around the sanctuaries. As noted, most of the early evidence for activity at the sanctuaries is related to feasting, which suggests a context geared toward communication and exchange. Most importantly, the sanctuary was serving as a context for institutions which would establish and perpetuate relationships between people from different communities. These relationships could be based on equality or inequality. The mechanism for these types of relationships would have been some sort of recognized gift giving.

Funeral Practices

For funeral practices from this period we can use the Homeric epics, Hesiod, and excavated graves to give us an image of what funerals were like and the range of differences among them. Homer describes the funerals of elites, so our knowledge of what funeral practices were like from his epics is somewhat biased. But the funeral of Patroklos (Homer, *Iliad*, Books 23–24), the friend of Achilles, gives us a lot of information. In this funeral, Patroklos was cremated on a pyre. The ceremony involved covering his body with strips of animal fat, sacrificing animals (dogs and horses), and even people to be placed on the pyre with the deceased, the pouring of libations, and the placement of hair cut from other men onto his body. His bones were gathered after the fire was quenched, placed in an urn, again wrapped in fat, and housed in a tumulus. Similar depictions are found in other parts of the *Iliad* and the *Odyssey*.

It would appear that elite funerals were often followed by institutionalized funeral games. The fact that Hesiod mentions that his sung composition, *Works and Days*, won a prize at the funeral games of Amphidamas supports this observation. Although there appears to have been no span of time between the actual funeral and the games for Patroklos, because all the competitors were already at Troy, we can safely assume that funeral games were held sometime after the funeral itself.

This would allow elite competitors time to travel from different communities to compete in the games. Homer's depiction of the games for Patroklos indicates that some of the contests in this period were chariot racing, boxing, wrestling, javelin throwing, foot racing, and archery.

While Homer provides us with a depiction of an elite funeral, the burial record of the Iron Age supplies us with a larger picture of funeral practices. However, while we have some relatively good information from a few well-excavated cemeteries from this period, it is difficult to extend that information to help us fill out what the *entire* range of funeral celebrations would have been. The burial record varied from community to community, with cremation or inhumation being a key distinction. There was, however, a general trend toward cremation in most communities. Furthermore, we know from eighth-century amphorai that the funeral celebration, at least in its idealized form, was a protracted process, which included much more than graveside behavior. Large amphorai and kraters which served as grave monuments at Athens depict some of the features of funerals at this time (Kurtz and Boardman 1971). Some of what is depicted on these vessels is the prothesis, or the laying-out of the body. This exhibition of the dead is attended by male and female mourners, often seen either beating their breasts or pulling out their hair. On some vases there are also depictions of children. We also see the ekphora, or procession with the dead to the cemetery. This is displayed as similar to the prosthesis, in that we often see mourners as well. The body appears to have been pulled on a wagon. There is also a shroud over the body. In a lower register on several of these vases is a row of chariots and drivers. This could well be a representation of a funeral game.

The burial evidence we have (excluding Knossos on Crete, which I will examine in Chapter 9) comes primarily from Athens (good overviews remain Morris 1990; Whitley 2003) and Lefkandi (Catling et al. 1991; Popham et al. 1980). Each community presents slightly different burials which must have reflected accepted burial customs at each community. At Athens we have a mixture of cremated and inhumed burials, with the inhumations being somewhat earlier than cremations. The cremations, which come after the sub-Mycenaean (late eleventh-century) burials, supply us with evidence of male and female differences in burial symbols. The majority of burial urns of neck-handled amphorai are male burials, while women were buried in belly-handled amphorai. The grave itself consisted of a trench and a lower pit for the placement of the urn amphora. Debris such as burnt animal bone and broken pottery often lie in the trench and indicate some type of funeral feasting. Graves were distinguished above-ground by either raising a mound or marking the burial with standing stone slabs, large amphorai or large kraters.

In Athens it also appears that subadults were not cremated but simply inhumed.

Box 8   Our First Centaur?

A centaur was a mythological creature who was half man and half horse. The ceramic centaur shown in Figure 7.4, dating to the tenth century BCE, was found in two tombs at the site of Lefkandi. The head came from the bottom of tomb 1, which appears to have been that of a female, and the rest of the body was laid on cover slabs on tomb 3, thereby indicating that it was used as a dedication. The creature stands approximately 36 centimeters high. Its left arm and tail are missing. The body itself is a wheel-thrown cylinder, which explains the hole at navel height in the front. Such holes served as vents during firing. It seems relatively certain that this centaur represents Kheiron,

Figure 7.4 Ceramic centaur from Lefkandi burial. (From https://commons.wikimedia.org/wiki/File:Centaur_Chiron_of_Lefkandi,_Archaeological_museum_of_Eretria,_Greece.jpg, CC BY-SA 3.0; accessed 7/17/2018.)

Box 8   (*cont.*)

the legendary wise instructor of heroes and children, who had six fingers, noted on the right hand of this artwork. A gash on the left leg further ties this statuette to Kheiron, who was injured by Herakles in this spot. Centaurs might well have had some association with the training of children in real life, and the head of this statuette may well have been part of a child's funeral. This may be one of the first representations of centaurs who became part of Greek mythology. Some similar centaur representations come from tenth-century finds on the island of Cyprus.

For further details, see Bremmer (2012), Desborough et al. (1970), and Langdon (2007).

The other sizable quantity of information we have comes from Lefkandi. Mortuary material indicates that there were some significant differences in graveside behavior between Athens and this community. The excavators were able to identify more than eighty pyres within the cemetery. Many of these pyres represent the burning of the dead within the grave, a custom rarely seen in Athens at this time. In addition, the use of a burial urn was not common, the ash remains of the deceased being placed directly in the grave, along with burnt grave goods.

The most striking information from Lefkandi is the large building at the Toumba (Figure 7.5), or burial mound, which was used as a burial for an elite man and woman (Popham et al. 1993). The building was extremely large for its time. Approximately 50 × 14 meters in size, it is the largest building we have from this early period in Greece. From a purely architectural standpoint this building is important, because it shows us that in this time, monumentality in architecture was achieved by elongation of a building, rather than increasing its height

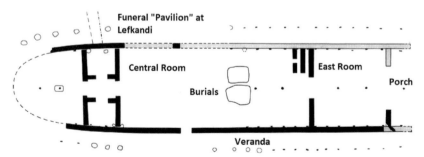

Figure 7.5 Funeral pavilion at Lefkandi. (Redrawn from Popham et al. 1993: plate 5.)

or breadth. The architect was obviously working within the technological limitations of the Iron Age.

That being said, the building was still impressive. Its outer walls sat on a stone socle (foundation course) of rubble masonry with facing stones. The wall itself, which was built of mud brick, was lined on its inner face with a row of wooden posts. All walls, except for that on the east side, were surrounded by a veranda of wooden posts, which gave support to the extension of a thatch roof. Along the center of the building ran a row of posts which must have supported cross beams in the roofing system.

This large building was also subdivided. On its east there was a porch, and an east room of similar size to its west. This room gave access to the central room, the largest space within the building. Continuing west from the center room, one would have come to two small rooms lying against the north and south walls, which provided a narrow corridor leading back to an apsed room on the western end of the building.

In its overall plan – use of a porch, a main room, and a back apsidal room – this structure incorporates spaces which we have already seen in domestic architecture, such as in the house at Nichoria. Finds from excavation, however, did not yield much information on the functions of these spaces at Lefkandi. Pits in the floor of the apsidal room might have been dug-out supports for pithoi, but we have little else to help us recreate the functions of the other rooms.

The great exception to this is the burials in the central room. In this room there were two pits which held human and horse burials. The southern pit contained the remains of a man and a woman. The man was cremated and his ashes and bones were stored in a bronze amphora, which was an heirloom, and probably came from Cyprus. Next to him lay a woman who was inhumed. Obviously an elite, she was buried with golden jewelry and even a golden breastplate. In a pit to the north of this couple were the skeletons of three horses. Their presence indicates that there was an elaborate mortuary ritual, probably involving feasting, where the status of the interred was created by the deliberate destruction of such prestige animals (also seen in Tomb 68 in the same cemetery; Popham et al. 1980). Since the construction was quickly covered over by a mound, which must have been the original intention of those conducting the funeral, I would argue therefore that the building was actually a very elaborate funeral pavilion, rather than a house or a tomb itself. In that sense, the large krater put next to the burial shafts, and the pieces of cooking pot, would also have been part of a mortuary celebration within the pavilion itself.

The people interred in this building were obviously members of an elite stratum in Early Iron Age society. And they had access to imported prestige goods. The burial amphora comes from Cyprus, is an heirloom, and was decorated with an elaborate scene of hunting on its rim. Contact with other cultures is not limited to evidence from the pavilion. Graves within the cemetery at large have yielded imports from the Near East and Egypt. As Antonaccio (2006) argued, this use of imported prestige items, coupled with the fact that some items are antiques, gives support to the conclusion that negotiation of status through the funeral context at Lefkandi was based on possession of foreign prestige goods and a claim on the past (the antiques). Notably here, the claim on the past is not one which seeks any identification with the earlier Mycenaean period. The claim is totally owned and created by the Iron Age elites.

Box 9   A Warrior Grave

Around 900 BCE a man in his mid-thirties was cremated, his ashes put into an urn, and the urn buried on a hill, the Aeropagos, next to the agora or eventual marketplace of ancient Athens (see Figure 7.6). This well-preserved

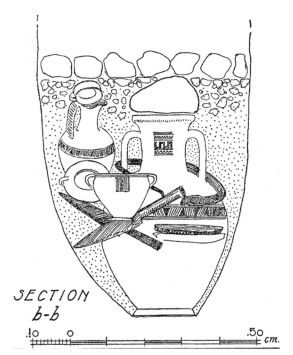

Figure 7.6 Areopagos warrior grave. (From Blegen 1952: figure 2, by permission of the American School of Classical Studies at Athens.)

Box 9   *(cont.)*

burial provides us with a window into what an elite male would have needed in the Greek afterlife. The grave goods were put into a cloth bundle and placed on top of the burial urn at the moment of interment. The character of the grave goods is both militaristic and commensal. The man took several fighting implements with him into the next world, socketed spear heads, a broad axe head, a javelin point, two knives, and an iron sword, which has been "ritually killed" by bending it around the top of the burial urn, thus making it useless. It was important that this warrior keep his weapons sharp, so there was also a whetstone in the bundle. He must have been rich enough to have owned horses, which he might well have rode in battle, because horse bits were also put into the grave. On a lighter side, those who buried this man also included in the burial an oinochoe, that is, a wine pitcher, and three kantharoi, two-handled drinking cups, which would have been used in the afterlife to drink wine with friends.

As a final, but important observation, we note that there was a close association of the institution of combat and that of funerals. The period from 900 to 700 BCE was a time of noticeable burials with men interred with two or three spears and elements of protective armor. These graves are referred to as "warrior graves," although there is no overwhelming need to see military prowess in the appearance of weapons within the grave (an important issue which lacks close study, but see Antonaccio 1995: 241–43). It looks to be more of a customary identity for men. The earliest example we have to date comes from Lefkandi. There are even whole suits of armor buried with some individuals. The cemetery at Argos has a number of them.

Institution of Warfare/Battle

The paucity of material from earlier periods did not allow us to discuss the institution of warfare/battle with any profit for their cultures. It is when we enter into the Iron Age that we can for the first time speak somewhat adequately about this institution, even if the picture is not as detailed as we would like. Here we draw on military artifacts and the descriptions of battle from the epics of Homer. Some weapons which have come down to us as artifacts do show that basic hand-to-hand fighting in battle was carried out with a sword. Individuals may well have protected themselves with body armor: greaves on the shins, helmets, and some type of torso protection. A famous grave from eighth-century Argos contained torso armor, which looked like a cuirass or breastplate from later Greece. The javelin was also used. This was not considered a spear, but was probably thrown in combat.

What the actual social institution of battle was is hard to tell. The *Iliad* is filled with depictions of combat. Until recently, the common opinion was that the manner of fighting was centered on one-to-one engagement. Elites would ride out to the field on chariots, dismount, and fight elite opponents. Careful study of the Homer's works, however (van Wees 2004), has shown that the soldiers, although they might have been led by leaders who would engage in this type of one-to-one combat, were grouped as infantry into fighting units, called phalanges (singular: phalanx). What form these units took is not knowable with any certainty. The fact that the soldiers were using javelins, however, strongly indicates that they were massed in open order, that is, with about an arm's length of space between each man. We have no good information on the internal strategy of battle between opposing phalanges.

Most of the combatants were massed in the infantry. While cavalries probably existed, and were even seen as the principal fighting method until 700 BCE by Aristotle, we have little evidence for their use in this period. In front of the infantry were probably stationed individual fighters, the heroes of the *Iliad*, who more than likely resembled skirmishers, advanced individuals who would fight ahead of the infantry's line. Within formation there was probably a sense of common purpose, with an allegiance to the reason for the conflict (revenge, dominance, family or other larger kinship ties, etc.), through the leaders who would have been fighting in front.

The purpose of warfare in this period was probably not linked to Homer's recall of a heroic fight with Troy, but, as men like the old king Nestor in the *Iliad* relates, to raids on other families and communities to secure cattle and other goods for profit. These raids might well have established regularized transfers of goods between different communities, and thereby cemented intercommunity relationships.

Institutions of Leadership and Power

As mentioned in the previous chapter, the construction of social power was no longer associated with connections to those in the palaces. With the palaces gone, the upper echelon of society was absent and communities must have resembled somewhat those of the Middle Helladic (first suggested by Snodgrass 2000: 385). A good term for understanding the creation of leadership and power after the palatial collapse is that of "reboot" (Antonaccio 2016; Galaty et al. 2016). Palatial hierarchy was gone, and what remained were less hierarchical reciprocal relationships between individuals and families. Intensification and manipulation of these relationships, often in feasting contexts, by the use of prestige goods and claims to important ancestry (Antonaccio 2002, 2006), produced unequal relationships of power and status. In addition to this mechanism, individual positions of leadership and power could also be enhanced by leadership skills themselves.

Possible community leaders are very hard to identify in the archaeological record of this period. The excavators of Nichoria (McDonald et al. 2013) have seen house IV as the house of a community leader, here specifically a chief, because of its large size. Yet the identification is extremely problematic. To single out house IV as exceptional requires that we have adequate knowledge of the variety in size of most of the houses from this period at Nichoria. It also requires us to have already established a firm equation between house size and community leadership. That vital equation is overlooked and has been shown to be extremely problematic (Souvatzi 2008; Wilk 1983). Mazarakis-Ainian (1992, 1997) claimed that he has been able to isolate the community rulers' houses in several communities by isolating features which would have made the houses places for religious gatherings for people in the community. But his argument is plagued by an overeager aim to identify religious functions in these houses on questionable reconstructions of the interiors of these "rulers' houses."

While our ability to reconstruct leadership institutions within Iron Age communities through architectural analysis is somewhat limited, important information on these institutions comes from the works of the seventh-century BCE singer of epics, Hesiod, and our somewhat earlier oral poet, Homer. Hesiod supplies us with a wealth of information on his century in his short epic poem, the *Works and Days*, which was written about daily life in Greece. The Homeric material is a bit different, in that it pulls images from times as early as the Mycenaean period, but also builds a world which is thoroughly descriptive in much of its social structure of the eighth century BCE (see Finley 1991; Morris 1986; Snodgrass 1974).

Both these epic singers provide us with several leadership roles, most often focused in the basileus (Crielaard 2011). He was probably a local leader who held power through a variety of means: two of the more important being the power of his estate and his personal ability to lead in various contexts. Society during this period was horizontally segmented, composed of similar units of basileus-led people (Drews 1983). Leadership among basileis was not fully instituted. For example, Agamemnon was the principal basileus among the Greeks at Troy, because his wife, Helen, was taken by Paris, but he apparently held no formalized rule over the other basileis. This is interesting, because he takes the title of wanax, which might well show that the earlier Mycenaean wanax's power was poorly felt outside the limits of his controlled estates. This basileus-type of leadership existed in the Middle Helladic period and is represented by the *qa-si-re-u* from Linear B texts (Palaima 1995). There were no hard institutionalized functions for the basileus. From Homer we recognize that the prominent basileis such as Odysseus, Agamemnon, and Achilles possessed no institutionally recognized competence or responsibilities. Leadership in arbitration or fighting came from personal skills.

Two other sociopolitical institutions are described in the epics as well, the council and the assembly. In both of these men would meet to discuss issues, often brought forward by a leader. The council was an assembly of leaders. The assembly was a congress of a larger group of men, most of whom were not leaders. It is important to note that in each case, the council and the assembly were actually more reactive than active. The council could be called by a leader to seek advice or to carry out the ideas of the leader, as in the council of the Phaiakians in the *Odyssey*, who were persuaded to carry out the will of the king to give Odysseus a ship with men so he could sail home. The council could also meet in conjunction with the assembly so that the assembly would be persuaded to give assent to the council's decisions. There is some evidence that meetings themselves were at least somewhat institutionalized. That is, they met in a regular assigned place, the agora, and they were usually called by heralds, who also controlled the behavior of the assembly. There is no evidence that the assembly was a group that could initiate action. It was mainly a reactive institutionalized body of men, a very important point to which I shall return .later.

Economic Institutions

In this period a great deal of economic activity was embedded in the institution of gift exchange. We saw that some early intercommunity meeting places, such as Olympia, probably served as loci for this type of behavior. Within the obligations involved in this exchange came ties which could be used economically later on. Subsistence assistance would have been part of this activity. While intercommunity settings such as Olympia or Kalapodi could have served as places for such institutions, we also have the field of battle. In Homer's epics, at least, it was an arena of gifting: there are several examples of gift exchange between elites in his epics (Donlan 1982, 1989a). From an anthropological perspective it is possible to argue that this was a reciprocal gift-exchange economy which existed probably primarily between ancient Greek elites. Morris (1989) has argued that the appearance of iron in early graves reveals a gift exchange relationship between elites.

The presence of overseas trade goods, which were not necessarily prestige items, shows that there were markets in Greece in this time period. In fact, a rather strong argument (Tandy 2000) has been put forth that people, such as the "warrior" we saw in the elite burial at the Toumba at Lefkandi, were engaged in trade and markets. The fact that there were markets, however, does not carry over to a conclusion that all or even part of the Greek economy was market-driven. Markets functioned, but were not principal players, in the driving force behind commerce.

Chaos and Change

What held these various institutions together was a social structure built on established relationships (defined community social roles) between various people within Greek settlements. But in the eighth century these established relationships could not deal with the rise of new wealth and new social statuses. This was a chaotic period, when various Greek communities were experiencing internal strife, which often resulted in community fissioning. This fissioning is seen in the spread of Greek communities throughout the Mediterranean and Black Seas. This exodus was an answer to the inability of the established social structure with its limited social relationships to deal with the rise of new wealthy households who had gained wealth and new status, and the resulting conflict between elite households this must have engendered.[3]

The situation in Greece paralleled similar social scenarios in other ancient cultures. One of the most common is the example of cycling chiefdoms among the Mississippian cultures of North America (Blitz 1999). Here factional leaders, fighting for limited community positions, often hived off with their retainers and founded new villages (Barrier and Horsley 2014). The situation in Greece must have been similar. Historians such as Lintott (1982) have noted that the force of violence between

---

[3] Tandy's analysis of this period (2000) sees the rise of new wealth and access to prestige goods as due to the rise of markets, where the creation of wealth and social position was not automatically embedded in any institutionalized relationship between people (formalized gift exchange, for example), thereby providing an opportunity for new households to become wealthy and make social claims. But the use of the market model might be applying institutional analogues which pertain more to the present than the Greek past.

powerful factions fighting for positions of power in polities within Greece provided an impetus for the exit of a rival leading faction. Bandy (2004) reconstructs a similar case for communities in the Formative period (1500–250 BCE) of Bolivia's Titicaca Basin. In those villages there was increasing intragroup conflict. Such conflict can, as Turner earlier observed (1957), stem from competition between ambitious leaders in a community. Since the social structure of these communities could not mitigate this conflict, the villages fissioned. It was not until later in the Formative period that new institutions, here those related to public ceremonialism, rose which could counteract fissioning, by providing a context for social integration between conflicting members of the community.

It used to be held that one of the chief reasons for the appearance of this fissioning in ancient Greece was population pressure in the eighth century and later. But recent work in ancient Greek demographics has challenged this concept (Scheidel 2003). The results of this study are also supported by further ethnographic observations that communities can fission from intragroup conflict before any fissioning threshold in population size has been reached (Rappaport 1968).

The reason for this chaos and strife was new wealth and accompanying new social statuses. Like the situation in Yoffee's early Mesopotamia, new wealth and new social status now held by people without a community-recognized privileged social position presented a significant problem to Greek communities for many years, as we can see in Hesiod's biting eighth-century observation that wealth precedes community status in his day (*Works and Days* 313) and Solon's sixth-century attempts to give the new wealthy a position within the power structure of Athens (for a good overview of the results of Solon's legislation, see Osborne 1985).

There were two sources for this wealth and new status. The first was the movement of people into uncultivated tracts of land, which were abandoned after the fall of the palaces. This would have produced new wealth for families who were expanding their agricultural holdings. The second is the increasing contact and exchange that the Greeks were having with other cultures in the Mediterranean. This would have been a situation similar to that of the era of the Mycenaean grave circles, when Mycenaean families were gaining in wealth and social status from contact with the larger Late Bronze koine in the Aegean. This contact would have produced wealth from the trade itself, but also higher status within certain contexts, from the display of prestige goods. Foreign contact itself played a major role in social life even shortly after the collapse of the palaces. The use of foreign prestige goods in status negotiation in funeral contexts is seen in a rather well-preserved cemetery, Perati in

Attika (Iakovidis 1980). This cemetery dates to LH IIIC (twelfth century), and the graves themselves include prestige goods, which were imports from the Cyclades, Cyprus, the Levant, and Egypt. As we have seen, excavation of the later cemetery at Lefkandi has shown connections between the Euboians and the Near East and Egypt. Many of the graves contain imported prestige goods such as lyre-player seals from north Syria.

Foreign trade must also have produced wealth, and this begins as early as the trading, perhaps even pirating, ventures of the Euboians, who were active in trade in the eastern Aegean and Near East at least in the ninth and eighth centuries BCE. In several communities in this region we have found traces of classic Euboian ninth-century pottery, notably the half-circle skyphos and plate (Figure 7.7). But there is also strong evidence that the Euboians were striking out as early as the tenth century. Early Euboian pottery is known from Skyros (Lemos

Figure 7.7 Euboian skyphos. (From Metropolitan Museum of Art, Accession Number 74.51.589, CC0 1.0; Public Doman Dedication.)

2002; Lemos and Hatcher 1986). More evidence for this early trade can be seen in the discovery of Euboian pottery – bowls and skyphoi, therefore feasting ware – in Cyprus as early as the later tenth century and a continuation of Euboian ware and Levantine ware at selected early sites in Greece into the next century.

It is highly likely that those who transported this ware were Greeks, although we cannot rule out the possibility of Phoenicians also sailing with Greek goods (the issue of merchants is debatable; see Papadopoulos 1997, 2011). The presence of lyre seals, however, which were produced in northern Syria and appear only in Greek settlements with no Phoenician ware, argues strongly that Greeks were involved in bringing eastern products to other cities in their own culture. Ancient historians tell of an Ionian migration, in which Ionians from Attika migrated to the shores of western Asia Minor perhaps as early as the twelfth to eleventh centuries. If so, then the Euboians at least either were part of the migration or were following already established cultural connections, in the islands and lands of eastern Anatolia.

This trade was an early stimulus to social change in Euboia. Crielaard (2006) has nicely outlined how, in the graves at Lefkandi, social differentiation increases along with the number of exotic eastern goods in the graves over time. Contact, and the distinct possibility that many of these "traders" were elites and possibly close to our sense of pirates, can therefore provide a stimulus to social change.

Euboia was early but it was not alone. There was ever-increasing contact, trade, and the incorporation of foreign materials into Greek life as time progressed. By the eighth century we have evidence for Greeks in close contact with cultures of not only Anatolia, but the Levant and Egypt. This contact, coupled with the use of Orientalizing (eastern-styled) materials by the Greeks, was to become one of the chief means by which Greek households were to try and distinguish themselves in the Iron Age (see Morris 1999 for a window into this issue).

During this period the sense of social uncertainty must have been high, and we can see several measures taken to reduce it. It was at this time that we have evidence for new attention being paid to funeral feasting, just as we would expect from our study of these similar periods among the peoples of the second half of the second millennium BCE. There is evidence for feasting elaboration in funerals at Athens and Argos during the eighth century. At Argos it has been noted that the greatest amount of feasting ware – obeloi (roasting spits), large kraters, and skyphoi – lies in the eighth century (Whitley 1991: 190–91, with mentioned references). At Argos elaborate funeral feasting might well have had a distinct connection to the ideology of battle, because this century at Argos also witnesses the highest number of pieces of military equipment in the burials. At Athens, there was a tremendous rise in the number of serving dishes deposited in burials during the eighth century, mirroring the case at Argos but in ceramics (Belletier 2003; Houby-Nielsen 1992).

Feasting elaboration is also matched by the appearance of tomb cults. Beginning in the tenth century, but seeing its greatest occurrence in the eighth, was the start of tomb cults where people of the Iron Age would honor the deceased in selected late Helladic graves, up to 400 years old (the best treatment is Antonaccio 1995).[4] There have been several explanations for this phenomenon, ranging from a move from pastoralism to domestication (making claims to land through honoring its dead) or colonizing portions of Greece such as Attika (making similar claims as people move out of an urban context to one which is rural), but one of the strongest is that which sees the use of early tombs in later funerals as means through which different families would enhance the power of the funeral to gain social or even political position in periods of fluid internal community structure. The fact that it occurred in the mid- to late eighth century, when the Greek world was in a "chaotic" state, cannot be held to coincidence. The work of Hayden (2009) is the most instructive here. He demonstrates the fact that of all the contexts of a society, that of the funeral is the most powerful in building alliances and creating social position.

Community Fissioning: The Start of Greek Settlement Expansion

This disjunction between social status and social position in the community engendered intracommunity conflict, and many Greek households left their communities. This must not have been limited to households of elevated social status alone, but to other households as well, who would have ties with these households. The product of this community fissioning was the overseas expansion of Greek peoples. From the eighth to the fourth centuries BCE Greek communities founded more than 140 settlements in the Mediterranean and the Black Sea (Figure 2.1). A large number of communities were involved, with families from Khalkís, Miletos, and Korinth establishing the greatest number of settlements.

---

[4] This is not to be confused with hero cult, which was an entirely different institution. Hero cult was not like tomb cult in that it was practiced by large corporate groups, such as the population of a polis. While it served to honor a legendary individual of the earlier Mycenaean period, it was not tied to any tomb and represents the intentions of a community, rather than those of a family.

But the Greeks were not alone. The history of the Greek settlements involves the Phoenicians at an early period (for research on Phoenician colonization, see Aubet 2001; Zalloua et al. 2008). A little earlier in their explorations than the Greeks, the Phoenicians, coming from cities such as Tyre, set up a trading colony on Cyprus, Kition, ca. 820 BCE, and there is evidence for a Phoenician presence on Crete in a ninth-century Phoenician temple excavated at the southern Cretan settlement of Kommos. In a larger picture the Phoenicians established settlements not only in the Mediterranean but also on the Atlantic seaboard, at the early towns of Gadir (Cadiz) and Lixus in Spain. But the Atlantic was only a piece of the picture, as the Phoenicians quickly set up settlements throughout the western Mediterranean. Carthage was the most powerful and best known of all the Phoenician settlements, but there were other important settlements on the North African coast, in Sardinia, and in the western half of Sicily. The Greeks were to follow suit.

Greek overseas settlements can be divided into emporia (trading settlements) and apoikiai, or poleis which had agricultural settlers, who divided up the hinterlands for occupation. One of the most famous of the Greek emporia was Naucratis in Egypt (Coulson and Leonard 1979, 1982). The city was founded in the sixth century BCE in the western half of the Nile Delta. It served as an important trading connection for commerce between the Greek world and Egypt. Several Greek polities, were instrumental in its foundation: Xios, Klazomenai, Phokaia, Rhodes, Halikarnassos, Knidos, Phaselis, Mytiline, Miletos, Samos, and Aigina. There may have been additional Greek emporia in the eastern Mediterranean. The famous British archaeologist Sir Leonard Woolley argued that the city of Al Mina in coastal Syria housed a sizable population of Greeks. The archaeological remains from this city indicate that it rose in the eighth century BCE, and Woolley identified a large quantity of Greek pottery, Euboian, Korinthian, Athenian, and others. The permanent presence of Greeks in this city has been questioned, however. There is no evidence for any burials identified with Greeks, nor has any of the domestic architecture been tied to ancient Greeks. For the moment, it appears best to consider Al Mina as an emporium for trade between the Near East and Greek lands, but not a site of lasting Greek occupation (a good review of the problem is Waldbaum 1997).

The situation in the western Mediterranean was quite different. Greeks here were starting settlements along the earlier sea lanes which they had begun to use in trade in the western Mediterranean. Many settlements were placed along strategic sailing lanes between the Greek mainland and the west. This suggests strongly that there must have been contact and trade before settlement, but solid evidence for this concept is not easily found (Graham 2001). The first evidence we have for the spread of Greek peoples westward is from the eighth-century community of Greeks at Pithekoussai, on the island of Ischia, just off the Campanian coast. The settlement on Pithekoussai was probably more of an emporium than an apoikia. The island itself is poorly suited to agriculture. Some evidence of Phoenician material in some of the burials at this site betrays a possible collaboration between the Greeks and Phoenicians here (Docter and Niemeyer 1994; Greco 1994).

Over the next three centuries the Greeks were to establish hundreds of apoikiai in the west in south Italy and Sicily, eastern Iberia, and southern France. The famous city of Marseilles was founded as the settlement Massalia by Phokaians. The spread of Greeks was not limited to the western Mediterranean. The northern shore of Africa, in what is now Libya, was settled with several apoikiai, the most famous being Kyrene. The northern Aegean and the Black Sea, as far as the Khalkis Mountains, were also to see Greek expansion (Tsetskhladze 1992).

There was a time when this expansion was simply termed "colonization," but we are developing a more nuanced understanding of the issue. First, the relation between an apoikia and any mother city does not fit our notions of common connections such as shared government or other institutions. Second, the act of settlement itself is better seen on a more private elite intercommunity level. The private pattern of kinship within leadership groups leaving a community to seek new power bases is seen in several historical examples. The private rather than governmental nature of these early away settlements has recently been argued by Osborne (1998). Again, the most useful explanation for this expansion at least in the eighth and seventh centuries[5] would be the fissioning of competitive leading groups within the Greek polities over access to political power

Some of these settlements were the product of linked efforts by leaders and factions from more than one community. An important node in that intercommunity network was Delphi, a sanctuary which was visited by elites from various communities and which provided a context for communication and the creation of alliances between elites from different communities. Delphi often gave its blessings and sometimes even directions for the settlement (Forrest 1957; Malkin 1989). There is also the fact that several apoikiai were settled by groups of people from different

---

[5] By the fifth century and later, there is clear evidence that several of these settlements fit the model of colonization, with the government of the mother city setting up a colony, often for economic interests, such as ensuring the supply of grain to the mother city.

polities, leading one to suspect that various intercommunity elites were leading factions from different communities in these settlements.

In several cases, such as Korinth, the actual founders of these apoikiai were relatives of powerful individuals, reflecting attempts to lessen competition within a settlement within one kin group. Such was the case with the sons of the tyrant Kypselos, who ruled over Korinth in the seventh century. An important parallel to this situation was seen by Southall (1968: 61–62) in his study of the Alur. The Alur are a people who live in parts of the Congo and Uganda and were, and still are, to a limited extent seen as an organized kingdom. Alur society, although it had achieved a relatively high degree of social complexity, exhibited fissioning. Several of those who left the original group were sons of the kings, who were often causing problems at home, weakening the hand of the ruler. This is very similar to the situation in ancient Greece, where we had examples of rulers' offspring actually hiving off to start an apoikia, probably at the insistence of their fathers.[6] The closest parallel we have to this period in Greece might be the late Post-Classic period (ca. 1300 CE) in the Yucatan. Here the Quiche Maya were expanding into new territory through community fissioning, where a settlement sends out a segment of its population to found new settlements (Fox 1987, 1989).

Creating the Context for Self-Organization and Phase Transition

The creation of a network of interconnected Greek polities, more than anything else, helped to create a self-organizing system, which was to lead to a new social structure for the Greeks, through what may best be seen as a phase transition. The ensuing evolutionary change for the Greeks was systemic rather than limited to one community. We will examine what the products of this self-organization were in Chapter 8, but in what follows I will briefly outline what these networks looked like and what some of their internal characteristics were.

The most noticeable feature of the Iron Age is the beginning of the creation of webs of relationships between different communities in the

---

[6] Herodotos tells the tale of Battos, a man from Thera who was "pointed out" to the oracle at Delphi to lead a group of Therans to found a new colony. He was also chosen by the state. At first glance this tale appears to be a simple story of a friend of the king who was given the go ahead to found an away settlement. But deeper inspection shows that what probably happened was that Battos was elite who could have challenged the king. He and his party were banned from Thera and prevented from returning, on the pretense that Thera could not sustain a larger population.

Greek world. In many ways the Greek world was beginning to create a number of networks which would connect different communities and peoples and survive until the second century CE in the establishment of a Greek League by the Roman emperor Hadrian (Malkin 1987, 2011). These networks were made up of nodes or communities, links between the nodes, and flows of information, goods, and people. The Greek world was crisscrossed with these networks, and many nodes functioned in multiple networks. Rather than conceptualizing this structure as a flat net, it is more helpful if we were to envision the networks in three dimensions, noting how the same node might sit on different networks in different planes and different scales. For the ancient Greek this meant that he or she would operate in various institutional contexts where the persona of the individual would be created along different scales. One might envision a citizen of the ancient Greek city of Syracuse in Sicily as performing within contexts which operated on different distinct scales – as citizen of the city, a Greek within the larger Mediterranean, a resident of a city founded by people from Korinth, a member of a distinct group of Greeks living in Sicily, etc.

Malkin (2011: 20–21) gives a good demonstration of networks by isolating the institution of the theoria. This institution was an outgrowth of several ancient Greek sanctuaries. That which was connected to Delphi supplies an excellent example. Delphi's theoroi were ancient Greek sacred ambassadors whose function was to travel from Delphi every four years to announce a truce between warring polities. The truce was necessary to facilitate the participation of all Greeks in the Delphic games. When the theoroi visited a community, they were hosted by special theorodokoi, or hosts, whose position was often passed down in families. This created a network of nodes within the polities, which connected to a larger interpolital (spanning different polities) web, with Delphi as its hub. Delphi was not singular in employing theoroi; other major sanctuaries such as Olympia did as well. In addition to the major sanctuaries, secondary sanctuaries such as Epidauros also used theoroi. As Malkin (2011) notes, the flow of theoroi was often reciprocal, with theoroi attending each other's sanctuary festivals. In the end, what was created was an interactive network, where widespread clusters, such as that associated with Delphi, would be tied to subclusters, such as the theoroi connected to a sanctuary such as Epidauros. That is, the network was active on different scales.

Early Examples

As early as the seventh century we can see various networks which tied together different communities. These networks typically employed a sanctuary as a hub, to which the communities would send delegates to discuss matters of communal political importance. The most visible of these were on the western coast of Anatolia (Forrest 2000). Our information comes principally from the Greek historian Herodotos, who came from Halikarnassos, a community lying within this region. There were three networks which he described. The sanctuary of Tropian Apollo near Knidos served as a meeting place for several cities on the southern part of this coast. It appears that Halikarnassos, Herodotos' own home, was eventually expelled from this group. Twelve cities sent representatives to discuss common political issues to the sanctuary of Poseidon at Mykale. There are indications that there was another cluster of communities, somewhat further to the north, who met at a center near Gryneion. To this early list we can also add the cluster of communities known as the Ionian league, who met at the Panionion, near ancient Priene. It was at this center that Balas, a prominent citizen of Priene, argued that the Greeks should abandon this part of Asia Minor because of the impending invasion of the Persian forces. Further to the west, in the Saronic Gulf, we have reference to the Kalaurian amphictyony (an association of neighboring states), whose members were communities around the gulf. One of the members was Athens. The hub for the cluster was the sanctuary of Poseidon on the island of Poros.

Measures of Social Complexity

This was an incredibly dynamic time. The period right after the collapse of the palaces encapsulated a society with the top level of administration removed. The social structure of this period was not in the palaces, but now located within the smaller communities, many of which could probably trace their own social structure back to the earlier years of the second millennium BCE. Without the old Mycenaean hierarchy, social positioning was sought in reciprocal peer relationships, where leaders emerged who could manipulate or intensify these negotiated connections.

In the early years of the Iron Age we can identify notable institutions such as those within the house, those connected to funerals, to religious practice, to warfare, and to political institutions. The picture is not as clear as we would like, but we can see structural connections between institutions within funerals and those within warfare and by reference to epic poems, between those which were political and those of warfare.

This structure was to be challenged by the injection of new wealth and new social statuses into Iron Age communities as the period progressed. The old social structure could not supply satisfying community social roles for these new groups and individuals. The result was community fissioning. We can even say that these communities almost exploded (Small 2018), with a rapid expansion of Greek people into the Mediterranean and the Black Sea. This expansion produced a new social armature of networking connections between people in these communities. The stage was being set for the next step in the formation of the culture of the ancient Greeks. We will visit this stage in the next chapter.

Readings

A good introduction to the Iron Age in general is Papadopoulos (2014). Those interested in survey results from the Iron Age should turn to Alcock et al. (2005). Donlan (1985, 1989b) has written quite a bit on anthropological models for Iron Age society. His view is decidedly neoevolutionary. For the Iron Age at Nichoria, McDonald et al. (2013) is the most thorough study. For good overview of housing, see Fagerstrom (1988), Fusaro (1982), and Lang (1996). Those interested in the houses of the Iron Age might also check evidence for the oval houses in ninth-century Smyrna. See R. V. Nicholls (1958). See also Nevett (2001: 197) for references to other early communities, such as Eretria, Athens, and Theologos on Thasos, where traces of apsidal houses have also been recorded. An excellent overview of sanctuaries from this period is Kotsonas (2017). The elite Toumba building at Lefkandi has been the center of much interest since its excavation. For an interesting look at the metrology and the planning of the building, see Pakkanen and Pakkanen (2000). A further look at the growth of the cemetery at Lefkandi comes from Lemos and Mitchell (2011) and Nightingale (2007), who looks at trade and prestige goods within the burials. The issue of the relationship between early political institutions and Homeric epic is well addressed in Seelentag (2014). The issue of the presence of Greeks or of Greek materials in the Near East in the Iron Age has produced numerous questions. Good overviews and some insights can be found in Waldbaum (1994, 1997). For a fascinating look at the traces of Phoenicians in the western Mediterranean, see Zalloua et al. (2008). For early views on colonization, see Boardman (2001); for the possibility of Greeks settling near Carthage, see Boardman (2006). For a look at the seldom-mentioned nonelites in Greek colonies, see Zuchtriegel (2018).

8   A Brave New World
The New Structure and Characteristics of Its Emergence

In the previous chapter we saw how an economic stimulus created conditions within Greek communities which could not be addressed by their current social structure. This resulted in a fissioning of these communities, with new settlements now seen in parts of Italy, the western Mediterranean, North Africa, and the Black Sea. In this chapter I continue the use of complexity theory as a frame, turning to what transpired after chaos hit, that is, after the fissioning. The focus now is on how the Greek world self-organized out of this chaos into a new social structure with several new institutions. The genesis of this structure and its institutions is seen in early social behaviors or attractors and, just as importantly, the people behind the creation and the repetition of these behavior patterns throughout the culture of the Greeks as they emerged from the eighth century. What emerged was a Greece which we are accustomed to regarding as emblematic of "Greek culture" itself. It contained institutions such as the assembly of citizens, the gymnasion, and the specialized poliadic or community cult. And these institutions were connected to one another within a recognized-as-Greek social structure which was to last until the later years of the Roman Empire.

The city of Megara Hyblaia was a Greek colony on the eastern coast of Sicily, founded around 735 BCE (De Angelis 2003). A plan of the central section of the city (Figure 8.1), as it was first founded, provides an excellent window into the stage of evolutionary development for the Greek polity at this time. The plan of the city shows that the founders left a large open central area which could have housed the principal institutions of the city. We can assume that this space was probably an early form of an agora, or central meeting space, and that it would have housed community institutions related to religion and civic functions, such as those of the assembly and council which we saw in our analysis of the Homeric epics. The important point in looking at Megara Hyblaia is that it gives us a window into the evolution of municipal institutions at this time. There was no attempt to build a temple and no attempt to construct any edifice which would have been used for political or

133

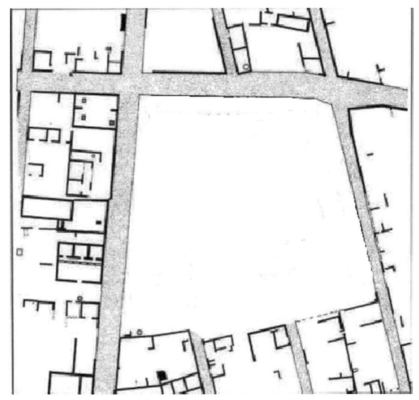

Figure 8.1 Agora from Megara Hyblaia. (Redrawn from Hölscher 2007: figure 5.1.)

bureaucratic functions. The Greek community had exploded in the eighth century, sending out settlements, but it had not evolved to the point that it contained the many developed institutions which we are accustomed to seeing in the later centuries of Greek history. The contexts of religious institutions were still simple, without temples, without dedicatory statues, etc. Political institutions were at the same level.

In the centuries which followed, Megara Hyblaia built temples, civic buildings such as a prytaneion (a type of council house), and a stoa (covered walkway with shops or offices). So did all the other Greek communities. Conditioned by the spread of settlements in the eighth century, the ancient Greeks were going to self-organize within this network of settlements and create new institutions. The amazing feature of this creation is that each community evolved along the same lines. Each community was to develop the same institutions. The tremendous interconnectivity of the settlements, plus the fact that the Greeks were now defining their own culture as they were coming face to face with foreign cultures in their cultural spread, produced a wonderful similarity in social structure in Greek communities. It is this evolution which we turn to in this chapter.

The Religious Sanctuary

By the eighth century new religious developments were taking hold. Several religious contexts had become strong fixtures in the Greek world. Formalized sanctuaries, within cities, as centers for ethne, as interstate places for gathering, as rural forms of celebration at the limits of territories of polities, were becoming fully developed as institutional contexts by the seventh century.[1] For the Greeks the sanctuary was the principal religious context within a community. There were three principal locations for sanctuaries: the intercommunity sanctuary (which we looked at in the previous chapter), the territorial sanctuary[2] (for sanctuaries in rural territories, see de Polignac 1995), and the urban sanctuary. Each sanctuary shared some common attributes with others. When we travel to the seventh century a sanctuary had evolved into a context which was composed of various institutionalized contexts of social interaction. In general these institutions were those at the altar and those within the temple.

Community Sanctuaries: General Characteristics

Greek polities commonly had a principal sanctuary, dedicated to the patron god or goddess of the city. Often called poliadic, that sanctuary was composed of an altar and, usually, a temple. We already saw the possible beginnings of an altar in Olympia's ashes. Yet the early history of temples is debatable. As mentioned, Mazarakis-Ainian (1989, 1997) has argued that the first Greek temples articulated out of the house of the community "chief." But I have described the problems with this analysis. Plus, as we shall see, the origin of the temple can probably be tied to

---

[1] To what extent the sanctuary had become a bounded-off area, with an official temenos and a distinction between sacred and profane, has become an issue of intense debate. Morris (1990), as part of an argument on the early articulation of the Greek community, argued that it had early, but was challenged strongly by Sourvinou-Inwood (1993).

[2] De Polignac (1995) advanced an argument that Greek poleis defined the territorial extent of their power by the placement of religious sanctuaries at the limits of their borders. Although this provides a new lens through which we may look at the function of these territorial sanctuaries, the application of the argument has not been able to stand up to data. See Greaves (2009: 12–15).

developments in larger, intercommunity sanctuaries, more so than in developments within sanctuaries inside communities.

The very early appearance of temples is not clear. Buildings which we quickly identify as temples, having recognizable features such as an inner naos (central room), peristyle or exterior colonnade, and porch, did not appear in polis sanctuaries until the seventh century, as seen by the early temple in Sicilian Syracuse. But there is some evidence for earlier temple presence, such as that of Hera at Samos, with temple construction as early as the eighth century BCE, also seen at Eretria.

Box 10   A Greek Temple

Actually secondary in importance to the altar, the ancient Greek temple nevertheless was to become the focus for sanctuary elaboration. The spatial composition of temples varied somewhat, but there are some general characteristics.

The temple of Ares, a mid-fifth-century construction in ancient Athens, represents what we might say was a typical temple plan (see Figure 8.2). The temple is composed of a large room, the naos, a porch (the pronaos), and a back porch (the opisthodomos), all enclosed by a peristyle. The naos itself contained the votives which were offered to the god, plus a statue of the deity. Its base would have been located near the end back wall of the naos. The pronaos was less important than the naos, but it appeared to have held a measure of importance in that one could swear an oath in the pronaos, presumably in view of the cult statue. The function of the opisthodomos apparently was to serve as an architectural mirror of the pronaos.

Temples served as important contexts for the development of Greek architectural traditions. Large early temples, such as that of Hera at Samos, Artemis at Miletos, and Apollo at Didyma, were built according to rules of the Ionic order. Many temples on the mainland were built according to the Doric order, which presented important problems in the coordination of

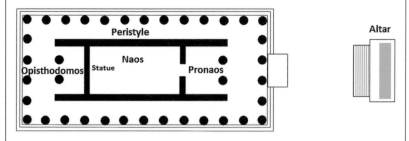

5th Century Temple of Ares in Athens

Figure 8.2 Fifth-century temple of Ares in Athens, moved to agora in Roman period. (Redrawn from https://en.wikipedia.org/wiki/Temple_of_Ares#/media/File:TempleofAresPlan.png.)

> **Box 10**   (*cont.*)
>
> various architectural features. For good introductory overviews on temples, see Berve, Gruben, and Hirmer (1973), and Spawforth (2006), as well as Coulton (1982), Dinsmoor (1950), and Lawrence and Tomlinson (1996).

And there is some evidence that eighth-century temples existed elsewhere. Small models, perhaps of temples, but just as likely of houses, were found at Perachora, which show a small building with a single door, an opening in the pediment to let out smoke, and a thatched roof.

A good example of a "typical" Greek community sanctuary is that of Athena Polias, from the polis of Priene in western Turkey (Carter 1983). The sanctuary was constructed in the fourth century BCE, but its components were the same as those of earlier community sanctuaries (Figure 8.3).

As we can see from the plan, the sanctuary is set off from the rest of the city by a wall, which demarcated a segregated, sacred temenos. There is an elaborate gateway, the propylon, which marks the transition from profane to sacred. The most important installation in the sanctuary is the large altar, which lies to the east of the temple of Athena. The altar area would have been a locus for singing, dancing, and the act of sacrifice itself.

Our knowledge of the ritual of sacrifice is now more complete than we had for the earlier Iron Age. Artistic depictions of sacrifice show that sacrificial activity was probably somewhat similar to what was described by Homer. The principal feature, which was becoming common after the eighth century, was the presence of a permanent altar, which formalized the activity and permanently marked the spatial center of the sacrifice.

The majority of sacrifices in ancient Greece were animal sacrifices. The most prestigious was an ox, its importance signaled by the energy it provided for agricultural labor. But the Greeks also sacrificed sheep, pigs, goats, chickens, and other animals. Sacrifices varied a bit, but the ceremony was held at an altar, upon which was a fire. The celebrants, who included women, men, and children, were usually washed and dressed for the occasion, often wearing garlands. There was a procession to the altar, with musicians, incense burners, and occasionally dancers. People gathered around the altar in a circle which marked the boundary between the sacred and profane. They sprinkled water on their hands and on the animal, raised their arms to the sky, prayed, and hurled barley groats onto the altar. Before sacrifice a bit of the animal's hair was cut off and burnt on the altar, then the animal was slain, with a cut through the throat to access a good blood flow. At the moment of the blow the women in attendance would shriek or wail. The celebrants used as much

SANCTUARY OF

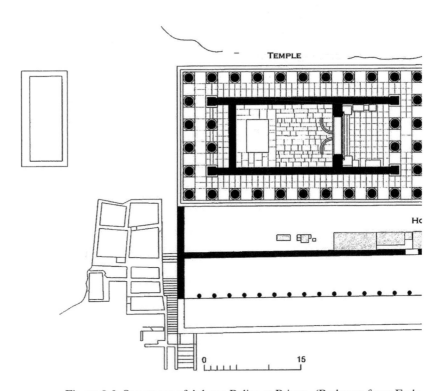

TEMPLE

Hc

0   15

Figure 8.3 Sanctuary of Athena Polias at Priene. (Redrawn from Ferla

blood as possible to cover the altar. With the death of the animal, some of the celebrants ate the entrails. The animal was then cut up, and bones, skin, and fat were burned on the altar as the gift to the god. In general the better parts of the animal were either boiled or roasted as part of a large meat-eating feast after the sacrifice itself.

ATHENA POLIAS

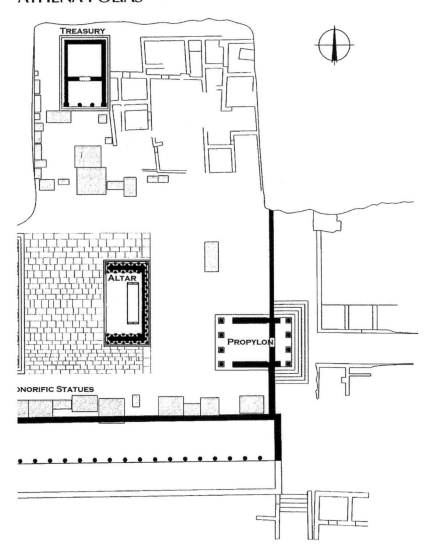

2006: 87.)

Most of our information on how any temple functioned in a sanctuary comes from literary accounts of people celebrating in sanctuaries, and the details mentioned by the second-century CE travel writer Pausanias. Temples often housed dedications to the god and served as loci for the god's statue. The temple of Priene fits into this description well. The naos housed the statue of Athena Polias, and by the period of the Roman Empire the pronaos housed statues of the Roman imperial family. We also know that the naos served as a city records office at one time, and, like any other temple, it was probably a repository for dedications and votives to the goddess. The temple thus contained several institutions. They would have been behavior before the statue (a good case can be made for the swearing of oaths; Torrance 2014) and behavior which would have signaled reverence for the imperial family within the pronaos. In its role as repository, it would have functioned as somewhat of a museum, with various votives possibly on display. Since the naos at one time also housed the city records, it was also tied to the political institutions of the city (Hollinshead 1999).

This sanctuary also contained an additional building in its northern section, a possible treasury. A treasury was a building, often almost identical to a temple, which also housed dedications and votives to the deity. This material could be dedicated by a specific group or even a polis (for analysis of treasuries as elite dedications, see Neer 2001, 2004).

This sanctuary and other religious sanctuaries served as contexts for the institution of community competitive display. Along the south wall of the temenos we find honorific statues. Most of the statues were erected by elites within the city, often representing them or family members and often recording their community status. The statues were just as prominent as the altar and the temple and provided an important contextual background for the other institutions contained in this temenos.

The presence of honorific statues appears almost universal in Greek sanctuaries. Work with these dedications on the akropolis in Athens gives us an invaluable insight into their significance. The Persians ransacked the akropolis in 480 BCE, and the remains of mutilated statues were thrown into a pit on the akropolis, which came to light in the early days of excavation. Analysis of the inscriptions connected to the remains of these dedicated statues gives us insight into the variety and purposes of dedications of honorific statues in general. In analyzing hundreds of votives from the akropolis, Keesling (2008) has outlined some critical features. Although there are many elaborate statues of women and men, the most important feature remains the inscription which usually appears on the statue base. The inscription does not refer to the statue itself, but to the person who dedicated it. A majority of the inscriptions are probably tied to elites, who would be using the dedication as a chance to advertise their success in athletic games or to just advertise their presence within the Athenian community. But a number of the votives were not dedicated by the elites, but by manual laborers and artisans. Their inscriptions mention Simon the fuller, Smirkos the tanner, a carpenter, a potter, Smikythe the washer woman, and Phrygia the bread seller.

The inclusion of these laborers and artisans is important because it shows that the sanctuary context was one where the elites could advertise their elevated positions, but also a context which nonelites could use for status aspiration. A very similar case comes from the work of Michael Parker Pearson (1982) in a study of modern English cemeteries. Marginalized people such as gypsies and carnival workers and lower income people were using the cemeteries for ostentatious display, in an apparent attempt at status construction which was denied them in other social contexts.

Box 11   Greek Sculpture: Humans and the Divine in Metal and Stone

Perhaps more than any other past culture, the ancient Greeks erected statues in various social contexts. Statues representing gods and humans were erected in cemeteries, sanctuaries, and public spaces, especially the agoras in different poleis. The early history of Greek sculpture takes us back as early as the ninth century, when we have examples of small dedications made at sanctuaries. Such is the case for the small bronze figure of a man and a centaur from the mid-eighth century BCE, which was probably a votive at a sanctuary (see Figure 8.4).

Figure 8.4 Early Iron Age centaur and human statuette. (From Metropolitan Museum of Art, Accession Number 17.190.2072, Public Domain Dedication.)

Box 11   *(cont.)*

It was not until the seventh century that the Greeks began to sculpt in stone. Perhaps following the Egyptian tradition of stone sculpting, the Greeks produced early examples of sculpture, such as the Lady of Auxerre, a standing female, found in Eleutherna Crete, and now in the Louvre. By the sixth century stone sculpture had truly taken off, with statues now erected in either cemetery or sanctuary contexts. There were three basic types: the standing male or kouros, the standing female or kore, and the seated woman. Early statues were somewhat blocky and oversized. The height of the famous pair of statues known as Kleobis and Biton (ca. 580 BCE) found at Delphi is approximately 7 feet 4 inches. An important focus in Greek sculpture was

Figure 8.5 Fifth-century bronze statues. (From https://en.wikipedia .org/wiki/Ancient_Greek_sculpture, WP- CC-BY-SA; accessed 7/6/ 2018.)

Box 11   (*cont.*)

male nudity. Female nudity did not appear in Greek sculpture until the fifth century and later. The male body was idealized, in both human and divine form. At first, the depiction of the body was somewhat undeveloped, with musculature not well indicated. As sculpture moved into the fifth century, however, the male body was depicted with full, sometime exaggerated muscles and idealized proportions, best fit for a god (see Figure 8.5).

Today we tend to think of Greek statues as either plain pieces of marble or bronze, but in antiquity they were painted (at least the marble ones) to represent, as far as possible, actual humans.

The habit of setting up statues was so intense that they often crowded out public areas within communities and sanctuaries. At Delos, for example, the pathway from the harbor to the sanctuary of Apollo had at least ninety statues.

Statues were active instruments in competitive display. Meant to represent the best men, who appeared like gods or heroes, these statues commemorated the person who was dedicating the statue. The habit was so strong that, when Athens outlawed elaborate statue display in its cemeteries in the early fifth century BCE, the number of statues dedicated within the akropolis sanctuary increased.

Intercommunity Sanctuaries

We often think of popular sites such as Olympia, Delphi, Nemea, and Isthmia as intercommunity sanctuaries. But we also have to include others. Many sanctuaries, even if not officially called "intercommunity," were intercommunity in function. One of the first and one which lets us look at some of the earliest developments within a Greek religious sanctuary is that of Hera at Samos (Figure 8.6). Although strongly tied to the city of Samos, the sanctuary itself had a Panhellenic and international profile, as witnessed by various dedications from individuals in different Greek communities in the eastern Mediterranean, and from people outside the cultural borders of the Greek world.

The sanctuary, whose earliest known activity dates to the ninth century, was quickly to develop institutions which were to become essential features to sanctuaries afterward (for a recent overview, see Kyrieleis 1993). The earliest material we have from the sanctuary dates from the ninth century. It is then that we see that the sanctuary housed a large altar, probably of ash, a long temple building, and, close to the end of the century, probably some small treasuries. The area around the altar was the focus of the sanctuary and probably the center of the sacred ground, or temenos, which might have been marked out before the construction of the altar by a willow tree.

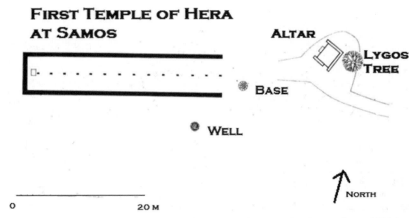

Figure 8.6 Early temple of Hera at Samos. (Redrawn from Whitley 2001: 7.2.)

While much of the religious service took place around the altar, our interest lies in the construction of the temple. One of the earliest temples to have been built in Greece, the first temple at Samos, probably betrays an important early function of a temple building, to house offerings or votives given to the deity at the sanctuary. In the design of the first temple, the representation of the goddess plays a secondary role.[3] In an early phase of the building, the statue of Hera is in fact hidden from axial view behind a pillar. The early interstate community which visited the sanctuary of Hera helped create the need for a temple, because of its numerous dedications, and the need to display those dedications required a building to house them. The votives or gifts to the goddess at Samos came from far and near. There is even a horse face-protector, which was dedicated to the goddess from the ruler of a Syrian city. The number of gifts from visitors from other polities who saw themselves as part of a larger network, which included the temple of Hera at Samos, must have been large.

So, the attention paid to interstate sanctuaries, seen materially in the numerous dedications from people within a religious network, created the institution of housing dedications at the sanctuary. One of the functions of the temple was to house the "products" of that institution. But

---

[3] Several textual sources indicate that the early "statue" of Hera was actually a wooden plank, or what is referred to as a xoanon. The recasting of her image came in the later archaic period. Just what a xoanon was is hard to say. The noun comes from the ancient Greek word "xeein," which means to scrape wood. So the word itself might refer to some sort of plank or piece of wood which was scraped and is a fetishistic representation of a deity. Although very dated, the clearest treatment still remains Bennett (1917).

intercommunity sanctuaries were soon to receive more attention from Greeks within the networks which they served. One of the most salient new institutions which rose out of this network was that of the intercommunity athletic contest. Such contests, while typically attributed only to the major four intercommunity sanctuaries of Olympia, Delphi, Isthmia, and Nemea, were actually more ubiquitous. They were integral to other intercommunity sanctuaries, such as the sanctuary of Zeus at Dodona, as well as some community festivals, which it appears were trying to become more intercommunal, like that of the Panathenaia at Athens.

Athletic Contests

Athletic contests were an institution in their own right, existing outside Olympia, and perhaps even earlier than the sanctuary. Therefore we need to examine this institution not only as a part of Olympia, but as a separate entity as well. Some would argue that the source of Greek athletics can been seen in the Minoan era (Miller 2006). Although it is quite likely that different individual sports, such as racing, boxing, and wrestling, did have a long history in Greece, our first piece of useful information on Greek athletics comes from the eighth century. Athletic contests are highlighted in the songs of Homer. The most famous are those of the funeral games of Patroklos (Homer, *Iliad*, Books 23–24), the friend of Achilles who died in battle at Troy.

These funeral games must represent an elite custom of the eighth century or earlier. The contests are quite similar to those we see later in Greek athletic festival celebrations, arguing strongly that funeral games were the source of the later activities. Like the situation at Troy, contests at the sanctuaries included a chariot race, wrestling, boxing, discus throwing, archery, and javelin competitions. Greek legend furthers this association by tying the athletic contests at Olympia to the earlier funeral games of the hero Pelops.

Athletic events of this sort were extremely popular with the Greeks. A tally of their number indicates that there were more than 150 *recorded* athletic events, of various sizes and importance. The event was always based on the individual athlete and not on any type of team sport. Although open to the participation of all who could claim to be Greek, not everyone could afford to compete. Competition required years of rigorous training, often with paid trainers, which narrowed the ability to compete primarily to the elites who could afford such measures. For the Greeks athletic prowess was a feature of "good breeding," an innate ability which was housed in aristocratic men.

The sanctuary of Olympia (Spivey 2004) (Figure 8.7) is perhaps the best known of the four most noted athletic sanctuaries, which included

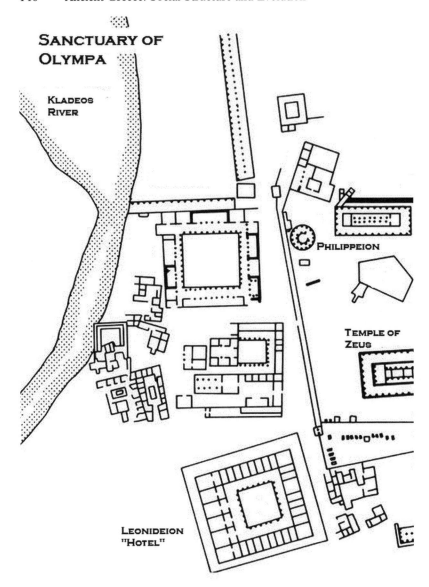

Figure 8.7 Sanctuary of Zeus at Olympia. (Redrawn from Lawrence

Delphi, Nemea, and Isthmia, and represents well the connection between institutions of religious practice and those of athletic competition (Swaddling 1999). Located in Elis in the western Peloponnesos, Olympia was first excavated in the later nineteenth century by the Germans and continues to be excavated to the present day.

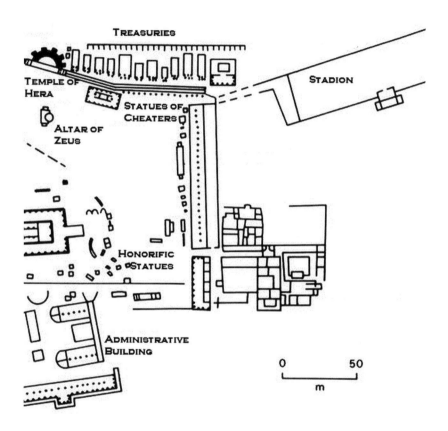

and Tomlinson 1996: figure 156.)

As in community sanctuaries like the Athenian akropolis, Olympia was to receive many honorific statues. It is conceivable that honorific statues were seen first in an intercommunity sanctuary such as Olympia, where their presence is seen as early as the late seventh century BCE with a continued custom of setting them up well into the period of the Roman

Empire.[4] At Olympia it is probably best to view the coming of honorific statues as a step on a continuum of a practice of dedication which started with small bronzes as early as the tenth century BCE. Snodgrass (1981: 52–54, 1989) has documented this continuum as a noticed trend in dedications from 750 to 470 BCE from an initial increase in dedications of figurines, fibulae, bronze pins, etc. to a decrease in this type of dedication and a change to dedications of statues, statuettes, bronze plaques, and others. Receiving recognition and using Olympia as a means to enhance your status included not only the use of statues. We also have evidence that some of the victors had poets, such as Simonides and Pindar, compose victory odes, which were sung in the hometown of the champion.

Similar to these personal dedications, of course, were the nine treasuries at Olympia. These were small, temple-like buildings which housed dedications from different poleis. The treasuries at Olympia were built along the north side of the sanctuary. Their position would have made them distinctly visible from much of the sanctuary. At Olympia we can see how the treasuries themselves clearly indicate the interest of people from different polities. These treasuries represent people from Sikyon, Syracuse, Byzantion, Sybaris, Kyrene, Selinous, Massalia, Metapontion, Megara, and Gela. The oldest, that of Sikyon, was built by Myron of Sikyon in 648 BCE in celebration of his victory in the chariot race.

The introduction of athletic contests at Olympia represents the earliest appearance of games at a Panhellenic sanctuary. According to a later Greek historian, Hippias of Elis (a town which had oversight of the sanctuary), the games began in 776 BCE and were held every four years. In all likelihood the start of the games was somewhat near that time, perhaps 100 years later. The games were not introduced all at once. There was a gradual evolution in the number and type of contest. By 400 BCE Olympia hosted various foot races, discus throwing, boxing, wrestling, and horse racing, both on back and with chariots. Participation was restricted to freeborn men. It was customary to compete in the nude, as a large reason for the contests was to celebrate male beauty. The winners of each contest were awarded a wreath of olive branches

---

[4] By the Hellenistic and Roman periods honorific statues had a much more narrow definition. They were usually erected in civic contexts, such as the agora, and they were tightly associated with powerful families within the polis. The more free-ranging function of honorific statues in the Archaic and Classical period had disappeared.

to be worn on the head. It appears that there was no recognition of second- or third-place winners, although they were well thought of (Crowther 1992).

Heralds went out from Elis before the festival to announce that it was coming and to hopefully nudge the different polities to call a truce in their wars with one another for the period of the festival, so that athletes could journey to Olympia. Participation in the Olympic Games, and presumably in other famous games as well, was widespread. Victory lists, which mention the champions only in the stadion (foot race), record participants from Messenia, Korinth, Megara, Sparta, Epidauros, Athens, Sikyon, Thebes, Syracuse, and Thessaly, in just the first two centuries of athletic competition. And this represents only a small slice of the participation, since it is limited to victors in the stadion, even after other contests were added to the games.

Victory in this type of athletic contest could be used by the victor as leverage to achieve some sort of position of power for himself back in his own community (Crowther 2014). Victors were honored by their own cities with free meals at public expense, statues commemorating their victories, and honorary seats in public assembly. A victory at the games was considered an advantage not only to the victor himself but to his city-state as well (Kurke 1992).

By the fifth century the festival at Olympia lasted five days and apparently drew quite a crowd of spectators. Excavated wells around the stadium attest to their encampments during the games. Punishments for trying to win illegally were stiff. If a man or boy were caught cheating in the contests, he had to pay for the erection of a statue which advertised his dishonesty. These statues were lined up along the north side of the sanctuary, just below the treasuries.

It is not certain whether women were allowed at the festival. The issue of male nudity might have been troublesome. While women might have been blocked from taking part in the festivities at Olympia, we do have evidence that women were competing at Olympia in the Heraean games, which were dedicated to Hera, the wife of Zeus, whose temple was just to the north of her husband's.

Other Sanctuaries

There were numerous interstate sanctuaries throughout Greece. Olympia, Delphi, Nemea, and Isthmia were the most famous. In Greece these four formed an athletic festival circuit. Their games were staggered on the calendar so that an athlete could compete in them almost annually. Several sanctuaries housed oracles. Dodona in northern Greece housed an oracle of Zeus. Didyma in Ionia was a famous oracle of Apollo. The most famous of the oracular sanctuaries, however, was Delphi.

Located on the slopes of Mount Parnassos in the Phokis region of mainland Greece, Delphi was essentially a neutral sanctuary like Olympia (for a good, but dated overview, see Marinatos and Hägg 1993: 203–6; see also Morgan 1990 for early Delphi and Scott 2010 for more recent treatment). The Greeks held that Delphi was the center of the earth and that it was once occupied by the goddess Gaia (earth) and her son, Python, a monstrous snake, until Apollo was to defeat the snake and claim his spot there.

We have already seen how Delphi played a significant role in the spread of Greek communities into the western Mediterranean, North Africa, and the Black Sea. The oracle at Delphi appears to be as old as the ninth century, when it was actually surrounded by the town of Delphi itself. In the sixth century, games were added to the sanctuary. These were known as the Pythian Games. The temple of Apollo was constantly being rebuilt, destroyed for example by fires in 548 BCE and by an earthquake in 373 BCE.

Unlike at Olympia, there was a stronger focus at Delphi on the representation of different polities. The Athenians built a treasury as well as a large display stoa to show off the war booty which they took when they defeated the Persian king Xerxes in naval battles in the second Persian War, 480–479 BCE. The Chians built a large altar, the Naxians an impressive sphinx on a column, and the Syracusans dedicated monuments to celebrate their victory in 480 BCE and 474 BCE over the armies of the Carthaginians and the Etruscans. The Greek communities as a group dedicated a golden tripod to celebrate their victory over the Persians at Plataia in 479 BCE. Delphi also seems to have attracted the attention of foreign kings, such as Gyges, Alyattes, and Croesus of Lydia, who dedicated elaborate gold offerings.

Important economic institutions were very much part of every interstate sanctuary. To take an example, one of the chief characteristics of these interstate sanctuaries was offering an opportunity for elites from different polities to meet. Control over the distribution of economic surplus could be used as a tool to negotiate for power within your own community, and the regularity of the festivals, and the fact that many were held after the year's major harvest, meant that elites would be traveling to the festivals with knowledge of the surplus and the underproduction of harvests throughout Greece. Trade in supplies of grain was locked into the world of the elites, and the festivals acted as nodes in larger networks of information, which were critical to grain flow. We know from inscriptional evidence that several elites were able to gain status and power within their own polities through engagement in this system (Gabrielsen 2015; Small 1997). This institution was heavily embedded within the institution of ritualized friendship between elite peers. Ritualized friendship provided contacts between peers in different polities. One of the principal contexts for the origination of ritualized friendship was attendance at the festivals, which would have brought elite men together from different Greek polities.

While this part of the economic function of interstate sanctuaries was embedded in an elite institution, there was probably a more open economic context which surfaced at the sanctuaries: the religious festival market. Numerous references to festivals describe their markets, which continue to exist in the Mediterranean world even today.

Warfare/Battle

By 600 BCE the institution of battlefield warfare had changed dramatically from the small raids of the Early Iron Age (for a thorough treatment, see Sabin et al. 2007, but also Hanson 2002; Kagan and Viggiano 2013; Rawlings 2007). Two significant new characteristics had emerged: hoplite-engineered battle and the ritualization of engagement. The Greek word "hoplite" refers to a soldier carrying a hoplon, or round shield. The hoplon was one piece of a larger set of armor (breast plate, helmet, greaves, etc.) which was now basic to Greek fighting. For a weapon he was equipped with a spear and a short sword.

This type of armor and weaponry dictated the battle engagement. The spear was meant to be thrown first into the ranks of the enemy. If there was further engagement, it was in closed formation combat. The soldiers were arranged in a block, or phalanx, where each was fighting in a line and using the shield not only for his own defense but for the defense of the entire line. This introduced a new element into warfare: the safety of the phalanx depended on the combined efforts of all soldiers to hold position and to use the hoplon to protect the phalanx itself.

This armament fit in with the pattern of engagement. If the spear bombardment was not effective against the enemy, the phalanx would charge ahead as a group to push the opponent back, with the goal of destroying the coherence of the enemy's phalanx, so that they would break formation and turn. If this happened, there could be possible hand-to-hand combat as soldiers who were successfully pushing an enemy would break their own formation to attack enemy soldiers who were now less defended as they ran individually to escape the enemy phalanx.

Between the Iron Age and the seventh century, battlefield engagement became more and more ritualized. For example, an oracle was sought before going to war, often from such famous sanctuaries as Apollo at Delphi. A battle was set for a preferred spot, and fighting was limited to that area. Before the battle omens were taken, a sacrifice was made and a sacrificial meal consumed by the soldiers. The spot where an enemy broke rank and turned was identified by the erection of a trophy. The bodies of the enemy were not mutilated, but their armor was removed. A truce was called and signified by the pouring of libations, so that the defeated party could remove its dead and bury them. Afterward, a tenth of the spoils from the battle was usually dedicated to a deity. Often these dedications were in interstate sanctuaries, and displayed in the treasuries of various polities. There was a close similarity in the ideals of the battlefield and those of the interstate sanctuary.

Funerals and Burials

By the seventh century and later we have a clearer picture of the processes involved in funerals (Garland 2001). The lion's share of our archaeological evidence comes from Athens, Korinth, and Argos. Cremation was becoming the more common treatment for the corpse. Cremation required a longer funeral than did interment. Recent study (Ubelaker and Rife 2007) has shown that some cremated remains from Greece indicate that the body was exposed to extremely high temperatures which required constant tending and a duration of not only hours, but even days. With this shift toward cremation, we note that there was also a general trend, starting in the seventh century, to put fewer and fewer items in the grave with the buried.

Another custom of burial, seen in the seventh century at Athens, was the construction of a burial mound. These mounds often contained multiple burials, presumably of people with kinship or household (kin and nonkin) connections. The construction of the mound, which would have taken place after the interment, must have taken time, thereby extending the presence of mourners at the graveside. Some graves at Athens had offering trenches. These were trenches which received offerings for the dead. Where they have been found, the archaeological material indicates that the offerings, animals, pottery, etc. were burned within the trench.

Box 12   Cheating the Dead? The White Ground Lekythos in Classical Athens

A cylindrical pitcher, the white ground (background) lekythos was produced by Athenian potters. This vessel was especially associated with funerals and marking the monuments of the dead. Its shape indicates that it was meant to pour a liquid, the best candidate being oil which was poured out as a libation during a funeral and for anointing the funeral monument. It was often left as an offering at the tomb. Many of the scenes on the lekythoi refer to death, with the image of the deceased often painted on the vase. To me, the depicted art on this lekythos is one of best representations of the finest pottery drawing in Athens. For the deceased, the meaning of the lekythos might well have been different, especially in the middle years of the fifth century (470–430 BCE) when attempts were made to reduce the amount of oil which the lekythos would have contained. It was during this period that the interior of the vessel was being fitted with a small container, which held the oil. This meant that one could use less oil to fill the lekythos, and less oil to present to the deceased. The reason for this deception is not clear, but the most logical argument is that the oil in the lekythos was probably quite expensive, and those pouring libations to the dead and using oil from a lekythos to anoint a monument were simply trying to spend less on this obligation. (A good overview is Oakley 2004.) See Figures 8.8 and 8.9.

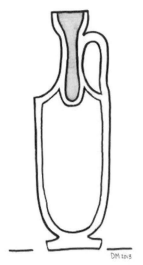

Lekythos with False Bottom

Figure 8.8 Lekythos with false bottom. (By permission of Daniel Mehlman.)

Box 12   (*cont.*)

Figure 8.9 Lekythos by the Achilles Painter. (From Metropolitan Museum of Art, Accession Number 1989.281.72, Public Domain Dedication.)

Two important new features related to funeral custom, which we did not see in the earlier Iron Age, were a tendency to monumentalize the grave and attempts to restrict such monumentalization. Athens supplies our best information for monumentalization. Some monumentalization can already be seen in the seventh-century trend to construct large mounds over burials. Around this time Athenians were also beginning a trend of setting stone monuments over the graves. These monuments could be elaborate, with large statues, some perhaps of the deceased, but several simply emphasizing male or female beauty, like those we saw being set up in sanctuaries. Other monuments were tall stelai (standing flat monuments), often with human reliefs or topped with decoration.

This monumentalization was part of a process of social competition through the display of elevated status or aspired status and was met by attempts to curb this behavior in the cemeteries (Small 1995b). We have several examples of laws which sought to restrict monumentalization and the ability of burying groups to have elaborate funerals. For example, Athens passed a rule which forbade the sacrifice of an ox in the cemetery. The ox is of particular importance because it represents the destruction of an extremely valuable item. Unlike a cow or a bull, the ox was an animal whose main function was not to supply food, but to provide a major source of energy for farming. The destruction of the ox therefore represents a bold statement that the family is wealthy enough to destroy an animal in an act which would otherwise seriously impact its ability to till soil in the future. With restrictions on funeral ostentation came a decrease in funerary games, which appear to have died out in the sixth century in places like Athens.

The current thinking on these sumptuary rules is that their restriction on extreme ostentation in the funerary context created cemeteries which displayed the concept of citizenship, and that they were products of the power of a "middling ideology" (Small 2015). In fact, several ancient historians (for example, Morris 2004) see this trend in restriction on ostentation in the cemetery as part of a larger evolution toward democracy. But this is a serious misreading of the context. These attempts to limit cemetery ostentation actually contributed to a crystallization of differences between groups. These groups were families who were able to use the cemetery for status display or aspiration before the rulings and those who would have used this context for elaboration, but were now prevented. In a serious way these rules were measures to apply the brakes to social climbing in the communities.

Political Institutions

By the end of the sixth century most Greek polities had a similar political structure. Their assemblies were now more proactive than those of the earlier Iron Age. There was an assembly, the ekklesia, where citizens (the demos) who were propertied men over eighteen gathered to vote on general measures of polity governance. They also had a boule, which was a small group of selected individuals who would set the agendas for the assembly. Many also had a gerousia, or council of older men (called the Aeropagos in Athens). Most also had public courts within which the citizens served as jurors. The courts were not like those we have today. Several thousand citizens could sit in judgment of a case. The basileis of the Iron Age were now replaced with various appointed and elected magistrates. There were often several to a city, and known as archons. They functioned as administrators, looking over issues such as those of finance or warfare.

A very important feature of this structural composition is that it did not determine how political power within the polis was constituted. The reader may be surprised to learn that poleis, which had large assemblies which would support democracies, could exist as oligarchies, monarchies, or tyrannies (see Hansen 2004: 1338–40, index 11 for a summary). A large assembly did not ensure that anti-democratic forms of government did not occur. The case of ancient Syracuse is a clear example. The tyrant Gelon, after defeating the Carthaginians in a battle at the Sicilian town of Himera, called an assembly to judge his actions (Burn 1984). He had usurped authority in his military behavior and, by rights, could have been deposed by the will of the assembly. But he cleverly manipulated the scene in front of the assembly to the point that it declared him a benefactor and savior. Gelon's actions were not singular. In the main, tyrants and other despots were clever enough either to play or bully the assembly to get their way and approval, not by formalized voting, but most likely through acclamation. Other twists of constitutions which dwelt within this internal political structure can be found in efforts to restrict the members of the assembly, by changing the requirements for citizenship. Restricted citizenship and therefore restricted assemblies were often referred to as oligarchies.

Economic institutions which were part of the larger governmental sphere were minimal and most not directly under governmental oversight. Taxation was minimal by modern standards and limited in the main to small fees on commodities. Few ancient polities had direct access to economic wealth. An exception was the city of Athens, which owned and used the proceeds of the silver mines at Laurion in Attika to finance part of its operations, but this case seems to be the exception rather than the norm. And even with control of these mines, Athens still had to rely on indirect financing of most civic institutions, such as dramatic festivals or even outfitting the military. That means of indirect financing was the liturgy. The liturgy was an institution whereby rich individuals in an ancient polity financed state institutions. In ancient Greece there were essentially two major types of liturgies: those which financed the military and those which financed nonmilitary events. The military liturgies consisted of private financing of the navy. Individual ships could be fitted out with men and equipment. Often the individual who fitted out the ship also had the responsibility of being the captain of that ship in battle. By far the most common liturgies, however, were nonmilitary. Many supplied funds for dramatic festivals. Often the choruses of plays were paid for by private funds. Private individuals also supplied financial support for important institutions, such as those housed in the gymnasion.

The fact that so much of the responsibility for the economic financing of the polity was in the hands of private individuals gave those individuals an important opportunity to use the liturgy for the advancement of their social standing within the polity. Often public monuments were erected to celebrate their financing of such institutions as the dramatic chorus. We also know that the liturgist could also be honored by the assembly with permission to wear a gold or silver crown in public assembly.

This institution of the liturgy appears to have had good antecedents. Lyttkens (1997) argues that it can be seen in the measures of the Athenian archon Solon at the turn of the seventh to sixth centuries to create various wealth classes in Athens. But there is probably little to stop us from conceptualizing that this institution existed in Greece even earlier.

Similarities of Internal Political Structure: The Result of the Codification of the Epics as an Attractor

One of the most salient features of the evolution of the Greek poleis was that, even with local twists, the internal composition of most poleis was very similar. We already saw that a tyrant, such as Gelon of Syracuse, could operate within a polis with an assembly. When we look at the whole picture, there are more similarities. Each polis, no matter what its power structure, to some degree had two additional assemblies which acted as councils either to decide what the principal assembly was going to discuss or to sit in judgment on special cases. Why did the poleis have such similarity in their internal political composition? If we see this within the frame of complexity theory, then we have to understand the power of various types of knowledge structure in determining how societies will self-organize. Early writing among the Greeks served to crystallize the institutions of the *Iliad* and *Odyssey*. Here I am referring to the assemblies and the councils in the epics themselves. The medium of writing and the fact that these songs were so sacred to the concept of "Greekness" helped to spread these institutions throughout the Greek world. This was important, but the popularity of political assemblies is also probably aided by peer emulation in the period of polis development. That is, not only was there a larger common notion of what a proper community should have as far as organizing institutions is concerned, but the similarity of these institutions from polis to polis was also a direct result of the active spread of information and specifically the proper image of a Greek polis active within the network. Important nodes within the network played a significant role in disseminating a common ideal for the Greek community. A good case in point is that of the Great Rhetra of Sparta. This was a constitution for the polis, which, by legend, was given to the Spartans by Lykougos, who was given the form of the constitution from Delphi (see Ogden 1994). A final point in all of this refers to the power of cultural contrast. The political structure of the Greek community was forming in the era of Greek migration, when the Greeks come into direct contact with other cultures, and the fact that they were defining themselves in contrast to other cultures in the Mediterranean must also have helped in creating a common image of the Greek polis.

Additional Institutionalized Public Assembly

In addition to periodic meetings for political purposes, the Greeks were expanding the custom of public assembly with the development of the ancient theater (Figure 8.10) (a good early overview remains Bieber 1961; but see Green 2013). Some of our earliest evidence for theater comes from the description of the installation of tragedies in the Great Dionysia in Athens in 535 BCE, and the remains of a theater from that date in the Athenian agora. But this type of public assembly, to watch some type of performance, probably had a much earlier history in Greece. For example, the polis of Metapontion in southern Italy had a large auditorium which was built in the seventh century BCE.

Greek drama was an Athenian invention in the late sixth century BCE and was associated with the festival of Dionysos. This is not the place to delve into the many ramifications of the study of Greek drama (but see Storey and Alan 2013).

Figure 8.10 Theater at Epidauros. (Photograph by the author.)

Box 13   Greek Drama

The creation of an institutional context for community assembly helped give birth to Greek drama. The unique characteristic of Greek drama was that it was the first institution in human history where critical questions of the human condition were explored through dramatic presentation in front of an assembly of people within the community. The possible precursor to drama was satyr plays, spoofs, often with ribald action during celebrations of Dionysos in Athens. Actual drama originated in the late sixth century in Athens, with the first recorded actor, Thespis (ca. 520 BCE). Staging was not elaborate for Thespis, who was the sole actor, changing costumes and masks to play different characters, and performing with a chorus of fifteen men who sang and danced, but did not have any theatrical lines.

Dramatic performances took off with the establishment of the Dionysiac festival in Athens as early as 508 BCE. During the festival there was a tragedy competition, when the plays of different playwrights would be performed. One of the earliest playwrights was Phrynichos. He wrote a play on the capture of Miletos by the Persians in the late sixth century. This play was poorly received by the Athenians, who actually fined him for writing it!

The three most famous playwrights were Aiskhylos (Aeschylus) (ca. 525–456 BCE), Sophokles (Sophocles) (ca. 496–406 BCE), and Euripides (ca. 484–407 BCE). Aiskhylos added a second actor to the play, and Sophokles added a third. These playwrights presented thought-provoking themes to the audience, such as the abuse of power, pride, fate, love, obligation, and the relationship between humans and the gods.

Staging in Greek plays involved a chorus of men who sang and danced and performed in the orchestra section of the theater (Figure 8.10). The principal actors were on a stage in front of scenery. The scenery wall itself had three doors for entrance and exit. The actors were all men who wore masks to depict the characters they were portraying (see Figure 8.11).

Aiskhylos, Sophokles, and Euripides wrote tragic plays, but the fifth century in Athens also saw the beginning of another theatrical form, comedy. The most famous comedy playwright of the fifth century was Aristophanes (ca. 446–386 BCE). Perhaps taking his cue from earlier satirizing productions in Dionysiac festivals, Aristophanes wrote plays which often had a chorus dressed in outlandish costumes, such as wasps. He used the comedy platform to make fun of and question the political and social makeup of Athens. Some of his more famous plays, such as *Lysistrata*, have the women of Athens attempting to end the Peloponnesian War by withholding sex from the men. In his play *Clouds*, he makes fun of the Athenian philosopher Sokrates (Socrates), who was his contemporary.

Greek comedy went through different stages of development. That of Aristophanes is referred to as Old Comedy. There may have been a stage referred to as Middle Comedy, but we know little about it. New Comedy, which began in the later part of the fourth century and lasted until the mid-third, differed from Old Comedy in that the plays were more like situational

Box 13   (*cont.*)

Figure 8.11 Mosaic of theatrical masks from the villa of Hadrian. (From https://en.wikipedia.org/wiki/Theatre_of_ancient_Greece, WP-CC-BY-SA; accessed 5/11/2018.)

comedies. Gone were the spoofs of famous political figures, and in their place were scenes based on family life and social mishaps. The most famous playwright for New Comedy was Menander (ca. 342–291 BCE).

For further information on Greek drama, see Gregory (2008), Hall (2006), Sommerstein (2003), and Storey and Allan (2013).

What is important for our look at social evolution in Greece is the fact that the audience for plays was different in its composition from that for the political assembly. The assembly was restricted to the citizens of the polis, but those watching a play were more than just the citizens of the polis. Metics, that is, resident foreigners, could be seen in the audience, as well as visiting foreigners and slaves. There was also a good chance that women, especially in the early constructions of theaters, where there was unofficial seating around the cavea, or rows of seats, were also members of this group.

At Athens many plays were performed as part of the Great Dionysia, or festival to celebrate Dionysos. Since this was a festival, many participants came from other poleis; in the case of Athens, most likely from other Ionian cities. What this foreign participation meant was that the theater was a central point on an interactive network of participation which included people from other poleis, playing a role very much like that of the intercommunity sanctuary.

As a final point in our look at public assembly we must be aware that, in its theatrical and political contexts, it provided a rather open context for status display and competition (Roselli 2011; Small forthcoming). Although the theaters look rather bare today, we know that in antiquity they were filled with people who were competing for status by wearing gold crowns, making purposefully delayed entrances, using heralds to announce their entrance into the assembly, perhaps wearing expensive clothing, owning retinues of slaves, etc.

The Gymnasion

Participation in the public assembly was a means by which one could identify with his or her own community. Identifying with the community was also integral to the institutions housed in another building, the gymnasion. The ancient Greek gymnasion was a building which held two parallel types of activities: physical training and education. I have shown that the Greeks were extremely fond of sports and athletic competition. They also held that a fit body was important for mental health. Most Greek gymnasia had a large interior colonnaded courtyard referred to as a palaistra, or exercise yard. Attendance in the gymnasion was restricted to men of the polis. But you did not have to be a citizen to participate. There is evidence of metics participating in the gymnasion as well.

The gymnasia which usually housed an exercise yard, or a palaestra, offered an opportunity for physical exercises, running, jumping, wrestling, and other activities. But there was also attention paid to the education of the young men of the polis. Young male citizens were referred to as ephebes, and they were educated in a special room in the gymnasion known as the ephebeion. Here they were instructed in various topics, the laws of the city, morality, courage, etc. The ephebeion probably spurred the development of formalized education and the later advent of the philosopher in history (Humphreys 1978: 241–73 provides an excellent introduction to this type of institutional evolution).

Economic Institutions, Principally Markets

By the fifth century there were a number of economic institutions which were playing significant roles in society. The reciprocal gift giving of the earlier Iron Age was still active with the intercommunity sanctuaries playing a significant role. Usually signified by the institution of guest friendship these contacts were set up by elites who would have met each other at various interstate celebrations, such as the games at Olympia or the festival of the Dionysia at Athens (see Herman 2002 for similar institutional dynamics). Inscriptional evidence points to the fact that elites were using these connections to both sell grain to areas in Greece where there was a grain shortage and to secure grain from other elites, if they were in a region of grain shortage themselves. The power of these contacts lay in the ability of various elites to use their own grain surplus, plus connections to other grain sources to leverage their power within their own communities. Often foreign elites were rewarded with honors, such as crowns, and the right to own land in the polis they had helped by donations or sales of needed grain.

We also witness an increase in the number and the importance of markets (Tandy 2000).[5] Every polis had by now an active central market, usually set in the agora. However, this is not to argue that the polis was set on a market economy. There are several very important differences between our modern market economies and that of the Greeks. For example, the profit motive and the relationships between people which were generated in the market were not the primary features which determined the economy, as they are today. The relationship between interpolital elites and reciprocal exchange was just as important a feature in determining the characteristics of the ancient Greek economy.

The Household

As a society becomes more institutionally complex, new cultural divisions are often reflected in the fact that domestic architecture will utilize more spatial distinctions within the house which correlate with the new institutions and roles being created in the culture (Kent 1993; for the Greek case, see Jameson 1993; Westgate 2015). We have evidence for houses with multiple rooms, but we do not have enough data to tell us very well what the different rooms were used for. But what little we have does tell us something. By the fifth century BCE and probably earlier, the Greek household had solidified around institutions which governed

---

[5] Tandy sees the introduction of markets as part of a struggle between established elites and commoners in ancient Greece. My own view is that the issue was probably more nuanced.

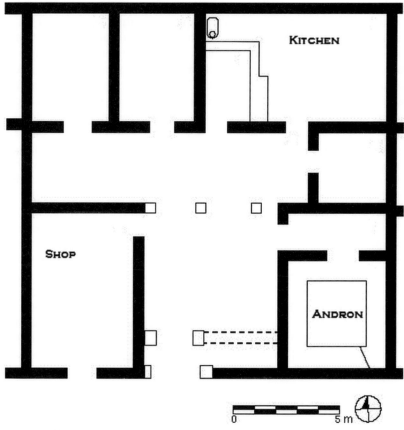

Figure 8.12 House from Olynthos. (Redrawn from http://historum
.com/ancient-history/25520-how-large- were-lower-class-houses-ancient-
athens.html.)

access to different sexes, placement of activities, and controlled interfaces
with the larger community (Nevett 2001, 2010).[6] (See Figure 8.12.)

There appears to be a connection between the rise of markets and the
household. An important feature which we find in houses of this period is

---

[6] Westgate (2015) outlines the possible relationships between domestic space and possible
increased craft specialization and the use of resident slaves within the household. While
the reader is encouraged to consider Westgate's assessments, these correlations can be
difficult because we do not know if evidence for industry within the house is actually tied
to specialization, and despite attempts to identify "slave space," we do not know enough
about the spatial presence of slaves within the household to accurately identify where they
would have been working and living.

the presence of shops within domestic space. Some houses had rooms on the streets which were shops. Sometimes a house had street-fronting shops with doors between the shops and the house, indicating that those who owned the shops were members of the household.

One of the most salient features of the Greek house in this period is control of access to household members, specifically women. Most houses appear to have had some sort of interior courtyard, where a great deal of activity took place. Weaving and other activities probably took place here, because of the light which the courtyard afforded. Since the principal workers within the courtyard would have been women, access and views into the courtyard were controlled by offset doors and alley entrances.

By the middle of the fifth century we have evidence that a separate space was being created for an interface between the household and the community. In many houses an andron, or room for entertaining, was included in the spatial arrangement. The andron itself was an extremely important addition to the household. It housed entertainment participated in only by the men of the household and men from the wider community. The institution of the symposion describes well what took place in the andron. With antecedents in the Iron Age, the symposion was an all-male gathering party. Women of the household were excluded, but outside female entertainers, might have been allowed access. In many ways the symposion can be compared to a male drinking party. Men in the symposion reclined on couches. They drank wine from a common krater and we have evidence of the effects of overimbibing, which could get out of hand.[7] There could be some sort of entertainment. Poetry was read, there might be dancing girls, and women for sex. There is evidence of homosexual activity in this gathering as well. With a gathering of men drinking, the conversational topics were not that distant from those in similar contexts today. Talk revolved around issues of sport, politics, sex, battle, honor, etc. As such, the symposion had strong affinity to the activities in the interstate sanctuaries, the assembly, and the battlefield. The symposion was an important context for the use of ritual friendship, which linked elites from different polities through

[7] In a fragment from his c. 375 BC play *Semele or Dionysos*, Euboulos has the god of wine Dionysos describe proper and improper drinking: "For sensible men I prepare only three kraters: one for health (which they drink first), the second for love and pleasure, and the third for sleep. After the third one is drained, wise men go home. The fourth krater is not mine any more – it belongs to bad behaviour; the fifth is for shouting; the sixth is for rudeness and insults; the seventh is for fights; the eighth is for breaking the furniture; the ninth is for depression; the tenth is for madness and unconsciousness." See Athenaios: *The Deipnosophists* 2.37c.

sacred bonds of mutual trust and friendship. There is a strong argument that the convivial drinking of the symposion matched that of similar drinking parties among soldiers (Murray 1991), and we can imagine that some of the guests to the symposion were men with whom one shared battle.[8] Since the symposion is also an example of ritualized feasting, it likely served as a venue for status or status aspiration display, with men negotiating for social hierarchy.

This control of contact between outside men and the women of the family was more of an ideal than a reality at times. Economic considerations would often necessitate that women of the household interact with outside men. Shop owners, for example, would have been hard pressed to maintain the ideal separation. We can see an example of this from the excavated site of Olynthos (Cahill 2002; Nevett 2001: figure 10).

Another Complexity: Structure within the Ethne

Up until this point our focus has been on the evolution of the Greek polis. But there was a large part of the Greek mainland which was not polis-centered. Thessaly, Lokris, Phokis, Doris, Aitolia, Arkadia, Boiotia, and Akhaia, which were identified as coterminous with different subsets of Greeks – that is, ethne – were organized by internal networks, which bound communities in these regions together along economic, political, and religious parameters. The identity of the region was not based on the polis as much as it was based on these networks. The networks between the different communities appear tied to the needs of the population within the specific region. For example, there were often rules establishing the right to own land in other communities and the right of inter-marriage, an obvious measure to buffer agricultural risk and general economic fragmentation within a region. These different communities which made up the ethnos often claimed common descent through a heroic ancestor. Nodes on these networks were the sanctuaries in the region. Periodic assemblies of representatives from the communities in the ethnos would be held at a sanctuary. It was here that political issues were discussed. One of the most prominent of these issues was how the ethnos was going to react to pressures from either other ethne or a polis.

---

[8] Most recently, Morris (1997, 2000) and Kurke (1991, 1992, 1999) have seen the symposion as tied exclusively to elites and actually a gathering which was anti-polis. This argument is too polarizing in its view of ancient Greek society, which was a subtle gradation of different interests in several different social institutions. Rather than seeing the symposion as linked to strictly aristocratic interests, it is best to view it as linked to male interests in the rest of Greek society.

By the fourth century BCE some ethne had formalized their internal networks to form a koinon, or league. These leagues can best be seen as regional power structures, which in form and function evolved according to the developing social interactions between the people and the communities which compose the league.

We know less about these ethne and koina than we would like (Hammond 2000; Mackil 2013). There has been some archaeological investigation into regions such as Thessaly and Boiotia, but understanding the regional structure of these entities from isolated excavations and survey is difficult in respect to the questions that we would be asking to understand an ethnos or koinon. For example, ancient historians such as Herodotos give us some information, such as the ethnos of Arkadia being divided into twelve parts. But exactly what this means culturally and how it might manifest archaeologically is not fully understood

Aspects of Emergence

Greek communities were strikingly similar after they emerged from this period of chaos.[9] Here again, complexity theory provides a useful analytical frame for looking at this similarity. Such similarities in complexity theory are often the result of attractors. I already described the similarity in the internal political constitutions of the Greek poleis as due to the codification of the epics serving as an attractor. I wish to use this frame again, and to emphasize the role of aggrandizers in creating these attracting patterns in Greek culture. In this post-eighth-century world we have individuals interacting in competitive strategies in the contexts of the cemeteries and the intercommunity and community sanctuaries. This was an age which saw aggrandizers acting to create new positions and institutions for themselves, but using methods which would give them an accepted Panhellenic recognition, such as erecting honorific

---

[9] The issue of interaction between Greek communities and their similarities was addressed by Renfrew and Cherry's edited volume, *Peer Polity Interaction and Sociopolitical Change* (1986). The book provided several chapters by authors who took a critical look at interaction and similarity. The book's shortcoming is that it treated the issue in too generalized a fashion, focusing on "polity interaction" rather than focusing at a closer range on the individuals who were interacting. Polities do not interact, individuals do, but often their interaction affects polities themselves. Highly recommended in this volume is Snodgrass's contribution, "Interaction by Design, the Greek City-State," pp. 47–58, which looks at the similarity in light of the development of the Greek polis. I would only add to his chapter by remarking that the competition was not the result of polities in competition with one another, but the result of individuals, aggrandizers, in competition, and not necessarily with the aim of building a polis.

statues or supplying funds for the construction of common buildings such as stoas, temples, and theaters.

In the cemetery we see the erection of elaborate tombstones which must have been part of larger social strategies, again correlated with funeral feasting, to create an elevated status for individuals and families in this period of social fluidity. But there were attempts to limit the ability of aggrandizers to change social structure, in that there was often legislation which sought to limit the ostentation of funerals themselves. But it was not only the funeral context which supplied opportunities for such individuals; it was the intercommunity sanctuary as well. Sport was becoming a powerful attractor. We have elites not only competing in athletic contests but erecting statues within these sanctuaries. Elites were also active in the civic sanctuary. Religious institutions were being "feathered out" with new institutions within which individuals sought community status through the erection of votive statues, and probably through the dedication of expensive votives which were also housed in temples. The Late Antiquity historian Peter Brown once labeled one of his chapters on the late antique "An Age of Ambition" (Brown 1993), that is, an age where the old order was breaking down and new people were seeking new positions and creating new institutions within society. We can use the same label for our Greeks of this period. These were ambitious people.

Some significant patterns were emerging among these institutional contexts as well. One very noticeable linkage was between the battlefield and the interstate sanctuary. The earlier custom of including military mementos in burials, thus producing the famous "warrior graves" of the Iron Age, was being replaced by a shift to dedicating arms to the interstate sanctuaries. This means that the ideology of the battlefield was shifting from a connection to the funeral to a connection to the activities of the interstate sanctuary. The ritualization of combat on the battlefield was now linking itself to the ritualization of athletic combat at the sanctuary. Linking to the sanctuary rather than the funeral would have provided aggrandizers who wanted to advertise their success in battle an institutional context with higher social visibility than that supplied by the funeral.

This new pattern was replacing the old association of funeral athletic games with funerals. That association was disappearing with funerals in the period after the eighth century and was being replaced with an association between the athletic sanctuaries and mythical funerals, such as that of Pelops, a hero of the Peloponnesos, whose funeral was said to have been the first instance of athletic competition at Olympia.

With this we must also mention the important pattern of linkage between the intercommunity sanctuaries and the communities themselves.

This pattern was forged by elites again, who were using participation in the sanctuaries to link to community institutions such as the symposion through concepts such as guest friendship to construct social, political, and economic power.

Measures of Social Complexity: Community Cohesion, Agency, and Political Economy

The final organization for ancient Greek civilization was a world of polities, poleis, and ethne with similar institutions, in their sanctuaries, funerals, gymnasia, warfare, etc. Additionally, there were contexts supplying institutions which were shared, such as those in the more famous interstate sanctuaries. It is important that we emphasize that this structure spanned various communities. To be Greek meant that you lived in a truly international world, within which you would participate in multiple institutional contexts, not only in your own community but in others as well.

No one lived in just one context. Negotiation of your social position meant that you operated and strategically played your roles in several arenas. Your hope often was to use your position in one context as leverage for raising your position in another. This is why we see victors at interstate games using their participation at the games and the success in a contest to gain leverage in the institutional contexts of their native communities. On the other hand, if you were locked out of participating in the institutions of a particular context, you could shift your energy to another context and use that to leverage social positions (see Papaconstantinou 2014 for an approach to this issue through sport). Models of the Greek past which see its dynamics through frames of class opposition, usually elites versus middling individuals (as exemplified by Morris 2000), have a very limited efficacy, because they miss this point. Elites and other classes were not locked out of social power construction in some Greek polities, as imagined. The Greek world was larger than the polity, and Greeks had numerous choices. The case of the Alkmaionidai is important. A powerful family, they lost their power base within the institutional contexts of Athens to the tyrant Peisistratos in the late sixth century BCE. But they were still operating on the Greek stage. They just shifted to a new context, and rebuilt the temple of Apollo at Delphi, which brought them intercommunity recognition. The institutional contexts of this larger networked world, to which the Alkmaionidai had shifted, were a network of the sanctuary, the andron, and the battlefield, and were just as real and just as active as some of political contexts within the polis.

A critical feature of these polities and their relationship to their networks was that their control of these networks was limited politically, militarily, and, more importantly, economically. Elites, who could afford to attend many intercommunity festivals, such as Olympia, and smaller ones as well, were able to construct alliances and connections through the institution of guest friendship (Small 1997). This gave them free range in a large intercommunity economic network.

This had a profound effect on the political evolution of the polis and the ethnos. The ability of elites to control an important economic sphere beyond the polis or the ethnos inhibited the internal evolution of a robust political economy within the polity. As Earle recently phrased it, political economies take on various forms, but "a political economy ... takes no special form, except the ability to mobilize and direct resources in support and extension of ruling institutions" (Earle 2011: 241). In most cases, except for Athens' brief imperial episodes, and the extremely unusual Spartan conquest of Messenia, the Greek polis was not mobilizing or directing resources in support and extension of ruling institutions. Financing many crucial institutions within the Greek polity was left to elite individuals with access to economies outside the control of the polis. Armies were structured so that equipping them was the responsibility of the individual, and navies, even in navy-focused Athens, were supported to a great extent by private funds. A great percentage of what we would consider public expenditure was under the aegis of private funding. Choragic liturgies paid for dramatic presentations, gymnastic liturgies for the development and running of the gymnasion, hestiac liturgies for public banquets, architheoric liturgies for sacred embassies, and arrephoric liturgies for community processions.

The ancient Greek community, as seen in Athens, was internally split by the interests of public and private economies. Analysis of the inscriptional record from fourth-century Athens (Gabrielsen 2015) documents how its elites were banding together in networks which focused around the grain trade. With connections within Athens, at principal ports in the East Aegean and Black Sea, and with grain-gifting rulers of non-Greek communities in these regions, Athens' elites were acting as double agents, procuring necessary grain for Athens, but also amassing grain privately, which they could use strategically to gain economic power and position within the polis.

This fourth-century case must have had several centuries of historic precedence in the economic world of Greek elites. At Athens this hampered the city's ability to develop effective economic policies. This underdeveloped state economic structure created a problem when Athens gained its empire in the middle of the fifth century, after the defeat of the Persians. The empire was new and very much an institution with which Athens had little experience. This can be seen in the barely nascent understanding of the Athenian assembly of the potentials of economically controlling its subject peoples. Rather than extending features of an already developed political economy to its territories to incorporate conquered polities, the assembly retained its myopic view of limited taxation, developed from the liturgy background, and leveled a tax on shipping in the empire. But the tax was not born from considerations of economic overlordship, because it was placed on Athenians as well as other peoples in the empire.

The condition of the Greek polis specifically, limited in its ability to manipulate an economic base for its own institutional growth, led Moshe Berent (2000) quite rightly to label the ancient polis as "stateless." His charge that the ancient polis does not fit state types elucidates well the issues embedded in the use of labels which mask unique cultural features as they attempt to fit a past society into their conceptual straitjackets. Unfortunately, debate over this issue has been limited to assembling trait lists which would identify ancient poleis as archaic states (Berent 2006; Hansen 2002; van der Vliet 2005). Such debate does little to inform us further on the nature of the internal structure of the community and its dynamics. The economics of the Greek polis were such that the polity falls outside our common state definitions. In a parallel study several years ago (Small 1995a), I pointed out the marked difference between islands in the Pacific which did not have important economic control beyond their shores and those that did. One example was the Trobriand Islanders' involvement in the famous Kula ring, an institution within which men would travel from island to island creating important social and economic connections. The communities on the islands themselves, however, could not control this network and not only suffered from an inability to employ the economic vigor of this network to build any ruling institutions but were also often subject to the maneuverings of these traders as they sought to gain social capital from their island network connections. In direct contrast to the Kula situation, the Yapese Pacific Islanders in their "empire" were able to spread out and control the networking between islands, which supplied them with the basis for developing ruling institutions.

In Greece, this underdeveloped political economy led to a weak arrangement of social contexts within the community. Usually communities with strong political economies have a tightly arranged hierarchy of community contexts, held in place by the power of the political economy. Such was not the case in Greece. Internally, the poleis were very fluid, with constant rearrangements of institutional contexts into various hierarchical arrangements. This was what often typified the Greek polities that had numerous internal political arrangements ranging from monarchies, tyrannies, oligarchies, and, importantly, democracies.

Readings

There are some very useful general books which deal with some of the topics I touched on in this chapter. In reference to hoplite warfare, the best book on the armor of the Greeks remains Snodgrass (1999). For burials, those interested in the protracted process of Greek burial, that is, the liminal state of the dead, should read Hertz (2013) and van Gennep (2013), two well-known studies on the anthropology of funeral practices. The issue of parallels in internal structure between various Greek poleis also brings up the issue of laws. I am not treating such issues in this book, but for timely observations on the issue of laws and lawgivers among the early Greeks, see Holkeskamp (1992) and Lewis (2013). Because my approach is structural, I have skipped close study of some excavated communities in this time period for Greece. For an example of an early town from this period, Zagora, see Cambitoglou et al. (1971, 1988) and Vink (1997). For more famous polities, such as Sparta, see the excellent work of Cartledge (1980, 2002, 2003). Athens has dominated historical literature for a long time, and it is difficult to select a single study of the city, but one of the best introductions to the polis is Everitt (2016). For those interested in ethne, a good evidence-based study is that of McInerney (1999), who examined the ethnos in the Phokis region of Greece, with its principal sanctuary at Kalapodi. Thessaly is an interesting case and was apparently controlled by powerful families who had power bases in the different communities. See Archibald (2000). For readings on the issue of the internal "constitutions" of the Greek polities, one needs to initially read Aristotle and Plato. A good overview of both of these authors is Barker (2012). This is a reprint of an earlier work, but the author supplies a comprehensive overview of ancient political thought. The theme of my book is the large-scale evolution the ancient Greeks in a structural sense, and I have eschewed teleological frames which put the evolution of the ancient Greeks into a model of ever-developing democracy. For those interested in the issue of this structure and the birth of democracies in such poleis as Athens, see papers in Morris et al. (1998), which is dated but still presents the salient issues in a constructive manner.

9   Developments after the Rise of Macedon

The structural reorganization of ancient Greek culture that occurred after the eighth century was set by the sixth century and was to remain rather stable for some time, at least until the later years of the Roman Empire. But this does not mean that the culture of the ancient Greeks remained static during this period. In this chapter I will look at how various institutional contexts, within and outside the community, were to continue and evolve as different polities were being absorbed into Hellenistic kingdoms and eventually the Roman Empire. But before we can do this we need to understand how the Greeks were living in a larger political world, unlike any that they had experienced previously (for good historic overviews, see Bugh 2006; Green 1990).

The Historical Context

The Greeks had resisted two attempts by the Persians to absorb them into their empire in the early fifth century, and enjoyed more than a century of independence, until an historic tragedy occurred in 336 BCE when the Greek poleis were defeated by the army of Macedon in a massive battle at Charoneia in Boiotia. This meant, to a certain degree, that the foreign and sometimes the internal policies of several of the Greek polities in mainland Greece were afterward controlled by the interests of the kingdom of Macedon.

However, the defeat of the Greek poleis did not have any immediate effect on Greek poleis outside the Greek peninsula. The immediate effect of Macedon's victory did not touch the Greek polities in Asia Minor. Macedon's rise did not touch the Greek poleis in the west, either. Their own political future would be determined more by the growth of the Roman republic, which was to dominate southern Italy, Sicily, France, and the Iberian Peninsula by the end of the first century BCE. What we understand of their operation after Roman domination, which began in the third century BCE, is unfortunately little. Some poleis, such as Syracuse and Massalia (modern Marseilles), have been continuously

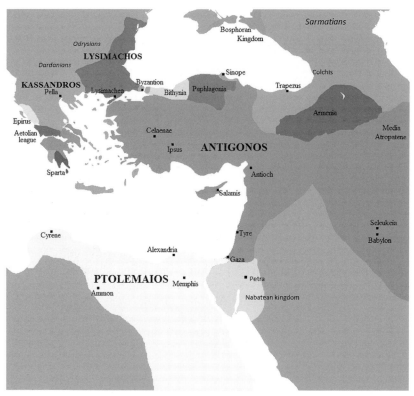

Figure 9.1 Map of Hellenistic Greece. (From https://en.wikipedia.org/

occupied and therefore it is difficult to excavate their pasts. We do know also that the Romans themselves altered to a great degree the internal structure of many of these poleis. There are good examples of Roman punitive colonies placed in cities which resisted Roman dominance, especially after the Social War, a disastrous attempt by Italian cities to throw off the yoke of Rome in 90–88 BCE. These injections of different types of internal governance and the desire by a number of the families within these Greek poleis to curry favor with Rome altered the original internal structure of these cities, leaving them poor examples of any continuation of the Greek experience (Lomas 2003, 2013). In many ways they were becoming small copies of the internal structure of Rome itself.

Looking toward the east, we must also turn our attention to the conquests of Alexander the Great. The son of the Macedonian king, Philip II, who defeated the Greeks at Charoneia, he conquered a territory

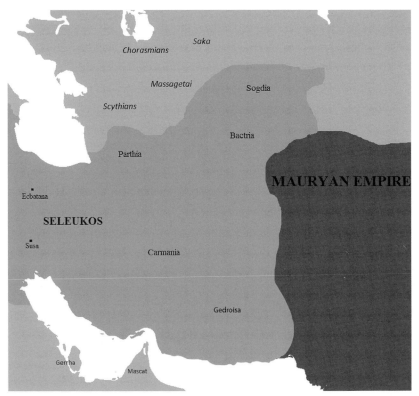

wiki/File:Diadoch.png, released into public domain.)

which was larger than the Persian Empire (Figure 9.1). On his death in
the swamps of Babylon in 324 BCE, his kingdom stretched from the
Greek mainland ("allied" states), south into Egypt and Kyrene, east as
far as northern India, and north as far as Bactria, modern Afghanistan.
When he died, his conquests were divided among his generals into
several powerful kingdoms. Alexander and his successors established
numerous cities, which were modeled on the internal structure of the
Greek polis, and often populated by Greeks and Macedonians, as well as
local peoples. Alexandria in Egypt was to become the most important city
among the Greeks, eventually rivaling the importance of Rome in the
Roman Empire. Founding all these cities increased the number of poleis
who ostensibly held internal structures similar to those which had existed
in earlier periods in other Greek territories. There were also a large
number of cities which were not Greek in origin, but which were to
adopt Greek customs and Greek political and social institutions. Such

cities were the rich communities of Asia Minor, such as Termessos, Sagalassos, and others. These communities were to eventually become poleis in their internal structure and customs, and I will turn to a few of them to exemplify some internal dynamics which were probably taking place in most all Greek poleis.

Considerations of Structure

I will approach the Greeks in this period by continuing with observations on the activities of important social and political institutions, both within the poleis and without. Much of Greece remained nonurbanized, occupied by the ethne which we discussed in Chapter 8. In the Hellenistic period several of these ethne were to develop leagues or koina. It appears that one of the principal reasons for this development was that the ethne were internally responding to military threats. Several of the leaders of the leagues were strategoi, or generals, a logical extension of the need of the league to coalesce for protection. The two principal leagues were that of the Aitolians (ca. 279–217 BCE) and the Akhaians (ca. 280–146 BCE). The Aitolian grew in reaction to military threats, such as the invasion of the Gauls into the Delphi area in 266 BCE. The Akhaian was the larger and stronger of the two. True to the character of an ethnos, the league, or we should say second league here, was born out of the Akhaian ethnos in the third century BCE, after the original koinon or league of the Akhaians disappeared after its erection in the fifth century BCE. The Akhaian league was to absorb some rather large poleis into its structure as it grew, Korinth and Megalopolis being just two.

Turning to the poleis themselves, the institutions which we identified earlier provide us with useful windows into the dynamics of these communities.[1] Greek polities continued to be very active, even though these were now absorbed into the larger sphere of Hellenistic kingdoms and later Roman Empire. The institutions contained in the assemblies apparently continued to be just as active as they were in the sixth and fifth

---

[1] Recent survey research in mainland Greece has opened up a new window on the state of Greece in the Hellenistic period and the early Roman Empire (best summarized in Alcock 1993). Survey evidence suggests that, starting in the Hellenistic period, the countryside was moving from being populated by small farms to being populated by large villas and nucleated farming settlements. This is an important observation on an apparent change in the economic structure of Greece proper. Unfortunately, other parts of the ancient Greek world have not been studied by means of the intensive surveys employed in Greece. We cannot therefore make a similar judgment for the rest of the Greek world.

centuries, but with a greater role for the wealthy. There is abundant evidence that individual poleis continued to have very active assemblies which passed quite a bit of legislation pertaining not only to internal affairs but to alliances and even declarations of war (Gauthier 1984; Ma 2000, 2003; van Nijf 2006; van Nijf and Alston 2011). We have a huge corpus of inscriptions from poleis in the Greek peninsula and Asia Minor which show clearly that the demos, the boule, and the courts continued their functioning much as they had before (for the standard work on cities in Asia Minor, see Jones 1940). People were to hold various offices, people were honored, treaties with other poleis were enacted, and grain was secured from regions outside the poleis.

While these functions were to continue up to at least the third century CE, there was an important internal change which was taking hold even though the functions of the poleis remained the same as they were in earlier periods. The change was that even though assemblies continued to function and the demos in many cases continued to debate issues (Ma 2000), power was now falling on selected families within the poleis, who were able to use the old functions of the Greek poleis to secure status and power which could be passed on to their progeny (for dynamic overview, see de Ste. Croix 1983). A classic case comes from Priene, where the family of Thrasybolos became one of the most prominent and presumably powerful families in the city (Small 2009, 2011).

The privileged position of elite families within the poleis was now actively celebrated more than ever. In many ways, the assembly, while retaining some of its original functions, was to function more and more as a stage on which nobles in the poleis could display status. The options remained the same. The assemblies often honored selected elites with the right to wear golden crowns during public assemblies, in both the theaters and the stadiums. Inscriptions also mention that these honors were announced during various public gatherings, most notably the festivals of Dionysos. The poleis were also now honoring their elites with processions which often terminated in the theaters, where the elite would enter before the demos and sit in honored seats in the front. We also know of civic banquets which were set up for similar honorific functions.

The city of Termessos in Asia Minor was not an original Greek city, but began to follow Greek custom extensively in the Hellenistic and later Roman periods. Its inscriptional record highlights the new role of elites within a Greek polis. Insightful research (van Nijf 2011, 2013; van Nijf and Alston 2011) on the city of Termessos has yielded some important observations on what was probably taking place in several poleis. The boule had now become the dominant assembly, with membership hereditary. It appears that there was a stable inner core of families within the boule, who numbered approximately twenty. Members of these families also held priesthoods, and would therefore have had elevated positions in city festivals and processions. They also appear to have funded up to twenty athletic contests within Termessos per year.

Other institutional contexts within the poleis show another dimension to this restricted control of the polis by a small number of families. The economic sphere, at least what was represented by the agorai, or market-places, apparently did not change significantly, with agorai continuing to fully function in the Hellenistic period and the Roman Empire, with some small exceptions, such as the reduction of the agora in Athens after the Herulian invasion of 267 CE (an invasion of peoples from Eastern Europe). But a significant additional emphasis appears to have been placed on the use of the agora as a context for status display. Agorai such as that at Priene in the Hellenistic and Roman periods provided the major contexts for the erection of honorific statues (Figure 9.2). These statues supplied an important ideological addition to the agora as a context for various social institutions. In the agorai, any business,

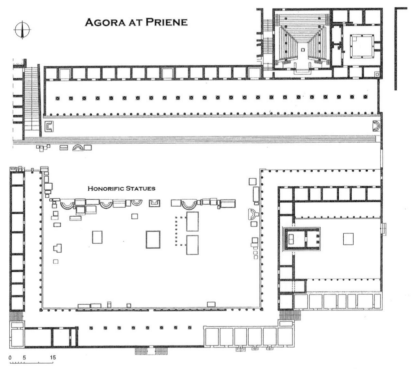

Figure 9.2 Agora of Priene. (Redrawn from Ferla 2006: 63.)

meetings, assemblies, and processions through the agorai had to operate within a context which was now highly honorific.

Close observations on the nature of the honorific statues reveal some important issues. Most dedications made explicit mention of the families of those receiving the honor, indicating that it was the family itself and its probable extensions into the fabric of the community which was being advertised. In addition, we have mounting evidence that more and more honorific statues were now being erected, not by the community through a measure in the assembly, as was common in earlier periods, but privately. Starting in the fourth century BCE, the display of power and position was no longer isolated to the recognition of the assemblies (for extensive review of the material, see Ma 2013).

Urban sanctuaries appear to have undergone little if any change in the Hellenistic and Imperial periods. They, too, were to receive new honorific statues, but the only really new function, seen in some urban sanctuaries, was the addition of an imperial cult. This was often seen in the addition of statues of the imperial families and in new religious institutions, which included offerings to the emperor and his family. In some poleis this cult was celebrated with an actual temple or shrine to the imperial family (see Price 1985). Thus the community sanctuary was to evolve into an important node in a larger network connecting the emperor with the cities of the empire.

In the domestic contexts, the institution of the interface between the family and the community was beginning to experience an important change, which was to accelerate tremendously in the later empire. As the Greek poleis continued into the Roman Empire, domestic contexts began to take on new institutional functions, which by the late empire were to challenge those which had been customary in other civic arenas. By the middle years of the Roman Empire (ca. third century CE) the houses of the rich in several Greek poleis were adopting new functions, which were previously embedded in the life of the polis itself (Ellis 1991, 2007; Ozgenel 2007; Small 2011). Houses continued to contain contexts for family/polis interface, but now these contexts were becoming more elaborate. Several houses now had special audience halls, where the notables of a polis would meet others from another polis or, more commonly, the nonelites of their own community. This new attention paid to the family and its interface with the community mirrors the rise of honorific dedications in the agorai and community sanctuaries.

While there was continual evolution of the internal functions of the Greek polis into the Hellenistic and Roman periods, the interconnected web between these poleis saw change as well. The multiscalar networks which grew out of the previous centuries were still vital to the operation of Greek economics and politics. But now Hellenistic monarchs chose to intertwine themselves into the fabric of these elite networks, seeking to control the poleis in that manner rather than interfering directly in the affairs of individual polities. The family of Phillip II and Alexander the Great were seen at important interstate sanctuaries such as Olympia. After Philip's victory over the Greek poleis in 336 BCE, he remained in the Peloponnesos and attended the festival at Olympia. His appearance at Olympia was a broad statement that Macedon was now the controlling power in Greece and that the elites of its various polities were to identify with his powerful position. He even built a monument to his family at the sanctuary, the Philippeion, which housed portraits of the royal family.

Box 14   The Philippeion

Built after the battle of Charoneia in 338 BCE, the Philippeion, or "monument of Philip," occupied a prominent position at Olympia (see Figure 9.3). It lay at the principal entrance to the sanctuary. This building was the first and the only building at Olympia dedicated not to a deity but to a mortal, Philip II of Macedon.

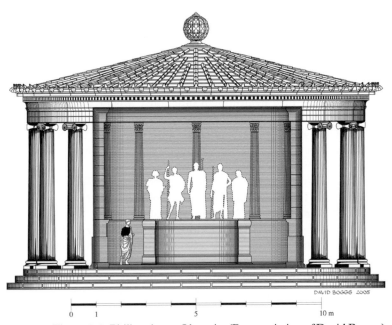

Figure 9.3 Philippeion at Olympia. (By permission of David Boggs.)

Box 14 (*cont.*)

Its architect, according to the Greek travel writer Pausanias, who visited Olympia in the second century CE, was the famous architect Leokhares. The Philippeion was a tholos, built in the Ionic style with an interior which housed the chryselephantine (gold and ivory) statues of Philip and his immediate family: Alexander the Great, his son; Olympias, his wife; Amyntas III, his father; and Eurydike, his mother.

In several ways Philip had set a trend with the construction of this monument. That trend was the symbolic connection of the Hellenistic monarchs with the intercommunity web of Greek elites. For the issue of the use of ruler imagery and political control and power in this period, see Denkers (2012) and Schultz (2009).

There were several important developments along this line which occurred after 323 BCE, the year of the death of Alexander the Great. First, the Hellenistic dynasts, that is, the Ptolemaic kings of Egypt, the Seleukids of Asia, the Antigonids of Macedonia, and later the Attalids of Pergamon, were using the major intercommunity sanctuaries as contexts for status competition and display (Thompson 1982). For example, the Hellenistic Greek king Ptolemy II of Egypt built a palaistra (building for athletic exercise) at Olympia ca. 270 BCE. Other sanctuaries were to receive similar construction from various kings as well. Of importance in relation to this issue is the fact that Athens, while no longer an economic or political powerhouse, had become a cultural center, where the elites of the Greek world continued to send their sons to be educated by its philosophers. Since this was the case, the city was now on an equal international footing with the sanctuaries, that is, a locus for interstate gathering. Several Hellenistic kings were to construct high-profile buildings in the city. The kings of Pergamon constructed two stoas, one in the agora and the other near the theater of Dionysos. Since these were buildings which served as gathering places within the city, they elevated the profile of these monarchs.

Although the interconnected web which tied the sanctuaries together was very active in the Hellenistic period, it was not until after the Greek poleis had been conquered by the Romans that the web was to see its greatest activity and a new function. Much like the Hellenistic monarchs, the Romans also advertised themselves in the international sanctuaries. Roman strongmen, such as Appius Claudius Pulcher, paid for the construction of architectural additions to sanctuaries, such as the monumental gate to the sanctuary of Asklepios at Epidauros in the mid-first century BCE. Athens, still the international city, even in the empire, was to receive several benefactions especially from the emperor Hadrian, such as the famous library of Hadrian, still seen today.

But the involvement of Roman rulers in the festivals and in certain cities was evidence of something much larger. The first three centuries of the Roman Empire witnessed the greatest participation of Greeks in the festival circuit. The inscriptional record shows that there was a tremendous spike in contestants, who were being honored not only for athletic wins but also for excellence in music, poetry, and acting. In many ways the function of the festival circuit was similar to what we saw at its inception: the construction of a Greek identity. Within the larger orbit of the Roman Empire, winning at these contests was a dramatic statement of being Greek. This was important, because of the desire of newly founded poleis, and of poleis which were not really ethnically Greek but had adopted the Greek forms of political discourse, to become more Greek-like in their internal institutions. It is not surprising, then, that we find numerous poleis offering citizenship to a large number of festival champions. The addition of these personalities would have served to strengthen the "Greekness" of the individual polity. The circuit also served as a means for mobility within the empire and as a means of connection between Rome and the Greek poleis in the east. This connection often functioned as a ladder to greater status and visibility within the empire. A famous case is that of M. Aurelius Demostratos Damas, who in the second century CE went from several early athletic victories at international centers to being offered citizenship from acclaimed cities such as Sardis, Ephesos, and Delphi. He wound up as the director of the imperial baths at Rome (van Nijf 2012: 56–58).

The Panhellenion energized this interconnected web. Established by the emperor Hadrian in 131/132 CE (Spawforth and Walker 1985, 1986), the Panhellenion was a league of poleis located in Thrace, Macedonia, Akhaia, Crete/Kyrene, and Asia. Koina were represented in the membership of poleis from Crete and Thessaly. The functions of the Panhellenion are not as well known as we would like, but the central community of the league was Athens. The league had an archon, chosen every four years (probably with the approval of the emperor), and a synedrion or council, to which the poleis sent representatives annually. It appears that some poleis, such as Kyrene and Sparta, had more than one representative in the council. The league did have its own treasurer, and maintained buildings in which it met in Athens. At times the council acted as a court. The league also had a religious center, Eleusis. The fact that poleis who were members had to prove their Greek ancestry, which eliminated important cities, such as Alexandria, points to a desire to link poleis who could advertise Greekness. The league probably also served as a principal means by which these poleis could interface with the emperor. For example, the participating poleis were represented by the archon of the leage when he met with the Roman emperor Septimius Severus in Antioch in 212 CE.

In many ways this spike in participation by Greeks in international contests, and the movement by Hadrian to establish a new Greek league, can be compared to the rise in Greek literature in the Imperial period up to the third century. Referred to as the "Second Sophistic," life in the Greek east at this time was actively punctuated by numerous writers and rhetoricians who were consciously archaizing, in that they would often make public declamations or reenactments of historical events and debates which took place in the early fifth century BCE. There was even an attempt to reanimate Classical Attic, the language of fifth-century Athens. It was at this time that we witness a rise in the number of Greek writers, coming from all over the east, not strictly from the original Greek poleis themselves. Some of the more notable were Plutarch, who wrote moral stories on Greek and Roman history; Pausanias, who wrote a travel guide to Greece; and Aelius Arestides and Dio Chrysostom, who were famous orators. It is important to note that several of these men had close relationships with the ruling men of Rome, who shared their enthusiasm for Greek rhetoric and philosophy. Aelius Arestides was taught by the Alexander of Cotiaeum, who was also the tutor of the emperor Marcus Aurelius and was later to have a close relationship with the emperor. Herodes Atticus, perhaps the most famous of the philosophers of the Second Sophistic, was brought to Rome by the emperor Antoninus Pius to be the tutor of his two sons, Lucius Verus and Marcus Aurelius.

Measures of Social Complexity

Compared with earlier periods, structural change in the Hellenistic and Roman periods was more of an addendum, some modifications and change applied to what had already been created rather than dynamic change. Structural collapse and chaos did not arrive in the Classical world until the third century of the Roman Empire. The principal forms of social structure which the Greeks had built by the sixth to fifth centuries set the foundation for society for the next 700 years. Only a few additional institutions appeared.

Hellenistic monarchs and Roman strongmen were to use the inter-community sanctuaries and their connections to control the direction of much of the Greek world. Religious institutions within the polis took on an additional connection to the Roman emperor. Coupled with this development, social institutions within polities were now more and more used by elite families to secure and maintain elevated social positions. Several of the institutions which were public in the past were now being absorbed into the houses of the wealthy as they and their interests were to eventually become more important than those of the polis as the Roman Empire moved into late antiquity.

Readings

Good historical overviews of the Hellenistic period can be found in Errington (2008) and Erskine (2005). A good introductory account of the Greek city in the Roman period is Millar (2006). An interesting treatment of the effect of their early incorporation into the empire can be found in Spawforth (2011). Excellent insights into the fascinating leagues of the Hellenistic era come from Grainger (1999) and Scholten (2000). On the inner workings of cities in Roman period Asia Minor, see Pleket (1998) and Zuiderhoek (2008). Survey is playing an important role in clarifying our knowledge of Roman Greece; see Stewart (2014) for good recent overview. A fascinating work on the issue of the cultural mix of athletics and literature is König (2005).

10   The Cretan Difference

Ancient Crete was part of an active koine in the Late Bronze Age, but after the collapse of palace society, it became isolated with its own distinct social structure and trajectory of development. Iron Age and later Crete was very much different from other "Greek" cultures. It maintained a pedigree which was traceable to the Minoans, a people who as we saw, although part of an interactive koine, differed in many ways from communities in the mainland northern limits of that koine. The Cretan Iron Age (1100–700 BCE) was a period of social change which produced polities with institutions not seen outside Crete: a restricted civic cult, a different institutional makeup for the house, non-mainland dining institutions such as the andreion, and a distinct lack of any type of institution similar to open assembly.

To understand this cultural development and to allow us to compare it with the rest of Greece, I am analyzing Cretan Iron Age polities with the same model of social structure I used for contemporary Greek communities outside Crete, and I again using the frame of complexity theory to provide a window into their genesis. More comprehensive data from the excavations at Azoria and the cemeteries of Knossos and Prinias allow me to discuss phase transitions in greater depth than I have been able to before. The best way to present the situation is to focus first on the communities of the eighth and seventh centuries, which were the results of Crete's unique evolution. I will unpack the structure of these communities, and then turn to issues of their development.

Azoria and the Different Institutions of Crete

We are fortunate in that we have an extremely well-excavated Cretan polis, Azoria (Figure 10.1), which supplies us with a powerful analytical view into the Iron Age Cretan polis (Haggis 2014a, 2014b; Haggis and Mook 2011a, 2011b; Haggis et al. 2004, 2007, 2011). The results of its excavations have shown that the community was established according to a predetermined plan for community social structure. The construction

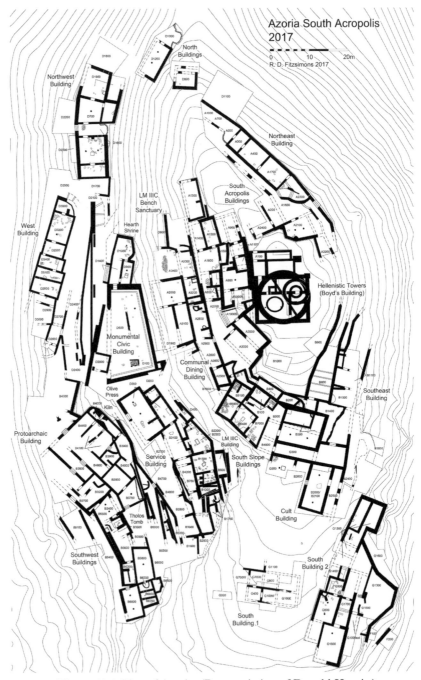

Figure 10.1 Plan of Azoria. (By permission of Donald Haggis.)

of spine walls on the site as an armature for various civic and domestic buildings indicates that whoever built Azoria was building a community which was the result of, if not top-down planning, at least a template of how the Cretans of this age would have liked to live within a community. All this fits well with our established concept of a phase transition, which has also been argued to have taken place in the Iron Age in central Crete (Kotsonas 2002).

Azoria specifically appears to have been the result of a nucleation of several smaller and earlier communities in its region, the Kavousi area. The communities are the Kastro (Coulson 1998; Gesell et al. 1991; Haggis et al. 1997), with occupation from Late Minoan (LM) IIIC to Late Geometric (LG)-Early Orientalizing (EO) (ca. 1150–650 BCE); Vronda (Day et al. 2009), with LM IIIC (ca. 1200–1100 BCE) occupation; and Halasmenos (Coulson et al. 1994), with LM IIIC occupation as well. The pace of evolutionary change in the Kavousi region was from a rather static settlement of clusters of small, spread-out, interrelated villages and a cemetery, to a point in the late seventh century when the community of Azoria, which is markedly different from the regional structure of these earlier villages and cemeteries, appeared (see Haggis 1993, 2005).

In terms of its structure, Azoria contains important examples of the principal institutions which made up an Iron Age Cretan community. It had temples which were exclusionary rather than presenting an opportunity for open participation in sacrifice or competitive display, as we saw with other temples in the Greek world. It had no space for open community assembly. It contained two exclusive dining contexts and had houses which lacked the typical interface between households and the communities which we saw evolving in the rest of Greece.

In reference to the context of a temple, excavations at Azoria were able to uncover a shrine and a temple which was used for community cult (Figure 10.1, D1000 and cult building). The exclusionary characteristics of the temple, restricted entrance, and an interior hearth or altar are matched by those of Azoria's shrine and parallel the structure of temples in other communities from this period on the island. A well-preserved example of this type of temple can be found at Prinias. Temple A (Figure 10.2) from that site was built in the latter half of the seventh century. Temple B, which appears earlier than A, still awaits more detailed publication (for bibliography, see Lefèvre-Novaro et al. 2007; Prent 2005: 283–89). There are other examples of similar temple design. The temple at Dreros is small, with an interior hearth or altar. In the southwest corner there is a bench or shelf, which probably served as a stand for three small statues of Apollo, Artemis, and Leto. Drinking cups

Figure 10.2 Early hearth temple at Prinias. (Photograph by the author.)

were also found in the temple, as well as animal bone, which indicate that some sort of feasting took place inside the building (Klein and Glowacki 2009; Marinatos 1936). At Aphrati, a seventh-century BCE structure fits our description of an exclusive cult building (Prent 2005: 278–80; but see Viviers 1994: 232–41), with wall benches and limited access. Smari also contains a cult building (Prent 2005: 276–78), probably dating from the seventh century BCE. The structure contains interior wall benches, a hearth, and small doors with controlled access. Other similar structures can be seen at Kommos and Sta Lenika (Klein and Glowacki 2009).

Azoria has little or no space set aside for open public assembly. The community had only a small area near the building of the town cult, not enough to fit our concept of public gathering. Azoria appears not to have been unusual. Several early town plans have few identifiable agoras. There is none yet seen at Prinias. That at Dreros is not fully understood. The original identification of an agora there was the result of excavating a set of stairs, which the excavators thought might have been seats for an open gathering area at their base. But no such area has been excavated. It has been shown to occupy a cistern (for an overview, see Sjögren 2007).

In a similar vein there is no contemporary Cretan development of a theater. Theaters themselves were transplanted into Crete during the

Roman periods (post 67 BCE), as seen in their presence in the Roman period at sites such as Gortyn. With incorporation into the empire, Cretan communities were falling in line with the trends of the larger Roman period koine of the eastern Mediterranean (Spanakis 1977). There is no evidence that the cultures on Crete, if left to themselves, would have developed any sort of theater.[1]

Instead of an open area for public assembly, the early Cretan polities had something more exclusive, the andreion. The andreion was an exclusive men's dining club, as described by Aristotle (*Politics* 2.10) and Athenaeus (4.143). The closest archaeological evidence we have for it to date is the communal dining building excavated at Azoria (Figure 10.1, andreion complex). Azoria also has another building which had a similar function. This was a large communal dining hall (Figure 10.1, D500, D100, and D200), with stepped seats around its interior wall to accommodate sitting at tables, which was the Cretan custom, rather than reclining, as seen in the rest of Greece. The andreion complex and the communal dining hall differed from one another in that the andreion complex was attached to kitchens which supplied food. Although it was also attached to kitchens, faunal material from the large dining building shows that some of its meals were probably less prepared than they would have been coming from a kitchen. Parts of animals were apparently roasted on spits here.

Good examples of domestic architecture on Crete come from the sixth century at Azoria. Excavations to date have identified houses in at least five areas. These houses contained several institutional contexts. One of the main contexts for the house was the central hall, which most often was next to a storeroom. The central hall, as evidenced by the material coming from room A400 in the Northeast Building, was broad and at least two floors high in its western section. Material remains from this context included a large lamp, a black-glazed skyphos, some long-stemmed cups, a krater, a table amphora, a hydria, and a lekane (a low, wide bowl with two handles). The excavators also report some food debris. The mix of dishes argues for some dining function within A400. The proximity of this hall to a large storeroom may well also indicate that whatever the commensal institutions of this space were, they were meant to take place within a context where the agricultural wealth of the family could be displayed.

---

[1] Arthur Evans found a few Geometric period sherds under the pavement of the theatral area at Knossos. But it is unlikely that the four sherds found – two amphorai, a krater, and a hydria – represent a public assembly function for the theatral area in the Iron Age. See Coldstream (2000: 272–73).

Box 15   Showing off Your Agricultural Wealth

Figure 10.3 Cretan Iron Age pithos. (From Louvre Museum, Accession Number CA4523; https://commons.wikimedia.org/wiki/File:Pithos_Louvre_CA4523.jpg, public domain.)

Box 15 (*cont.*)

The Cretan Iron Age storage pithos was meant to impress. Its antecedents were the storage pithoi which we encountered in the storerooms of palaces such as Knossos. But this Iron Age pot was different. It was impressive not only in its size, often at least 6 feet tall, but also in its decoration. While the earlier pithoi at Knossos did not have decorated scenes on their surface, those in Iron Age contexts on Crete often did. The one shown in Figure 10.3 comes from the Louvre and probably depicts a scene from the story of Bellerophon and the horse Pegasus. You can see a man, Bellerophon, having fallen off the horse, in the band of decoration on the belly of the pithos. The use of such a decorated pithos, possibly visible to those dining in the house, would have been somewhat similar to the use of serving and drinking dishes with mythological scenes, in the androns of houses outside Crete.

This hall would have served for dining both within the household and with others in the community. In the Northeast Building this hall is separated from a courtyard by a vestibule. Since the dining in A400 was connected to part of a contextual interface between the household and the community, the vestibule would have served as a noncommensal and probably more formal household–community interface. Food processing was located in A2100, which contained a hearth. Other remains within this room were materials from food processing tools, such as cook pots, a spouted mortar, coarse bowls, and a strainer. There is some variation in layout between these houses, but I would emphasize the important similarities of commensality for both the household and household/ outsiders, within a context of a display of agricultural wealth and the lack of accommodation for male sympotic activity, as we saw developing elsewhere in Greece.

Westgate (2007) outlined that much of the residential evidence we have for Crete is similar to what we see early at Azoria and can be seen in houses as late as the Hellenistic period. The city of Lato, for example, has houses from the Classical and Hellenistic periods with a linear arrangement similar to houses at Azoria. The Hellenistic houses from Trypetos are similar, with a linear arrangement and a hearth room, as the possible household and household/outsider focus.

Unfortunately, Azoria does not present us with a burial context. Although there is a very important earlier burial site within the LM IIIC community of nearby Vronda (Day 1995), the location of Azoria's cemetery is not known. Our best information on cemeteries comes from well-excavated sites like those from Iron Age Knossos (Brock 1957;

Coldstream and Catling 1996).[2] Here, people were buried in communal tombs, often in large pithoi. The burial goods on Crete are the same as in the rest of ancient Greece: goods connected to funeral ritual, some personal items, and some military equipment. But as we shall see, the Cretan burial context differs from that on the mainland in its connection to sanctuaries.

As we saw with the rest of ancient Greece, we cannot understand the social structure of the ancient Greeks based on an analysis of communities alone. We needed to nest the communities into a larger intercommunity network to understand the configuration of social structure in the Greek world. We need to do the same on Crete. There was a Cretan intercommunity web, which, like the rest of Greece, included the polities and intercommunity sanctuaries.

Cretan intercommunity sanctuaries (Prent 2005) were sanctuaries that, like interstate sanctuaries on the mainland, would have drawn people from different communities throughout Crete. In the Iron Age, Crete had at least twenty sanctuaries, of which fourteen have functional ancestry extending back into the earlier Minoan period, unlike those on the mainland, with the possible exceptions of Mt. Lykaion and Kalapodi. Ten of these sanctuaries have strong Late Minoan connections: Patsos, the Idaean Cave, Tylissos, Mount Jouktas, Ayia Triadha, Mount Kophinas, the Phaneromeni cave, the Psychro cave, Palaikastro, and Syme. Of these sanctuaries, three were exponentially more active as intercommunity contexts than the rest and provide us with a good window into what an intercommunity sanctuary on Crete in this period would have looked like. They are the Idaean cave, the cave at Tsoutsouros, and Syme. The sanctuary at Tsoutsouros appears especially associated with an emphasis on women, fertility, and sexual coupling and is outside our interest.

The Idaean cave, below the summit of Crete's tallest mountain, ancient Mount Ida, has been associated with the birth of Zeus since Hellenistic and Roman times (Prent 2005: 158–61, 314–18). Terracotta fragments of bull statuettes and horns of consecration highlight material

[2] For a nice overview of Iron Age burial on Crete, see Eaby (2007). But full use of data from Iron Age cemeteries is frustrated by lack of detailed publication. As we shall see, Knossos presents the archaeologist with a useful database for research on Iron Age burials, but other Iron Age sites do not have publications of equal utility. This is especially frustrating in light of the importance of understanding mortuary ostentation and the visibility of any burial monuments. See an early overview by Lebessi (1974) and references further on in this chapter. Eleutherna is especially vexing, because it appears to have had an elaborate cemetery dating to the Iron Age, but we still await final publication of excavations which began in 1985. See Stampolidis (1990, 2004).

from its Minoan period use. Later period finds within and just outside the cave include bronze shields, stands and cauldrons, tripod cauldrons, gold discs, bronze jugs, cups, possible urns, bowls, fibulae, pins, a range of ivories, and various small terracotta figurines.

The character of Syme was somewhat different (Erickson 2002; Lebessi 2009; Lebessi and Muhly 1987; Lebessi et al. 2004; Muhly 2008; Prent 2005: 342–48). Like the Idaean cave, it has connections with earlier Minoan activities. Remains indicate that there was considerable activity in the Minoan and early post-Minoan era, while a later (ca. 600 BCE) identification of the sanctuary tied it to Hermes and Aphrodite. What marks the sanctuary at Syme is the abundance of artwork with depictions of nude men and youths, nude male couples, and scenes of hunters. Lebessi and Muhly (1987) claim, with justification, that this site functioned as a locale for the main Cretan ritual of initiation into manhood. As described by the ancient Greek historians, Ephoros (in Athenaeus, fragment 149) and Strabo (10.4.16–22), an adolescent boy was "abducted" by an older man. The two leave their community and go off into the forest for two months of hunting. The relationship between the two was that of a young man and his older lover. After the stay in the forest, the boy would be reintroduced to his community as a man. He was presented to other men in the andreion and given clothing, a drinking cup, and an ox to sacrifice. The fact that an ox was sacrificed indicates that the participants were probably from the Cretan elite.

One important function of the sanctuaries was to serve as contexts for military display. Both of these sanctuaries contained dedications of armor. This ties them closely to the context of community cult within the polities, which contained dedications of armor, and probably to the andreion, which, at Azoria, has given us pieces of a bronze military helmet. This particular function of the sanctuary at Syme was probably present in other sanctuaries as well. Bronzes with similar themes of man/boy connection have been uncovered at Ayia Triadha (D'Agata 1998), which led Lebessi (1991), the excavator of Syme, to postulate that Ayia Triadha housed a similar custom.[3]

---

[3] The famous Chieftain Cup, discovered at Ayia Triadha, depicts a man and a youth on one side for symbolic decoration. Koehl (1986) has seen it as an earlier Minoan example of the same process of male initiation seen at Syme. The custom was no doubt at least Minoan, yet Lebessi (2002) argues for its origin in the Early Iron Age. Given the strong cult connection to the Minoan past in the beginning of the Iron Age and later (Prent 2008), it is probably attached to more sanctuaries than we know.

Armature of Institutions at Azoria

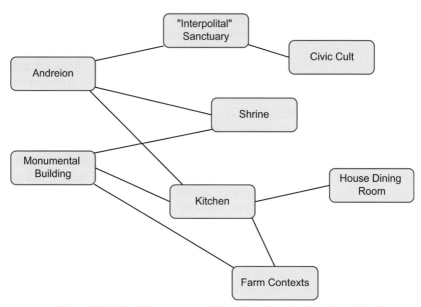

Figure 10.4 Social structure of Iron Age Azoria. (by the author.)

Having reviewed the basic institutions of the Cretan Iron Age polis, let us turn to a structural picture of Azoria within the larger Cretan institutional network (Figure 10.4). The units in this diagram are institutional contexts, not only in Azoria itself but in intercommunity sanctuaries as well, with which Azoria must have been communicating. They are linked to one another by evidence of important functional connections. In the early sixth century Azoria was a web of various interconnected contexts. The intercommunity or "interpolital" sanctuary was connected to the andreion and the civic cult by shared roles in male initiation and dedications of armor. The andreion was exclusionary, as was the civic cult. More recent publications on Azoria allow me to link small shrines (Figure 10.1, D1000 and A1900N) and kitchens to the andreion. The monumental building was also a context for gathering, although it was probably not as exclusionary as the andreion or the civic cult. It is now clearly connected to a small shrine also and to kitchens which must have been engaged in food preparation for dining. This link at first did not appear very important, but it has become so, with the andreion linked to kitchens, as well as their use in houses. All the kitchens at Azoria communicated with what we can only describe as farmstead contexts. Although we have no direct evidence for their existence, we do know that they were producing foodstuffs for kitchen-based processing. In an important deviation from this standard link, the monumental building appears to have also directly connected with farmstead contexts. Finds within the building indicate spit roasting in addition to kitchen-processed finds, with the meat most likely brought directly into the building, supplied from farmsteads rather than from a kitchen.

Azoria exhibits an attractor. But rather than an attractor like sport, as we witnessed for other parts of Greece, the attractor for Azoria is the behaviors associated with food preparation and dining (often exclusive), which appears to have acted as a cohesive force in the evolution of its community structure. The houses highlight this issue. When compared with earlier houses in the region, those at Azoria differ markedly not only in the separation of dining from food preparation, and the separation of food production from food processing and dining, but also in their storage of foods in excess of what would be used by a single family. The contextual units – kitchens, formal dining, and farmstead contexts – which were arranged to produce this type of household were creating something larger than the sum of their parts. The same type of units were also used to create the multicontextual andreion and monumental building complex, whose character was altered by the association of the dining, food processing, and off-house food production units with shrines and sanctuaries. The monumental building is interesting in that it also represents a different structure, with feasting within the building probably connecting directly to farmsteads rather than always to community processing. This would have created a different ideology for those dining within its walls. The focus on commensality and its extensions into agricultural production indicates that one of the chief contexts for the role of aggrandizers was this type of feasting.

Modeling Azoria as part of a larger web also allows us to see how some of these extra-community ties within the larger network helped shape the unique character of the Cretan polis. The role of the sanctuary on Crete was different from that on the mainland. The sanctuaries on Crete were not centers of athletic competition. This goes far to explain why the houses on Crete did not have the characteristic andron, where men would convene in an atmosphere which glorified athletic achievement and private connections to others through interstate sanctuary participation.[4] The sanctuaries on Crete were not places of athletic competition,

---

[4] Westgate (2007: 452) ties this particular spatial syntax of the Cretan house to distinctive characteristics of the Cretan polis that downplay the profile of the individual and

as on the mainland. The sanctuary did not play a role in the development of individual goals (as opposed to the state), as it did on the mainland. As we saw from our textual evidence on the relationship of the sanctuary to the community, its role was to prepare a boy for entrance into citizenship in the polis. This is why a boy would be presented to the community after his abduction as a newly minted adult.

Looking further at the relationship between the sanctuaries and the polities we can turn to the issue of their relationship to funerals and burials. On the mainland the sanctuary was to become the new context for the advertisement of military activity, as we saw with the shift in armor dedication from the burial to the interstate sanctuary. This was not the same on Crete. We do not have evidence from Azoria's cemetery, but data from burials at Knossos and Prinias indicate that military equipment was not shifted from burials to the sanctuaries, nor was there a general shift in dedications of other objects from burials to the sanctuaries.

A View into the Evolution of the Cretan Polis

Azoria represents the development of an established way of community living on Crete as early as the seventh century. Our understanding of what existed on Crete prior to this development is not as clear as we would like. We are limited to just a few known settlements in the period shortly after the fall of Minoan palaces, such as Karphi. But if we take a close look at the institutions evident at Azoria, we might be able to flesh out some salient observations. I will elaborate on three.

The first is cult. What earlier examples we have of community cult on Crete indicate that its defining characteristic, exclusion, was present in early cult buildings. The twelfth-century cult building at Karphi is small and would naturally have been exclusionary. This characteristic probably went further back into Cretan history. The cult building at LM IIIC Vronda was also exclusionary, with two rooms, benches, and an interior hearth, very much like we see later in the hearth temple (Klein and Glowacki 2009).

emphasize the communal system. Accordingly, the communal system, that is, the role of the andreion, on Crete would have created a society with less need for the control of women within the household. They therefore had a greater degree of independence in Cretan society, and there was thus less need to actively segregate women from male visitors to the house. Westgate makes a valid point, but she takes into account only *part* of the total network in which the Cretan polities were operating and omits an important additional point: the absence of intercommunity sanctuaries which were like those in the rest of Greece.

The second is community feasting. There is some evidence for this type of commensality as early as LM IIIC. Wallace (2010: 129–30) identifies three contexts at Karphi where there is evidence for feasting which does not appear closely connected to a family: the megarons complex, the priest's house, and the Great House (see also Day and Snyder 2004). She also rightly notes that there is a connection between feasting, ritual, and domestic life at Karphi. But when we pick up the thread of public feasting again, as at Azoria, the character of feasting is quite different. It is now tightly connected to display at interpolital sanctuaries, such as Kato Syme, and now has exclusion as a primary feature. This is a significant difference, and I would argue that it probably occurred in various communities rather quickly, as a new combination of institutions generating from a phase transition.

Our third case is domestic institutions. A community like Karphi can supply us with some information from the twelfth century. Here the houses were small, without spatial elaboration which would have set the members of the household a step away from the community. The LM IIIC houses at Vronda were very similar (Glowacki 2004). Houses in this period displayed a dynamic characteristic, in that they grew by agglutination; that is, new rooms were often built onto a house core, thereby expanding the house. It is most likely that these new rooms represent the inclusion of new kin units into the original household which would have occupied the house core. The houses we have at Azoria are distinctly different, however. Gone is the ability to expand and include new people. Another crucial difference is that the houses at Azoria appear to be a part of a larger system of food production. Storage areas in the houses were larger than needed and must have represented the fact that the house was now part of a food procurement and processing system which connected it to food-producing landholdings and, as we already saw, a community-wide focus on food preparation in general.[5]

Features such as these in the Iron Age Cretan polis show that it differed dramatically from what had preceded it. The fact that Azoria was a planned community which was settled quickly points sharply to the fact that the changes in these two features of Cretan community structure occurred rapidly, fitting well our understanding of a phase transition. But

---

[5] It is now thought that the houses are Azoria were "town houses" replicating the estate houses of wealthy individuals in the Azoria community. They would have been used when families from these estates were engaged in the activities of the community, such as feasting in either the andreion complex or the monumental building (Fitzsimons, personal communication).

there are at least 300–350 years between the communities of Karphi and Vronda. Can we understand this period of time any better?[6]

Here I turn again to complexity theory and its tie to elaboration in feasting. In a situation similar to funeral elaboration in communities outside Crete in the Iron Age, and on the island itself earlier, it is possible to isolate elaborate funeral feasting to point to possible periods when Cretan culture was in some sort of social chaos. For an entire island, our mortuary record is actually meager, but its dynamics do suggest periods when we might be able to illuminate some sort of period when aggrandizers were actively working to create a new social structure to their benefit. Three sites provide us with enough mortuary material to allow us at this moment to suggest possible dates for such community changes. They are Knossos, Eleutherna, and Prinias. There are two cemeteries from Iron Age Knossos, one exposed in the Fortetsa (Brock 1957) and the other in the North Cemetery (Coldstream and Catling 1996) excavations. The material from Eleutherna is currently limited to the ceramic and human bone publications of an Iron Age tomb, A1K1 (Anagnostis 2005; Kotsonas 2008; see also Stampolidis 1990). Prinias has a large cemetery which contains burials from the Protogeometric to Archaic periods (ca. 1050–700 BCE). Its current publication (Rizza 1978) is somewhat lacking, but it does supply enough information to make looking at it worthwhile.

Unlike the case seen earlier with the presence of numerous cups outside the earlier tholoi of the Messara, the much better state of burial preservation in the burials at Knossos allows us to more fully consider what evidence for elaborate funeral feasting might be. Ethnographic research (Hayden 2009) has indicated that elaborate funeral feasting differs from other forms of funeral feasting in the size of the funeral and in the cost spent on the feast, sometimes even including the slaughtering of expensive animals. From an archaeological perspective this would mean we would be looking for a large number of serving utensils associated with the burial, the richness of any related material, and, as we saw at Lefkandi, evidence for the destruction of costly animals.

Turning to Knossos first, the British excavations in the Fortetsa cemetery (Brock 1957) indicate that its tombs fall squarely within our time period, with a majority dating to the Protogeometric (ca. 1050 BCE). The other cemetery is the North Cemetery, which was excavated, again

---

[6] The results of excavations at Prinias could help fill in the gap. But the publications have some drawbacks in their lack of attention to stratigraphy, omission of various types of material, and delay of interpretation until future publication. See Rizza (2008).

by the British (Coldstream and Catling 1996), as part of a rescue operation in light of the expansion of a local hospital. It has burials which run
from the Protogeometric to the Orientalizing period.

How can we look for elaborate funeral feasting in these cemeteries?
I am assuming that some type of funeral meal was occurring at most
interments, as seen in the ubiquitous presence of kraters and drinking
cups in association with various burials. But identifying evidence for
elaborate funeral feasting is different. In examining tombs for evidence
of elaborate funeral feasting, let me return to the observations of Hayden
and others. Of the three characteristics Hayden highlights, I am removing the food-gifting category, simply because there is little in the archaeological record in the Knossosian cemeteries which would correlate
with that definition. Trying to kill as many valuable domestic animals as
possible can be visible in the archaeological record in two ways. If the
animals were eaten, then we might be able to find some evidence for it, if
we have animal faunal evidence in the tomb. On the other hand, if the
killing of domestic animals is not meant for food but to show how rich the
family of the deceased was, we might be able to observe this if the animals
were buried. Hayden's other distinction for elaborate funeral feasts –
inviting as many people as possible, from as large an area as possible, and
as high a rank as possible – might be seen in the number of feasting dishes
left in the tomb, the presence of imported materials left in the tomb as
tokens from members of the funeral feast who were not within the
community, or materials from the preparation of food for the feast.

With these observations in mind I examine two categories of evidence
from Knossos which might be related to elaborate funeral feasting. The
first is that of materials related to large feasting celebrations. For Knossos
this category includes obeloi, or roasting spits; firedogs which would have
been used for roasting meat; and fire baskets. These objects were made of
iron, which might present problems when it comes to quantification of
their presence within the tombs. There are two things which could affect
the record of iron in the tombs: tomb robbing and corrosion. Having
gone over the reports from the tombs, it does not appear that thieves
sought iron. Undisturbed tombs and pillaged tombs each contained a
wide variety of iron objects. Corrosion does not appear to have been a
factor, which would bias the data as well. For the North Cemetery it
appears that the rate of corrosion was somewhat consistent between
tombs. My own examination of the iron objects from these tombs, now
in the stratigraphical museum at Knossos, indicates that there was little
difference in the preservation of iron objects, such as swords or spear
points. Therefore it is quite likely that the frequency of obeloi, for
example, is indicated by the remains in the tombs.

The second category is evidence of killing prized domesticated animals. We have some faunal evidence from the tombs which indicates that some sheep, goats, and pigs were consumed in the funeral meal. But we also have strong evidence for the destruction of prized animals, horses and dogs. For Knossos, the bones of these prized animals were found in separate burial pits. If we can assume that the work in the North Cemetery was extensive enough to have not missed any other horse burials, which seems likely, we can isolate this material to early and middle Orientalizing period (ca. 700–650 BCE).

Analysis of the tombs and artifacts shows that feasting tools cluster in a few tombs in the period 750–700 BCE. An excellent example comes from tomb 219. As best that can be determined, pithos 45, dated to this period, represents a burial which had a funeral feast which used obeloi, firedogs, and fire baskets. The feasting material from tomb 285 was bundled together in the tomb. It contained obeloi and firedogs. Unlike the case in tomb 219, it is impossible to associate this material with a single burial. There are six urns which should be candidates, dating from the close of the eighth century BCE. Five horses and four dogs were killed as part of probably three funeral feasts between 750 and 700 BCE. The sacrifice of a horse is costly enough, and the material here indicates that these horses had just reached their full maturity, having been killed when they were between two and three and a half years old.

The material from the Fortetsa cemetery, while not as rich, is similar in indicating elaborate funeral feasting from 750 to 700 BCE. As reported by Brock (1957) in his inclusion of material excavated earlier by Platon, tomb P contained two "bundles" of obeloi associated with burial urns of the late eighth century.

What should we make of this evidence? There are some important points. First, the chronological span of both cemeteries allows us to isolate a period in the late eighth century when at least eight families found it to their advantage to host elaborate funeral feasts (Figure 10.5). I would therefore extend this to argue that the late eighth century at Knossos strongly suggests that it was period of social structural change, a period of chaos when different families were trying to establish themselves within the new structure which was developing. The families were the aggrandizers, and it was they who were agents in the creation of emergent properties which were to have a strong influence on the final evolution of the community of Knossos. New material which comes from the British urban survey of Knossos shows that this is the period of its greatest expansion. Thus its most rapid growth in population is in the tenth or ninth century. Our mortuary data, however, indicate that there might have been little internal structural change in Knossos until the

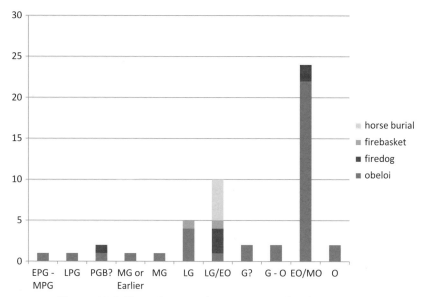

Figure 10.5 Use of ostentatious mortuary feasting material at Iron Age Knossos. Y axis indicates number of objects. (by the author.)

eighth century, when we can identify a phase transition. This lag time fits well with our concepts of a phase transition, whereby social conflict, which might correlate with an increase in population, might not be addressed until later and then in a rapid fashion (but see caveat in the case of stimulus and chaos in Iron Age outside Crete, page 123).

The case of Eleutherna is interesting in that the analysis of the pottery from tomb A1K1 indicates that there was a rise in feasting (Kotsonas 2008: 340) in the Late Protogeometric to Early Geometric phases (ca. 950–850 BCE) of the tomb. This could provide a window into a condition similar to that witnessed at Knossos, but we need the results of the study of the rest of the Iron Age burials at Eleutherna in order to carry this argument further.

Our third cemetery is associated with the city of Prinias. The city has a long history. While not as old as Knossos, there is archaeological evidence for some sort of LM IIIC (ca. thirteenth century BCE) occupation. The best estimate for its last days is the mid-sixth century. My interest here lies in its necropolis. It consists of at least 680 tombs and spans the time period from the thirteenth to the mid-sixth century BCE. The cemetery was excavated in the late 1960s and there is a short report on the results of the excavation by Rizza in 1978. For such a large cemetery, however, the current publication is inadequate, lacking much detail on tombs and finds (no details on the pottery have been published, for example). An attempt to recreate our work at Knossos is therefore impossible. We do not have adequate knowledge of associated obeloi, for example.

However, the excavators did uncover twelve horse burials, which, as in the case of Knossos, are associated with six canine interments. There are some close parallels to the horse burials at Knossos, which would indicate that this type of burial was an established institution on Crete. One of the Prinias burials holds a horse with its neck extended backward, as also seen in Knossos. Like the situation at Knossos, six of the horse burials were closely associated or even buried with dogs. Unlike the situation at Knossos, however, the dates for these horse interments fall within the Subminoan-Protogeometric B phases (ca. 1100–810 BCE).

The burials indicate that within this roughly 300-year period, the community of Prinias was undergoing significant structural change. This can be significant, because the construction of the hearth temples in the eighth and seventh centuries (temples A and B similar to that of the civic cult at Azoria) on the akropolis indicates that at least one institution which was to become somewhat ubiquitous in later Crete had already been established by the end of this early phase transition. Excavation under buildings on the akropolis of the community shows that there was already some sort of a LM IIIC presence. Taking into account the information from the elaborate funeral feasting in its necropolis, we are held to ask, what type of structural change might there have been before the establishment of the institution of the poliadic deity in the eighth century? It is interesting then that Italian excavations on the akropolis (Palermo et al. 2008) are just now beginning to expose evidence for what might have been earlier religious worship in the presence of what appear to be three standing stones, similar to the stones identified by Shaw in an early "Phoenician" temple at Kommos (Shaw 1989). The later hearth temples completely obliterated this earlier construction. This feature of the phase transition for Prinias could very well be similar to that at Azoria. There an eighth-century shrine/temple was covered over in the construction of the sixth-century community.

The observations at this point would indicate that it might not be wise to view phase transitions as taking place at the same time throughout the island. These transitions at Prinias and Knossos were not contemporaneous. Different communities would have different thresholds to phase change. This was probably similar to the situation in the rest of Greece. As the culture was moving to a new level of structure, each polity was probably undergoing its own "phase transition," which eventually interfaced with multiple polities to create a unified structural change for the polities as a group. A possible reason for the different periods of phase transitions at Knossos and Prinias could have been local cultural history. Knossos is a community with a history extending deeply into the early Minoan past. Prinias has a different early history. It was not part of a tradition as powerful as that of Knossos. It was a new settlement, like Karphi, dating from the end of the Cretan Bronze Age.

Measures of Social Complexity

The application of our structural model and the analytical frame of complexity theory has highlighted the unique culture of Crete in the Iron Age. The social structure of Cretan Iron Age communities was unique. Limited to the island, this structure was composed of various institutions, exclusionary civic cult, the andreion, etc., which were tied together in a social structure which was engendered by the force of early attractors associated with food preparation and dining. Complexity theory's frame would indicate that structural change was not even throughout the island, but that it began to coalesce in the eighth and seventh centuries.

Readings

Studies which concentrate on the Iron Age on Crete are not as numerous as they should be. But see Willetts (1965), who wrote an influential social history of Crete, based principally on textual resources. Willetts also chose a broad historical spectrum and did not focus exclusively on Crete's Iron Age. There are also some important problems related to our understanding of the archaeological record on the island in this period. An "archaic gap" has been noticed, where there appears to be a loss of ceramic evidence in the sixth and fifth centuries, which would imply a significant demographic downturn. See Coldstream and Huxley (1999), who approached the problem by using the ceramic series from Knossos. Erickson (2010) has also reviewed changes in Archaic and Classical Crete through ceramic analysis. He argues that, rather than some sort of demographic catastrophe hitting Crete at this time, the issue is probably a problem with our ceramic identification and chronology. The inscriptional record from Crete is unique, supplying us with some very early examples of community laws. See Chaniotis (2005) for analysis of the famous inscription from early Gortyn. An excellent survey of the settlements and territory around Azoria can be found in the work of Haggis (1993, 2005), who describes a particular pattern of settlement clustering, which probably appeared elsewhere in Late Minoan and Iron Age Crete.

11 The Sweep of Things
The Larger Picture of the Evolution of Ancient Greece

At this point I have discussed all the major features in the development of ancient Greece. In Chapter 12, I intend to show how the results of the study of ancient Greece can assist us in understanding other similar cultures. So, this would be a good point to sum up what we know of the evolution of ancient Greece before we move on.

Let us focus on the essential points of social complexity and social change. For the Neolithic period there are no real surprises. Communities in Greece were basically centered on households. Institutions were embedded in the households themselves, and there was probably little, if any, organization above the household.

For the first millennium after the Neolithic there is evidence that society was changing. But our understanding of what was new in comparison to the Neolithic is uneasy. Feasting ware shows some sort of social hierarchy. At issue, however, is whether or not society in Greece had some sort of developed organization beyond the household and, if so, what. Arguments for a political economy are not as clear as we would like. Seals found in the House of the Tiles could represent some type of economic oversight between households, but could just as well represent the interests of those bringing goods to the house itself. The construction of a defensive wall at Lerna might indicate that goods and labor were collected from different households to support its construction, but we cannot dismiss the possibility that it was built within the material and labor resources of a single large household.

In the Cyclades, several island communities were joined with those on other islands to create a common material culture. Oared boats tied these communities together and gave access to a common religious sanctuary on the island of Keros, which probably served as a neutral focus for interchange of ideas between island and possibly even northern Cretan communities. We know little more of these communities other than that there was possible social differentiation in funerals.

Crete at this time was an island of various different localized cultures, with communities on its northeast coast actually part of a larger Cycladic sphere. Burials suggest that there was some sort of competition between households. But we are still left with little knowledge of what might have existed above the household level. Evidence for community structure is limited to Myrtos, where our knowledge of what existed beyond the interests of households is limited.

The period around the beginning of the second millennium was one of dramatic social change. On Crete we have used complexity theory to frame dramatic changes in communities, such as those in the Messara, and at important centers, such as Knossos and Malia. Spurred by some sort of stimulus, the old social order of the early centuries of the third millennium was not meeting new social needs. We see aggrandizers operating within feasting contexts to create new institutions and links between them, with a resulting new social structure by 2000–1900 BCE. The results can be seen in administrative centers and several communities. Knossos and other palatial centers emerged with important economic, administrative, and religious institutions. Large communities, such as Gournia and Palaikastro, show us additional institutions tied to households of lower status. Centers like Knossos must have served as administrative hubs for polities.

In the islands the development of centers such as Phylakopi argues for some sort of administrative level above the household. Funerals become important with new feasting behaviors. The most important innovation in the Cyclades was that of the sailing ship, which increased the ability of the islands to contact other cultures in the eastern Mediterranean.

For the mainland there is still little evidence for any elaborate institutions beyond the level of the household, very much similar to the situation in the previous millennium. Funerals were active institutions and probably used for social competition and cohesion.

All three regions entered into a common koine by the middle of the millennium. An active region within this koine was western and central Crete, the western Cyclades, and the southern Peloponnesos. Its common language was probably an early form of ancient Greek.

Changes were to continue into the latter half of the second millennium. The island of Thera exploded, which had a damaging effect on the cultures of Crete. By 1400 BCE Knossos was apparently one of the few administrative centers remaining. Evolutionary developments were rapid on the mainland. Incorporation into the Aegean koine destabilized society in Messenia and the Argolid, as different households grew wealthy due to interaction in the koine, and aggrandizers were operating within elaborate funeral contexts. The result was a new social order, which was made visible in the Mycenaean polities, where earlier domestic institutions changed to become institutions of political and economic control.

By 1100 BCE the palaces and their society had collapsed. What was left was a Greek world somewhat similar to that which existed before the rise of the palace polities. Here our social modeling is most useful, as it supplies us with a model of an actual spectrum of social institutions: those of the household, funeral practices, religious practices, warfare, and politics. Most of these institutions are rudimentary. Religious behavior did not include temples; warfare was basically raiding and attached to household interests. Politics was encapsulated in the play between leaders and early forms of assemblies and councils. By the eighth century new wealth was creating problems, as the old social order did not mitigate the social disruption which this new wealth engendered. Aggrandizers were using elaborate funeral feasting, as seen in an increase in funeral feasting ware in tombs and an interest in marking Late Helladic tombs, to create an order which matched the distribution of this new wealth. But the stimulus of wealth was too strong, and communities lost their cohesive structure and fissioned. Greeks now spread out to other areas in the Mediterranean and Black Sea, building a network of connections between these communities which set the stage for the next evolutionary phase, the reorganization of the community.

The changes brought by the eighth century produced the social structure and the institutions which we recognize as typical of ancient Greece. Modeling social structure and using complexity theory as a window into social change highlights some salient points. An important feature of these institutions is that they were very much the same in all the Greek communities in the Mediterranean, except for those on Crete. Pre-eighth-century institutions became more complex. New institutions were created, such as those of the gymnasion. Ties between various institutions became regularized, such as those between the institutions of the battlefield and those of the interstate sanctuary. Old ties disappeared. The funeral was no longer as closely connected to the institutions of the battlefield as it had been. Many of these changes were brought about by competition between elites, both within the same polity and across polities. There were various attractors, the epics of Hesiod and Homer, athletic competition at the interpolital sanctuaries, and the similar competitive behavior of these elites as each sought a distinction – an honorific statue, support of theater construction, etc. – which was recognized by others. The social structure which resulted from the reorganization of Greek society in the eighth century and later was stable and lasted into the third century of the Roman Empire.

Looking at social structure and our use of complexity theory exposes critical differences between Iron Age Crete and the rest of the Greek world. Many of its principal social institutions were different from others elsewhere in ancient Greece. Its unique religious, dining, and domestic institutions were coupled with an intercommunity sanctuary tradition which did not match those in the rest of the Greek world. Rather than athletic competition at interpolital sanctuaries, and competitive behavior which sought distinction in the placement of statues or liturgies, the attractors on Crete were centered on restricted, exclusive dining.

The outcome of the reorganization of Greek culture after the eighth century was that the Greek world was made up of numerous independent polities. This weakened the development of a strong political economy, since no polity, because of its limited territorial control, could control the economic and sometimes political actions of elites who would and could operate on a pan-polity level. That problem, and the fact that Greece can help us understand its place in other small polities' cultures, is the topic of our final chapter.

12   Greece Is Not Alone
The Small Polity Evolutionary Characteristics of the Ancient Greeks and Other Past Cultures

In the first chapter I related how analytical frames which were developed in other archaeologies have been applied to the analysis of the ancient Greeks. In this chapter I want to turn the tables and show how observations we have gained in looking at small polities in ancient Greece can be of utility in cross-cultural analysis. I am looking specifically here at a comparison between the ancient Greeks and the ancient Maya. I am not the first person to suggest that there might be some benefit in cross-cultural analysis between the Maya and the ancient Greeks. Tartaron (2008) and Parkinson and Galaty (2007b) have suggested that there were important parallels between the cultures of the Classic Maya and those of the Late Bronze Age on the Greek mainland, which would facilitate useful comparative analysis.

Characteristics of Greek Small Polities

From our previous observations we can point to a number of salient characteristics which we outlined to describe the small Greek polity which existed from the collapse of the Minoan and Mycenaean palaces to the advent of the rise of Macedonian power. The Greek example has a rich database which allows a somewhat fine-grained analysis of its past and allows us to isolate some concepts inherent in clusters of small polities which would be applicable to the analysis of evolution in similar small polities in general. To explore this issue I am going to compare the situation seen among the ancient Greeks with the Classic Maya.

As I described, Greek polities after the eighth century evolved in a larger network of preexisting pan-polity elite economic and political connections. Because the polities were territorially limited they could not control the activities of these extra-polity networks. This left them subject to internal conflict, which was often abetted by the extra-polity connections of its resident elites. It severely limited the growth of an actual political economy within the polis. Much of the economic activity of the elites was beyond a polity's control. A dramatic result of this inability to develop a political economy is seen in the inability of Athens to economically absorb its fifth-century empire into a cohesive entity.

The Classic Maya

Located in the Mesoamerican countries of Mexico, Guatemala, Belize, and Honduras (Figure 12.1), the Maya peoples have had a tremendously long history, which reaches back to at least 9000 BCE when lithic tools and mammoth bones were somehow deposited in the Lotan Caves in the Yucatan.

To what degree does the cultural situation of the Maya compare with that of the Classical Greeks? The Classic period Maya (250–900 CE) evolved in an active interpolity network (Reese-Taylor and Walker 2002) very much like that of Classical Greece. There is mounting evidence that the Late Preclassic (400 BCE to 100 CE) witnessed the disintegration of large regional polities, like El Mirador, a large polity in the Peten region of Guatemala (Dahlin 1984; Matheny 1980, 1986), and the transformation of the landscape into one of smaller polities, with smaller controlling territories. One of the reasons for this change was increasing instability which arose from competition over long-distance trade routes, after El Mirador's collapse. This competition was between elites who were trading in commodities such as jade, shell, obsidian, and pyrite. Kinship was most likely fluid during that period and negotiated between elite lineages. Tokens of these connections were most likely high-value pottery such as Ixcanrio Orange Polychrome (Reese-Taylor and Walker 2002: figure 4.9), which is found principally in burials and caches and was probably associated with the moon goddess, Ix Chel. Such pottery was most likely exchanged between elites from different polities as various elites would gather at different polities for feasting events. In looking at the presence of this pottery in a frame of social dynamics, it was probably used by powerful lineages and nascent dynasties who were constructing powerful relationships by means of ceramic production and exchange. Reese-Taylor and Walker (2002) also contend that a later pottery, Dos Arroyos Polychrome, was associated with the rise of ruling elites in Tikal, who were developing alliances between elites from various polities as they were cementing their power at Tikal, the largest of all the Mayan polities.

Figure 12.1 Map of Classic period Maya centers. (Map outline from *The Electronic Atlas of Ancient Maya Sites*, © 2001, 2002, 2005, 2008, 2009, 2010, Walter R. T. Witschey and Clifford T. Brown; by permission of Nicolas Carter.)

As Mayan polities moved into the Classic periods, especially toward the Late Classic period (600–900 CE), evidence for this exchange becomes even more pronounced with the appearance of high-quality Late Classic pictorial polychrome. Decorated often with depictions of rulers, feasting, or just well-designed art, these pots were presented to visitors at feasts, as tokens of political and economic ties between lineages from different polities. They were taken back to home polities by elites and must have held a high importance in the profiles of different lineages, because there are several of these nonnative elite pots excavated in foreign contexts (Coggins 1975; Reents-Budet 1994: 164–233; Reents-Budet et al. 2000; see also Halperin and Foias 2010; Tokovinine 2016).

So, Maya polities of the Classic period must have been nodes on a larger interactive network such as we have seen for the Greeks. Important connections were made between elites from various polities. The connections were created by participation in feasting contexts, and gifted pots were powerful tokens of those connections. These connections were not limited to the ruling elites but were part of the generalized elite network altogether. Mayan polities were assemblages of multiple elite lineages. Not all lineages were ruling lineages, but many were negotiating for increased power, possibly even rulership, and these interpolital connections must have played an important part in this negotiation.

An important example of the ambiguity of relationships between rulers and elites within a polity, which these connections created, comes from late Classic El Palmar (Figure 12.2). The Guzman Group, which was an elite compound within the polity, was connected to the Main Group of the polity, which is identified as the compound of the ruling lineage. Recent work at El Palmar (Tsukamoto et al. 2015) has uncovered a hieroglyphic stairway in the Guzman Group which ties the ruler of the group's lineage to the ruler of Copan and that of Calakmul (two large, powerful, but distant polities). The stairway further identifies the ruler of El Palmar, but does not list the lineage head of the Guzman Group as his subordinate, even though the group is tied to the Main Group by a causeway, a raised roadway which usually indicates that such a group is actively tied to the polity (Cheetham 2004; see also the Caracol case mentioned later). It is evident that El Palmar's ruler was not able to control the trajectory of the lineage in the Guzman Group, which had important connections outside the territorial limits of El Palmar. The layout of the Guzman Groups shows that it contained an internal plaza which would have been the location for feasting (Wells 2004), indicating that the group itself was a context for feasting which would have challenged the hegemony of the lineage of El Palmar's Main Group.

This must also have been the case with the elites at Las Sepulturas (Sheehy 1991; Webster et al. 1989). Las Sepulturas was an outlier elite

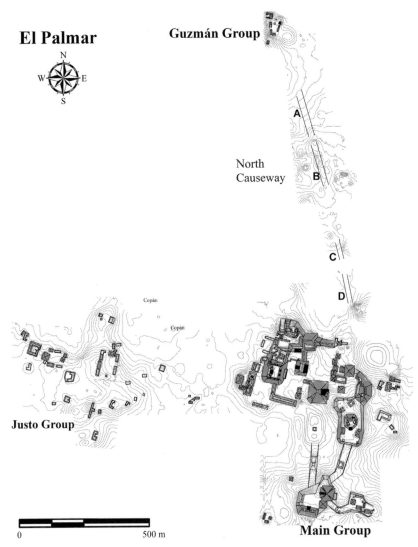

Figure 12.2 El Palmar. (From Tsukamoto et al. 2015: figure 2; by permission of K. Tsukamoto.)

compound in the Copan polity. Its elites were beginning to usurp the ideology of the ruling lineage of Copan in their use of the "skyband" motif, an image closely tied to rulership, on presentation benches in their houses toward the end of the Classic period.

Box 16   Usurping Symbols of Rulership: The Skyband
in the Elite Compound of Las Sepulturas, Copan

The skyband, also known as the celestial monster, was a representation of the
cosmos or, more specifically, the Milky Way (Figure 12.3). It was used by
Mayan royals in ceremonies associated with royal power and presence. The
ruler, or "ahau," was often depicted as standing within the cosmos, surrounded by the skyband, and thereby centered in the power of the universe.
A classic example is the skyband surround for the entrance to building 22 in
the Copan akropolis. This was a presentation doorway for the ruler himself.
Although a symbol of royal power, the skyband was incorporated into the
design of elite benches in the non-royal elite compound of Las Sepulturas at
Copan. This use occurred late in the history of the polity and represents a
symbolic challenge to the ideological power of Copan's ruler.

This ruler/subelite relationship of partial independence is also documented well in other Mayan settlements. A dramatic example of compounds with semi-autonomous elite residences comes from the Lower
Montagua Valley in Guatemala (Shortman and Ashmore 2012). In this
valley several settlements were apparently occupied by different elite
families, each of whom had an apparently different interpolital network
within which it would operate. Factional distinctions can be seen at
centers such as Las Quebradas, where its different elite compounds
had distinctly different symbols of authority. The elites in these compounds were cooperating with factions through an intercommunity network larger than one would expect. This is signaled by the fact that
people within this valley system apparently did not succumb to allying
with either of their close neighbors, Copan or Quirigua, after the apparent regional political instability launched by the beheading of Copan's
ruler Waxaklahun-Ub' ah-K'awil by the Quirigua ruler K' ak' Tiliw' in
738 CE, after Copan raided that polity.

This manner of networking created a great danger of internal instability within the Mayan polity. As we saw in the case of the Greeks, ruling
elites, because of the limited size of the territory of their polity, could not
control or dominate the economic spheres of nonruling elites, who had
connections outside the polity and who could use these connections to
destabilize the internal cohesiveness of the polis, making the construction
of a political economy difficult at best. As Cioffi-Revilla and Landman
(1999) have demonstrated, most of the Mayan polities were highly
unstable, and it was only a few of the older polities, such as Tikal or
Copan, who having perhaps cemented internal hierarchy early on were
able to enjoy any measure of internal stability. Polities without such a

Figure 12.3 Skyband on elite presentation bench from Las Sepulturas,

historical pedigree, such as Bonampak or Uxmal, were not able to withstand the force of networking outside the polity.

As successfully argued by multiple Mayan scholars (Rice 2008; Stuart 2005), the basis of Mayan royal rule does not lie in an accepted concept of political economy, where a ruler would extend his economic power, be it based on the ownership of large tracts of land or slaves, over other lineages within a Mayan polity. Instead, these other lineages were tied into interpolital relations. Rather, the power of the lord, or ahau, lay in

Copan. (By permission of Robin Heyworth.)

his role in the larger religious context of the polity. In an important way he created power over others when he let blood, burned incense, and danced. In each action he was creating divinity and creating connections to powerful deities who would ensure the good fortune of his kingdom, whether it was in agricultural abundance or in military victory. These observations have led some scholars such as Demarest (1984, 1992, 1997, 2004: 215–17) to underline the unstable internal structure of the Mayan polities and to describe this internal composition with models such as "galactic polities," a term coined by Tambiah (1976, 1977) to describe polities in Southeast Asia with rulership based primarily on ideology and a great degree of internal instability.

Benefits from Employing the Greek Model

The disjointed structure of many small polities in Greece was similar to the situation for the small polities among the Maya. The material evidence for ancient Greece, however, is much richer than that for the Maya, which prods us to ask if the richer observations gained from our study of the ancient Greeks can aid us in work with the Maya. The answer is an obvious yes, in that it helps us place issues stemming from the Maya into useful analytical frames.

There are two ways in which we might take into account this observation when we look at the Maya. The first is in challenging the common assumption of strong bureaucratic oversight within a Mayan polity. Chase and Chase (A. Chase 1998; A. Chase and D. Chase 1996, 1998, 2001, 2004; A. Chase et al. 2015; D. Chase and A. Chase 2015) have repeatedly made the argument that Caracol internally developed a large bureaucracy in the Late Classic period. They point to the archaeological record, which contains evidence for causeways which connect numerous architectural groups like those at El Palmar to the main group at Caracol and the presence of compounds near these groups which could have been used as markets, controlled by the royals of the main group through taxation. Chase and Chase would see these features as indicating that some sort of bureaucracy was controlling the distribution of goods in the polity. The application of observations gained from the study of the control of economics in ancient Greek polities can be of some assistance here. Rather than assume these markets were controlled by Caracol's ruling elite, the case of the ancient Greeks should lead us to be cautious. Another model needs to be taken into consideration, that which considers economically independent elite groups, like those in Classical Greece. Markets dispersed at the end of causeways might not fit into a model which suggests control from central ruling elite, but instead localized control, with economic connections outside Caracol, which might even be used to challenge attempts by the ruling faction to control the affairs of the subelites. Like the economic situation in Classical Greece, there is a case to be made that Caracol might have been a polity with distributed economic power among its elites rather than a tight central control.

My second point relates to the inability of small polities to integrate conquered lands through some sort of economic control. The last twenty years of research into the ancient Maya has seen an increasing awareness of political alliances and sometimes outright conquest of different polities in the later part of the Classic period. At least by the Late Classic there was noticed inequality between many Mayan polities, with several polities in relationships of overlordship and subservience (noted by Marcus 1976). Hieroglyphic references to war from this period tell us that there were at least four types of aggression and conquest between different polities (A. Chase and D. Chase 1998). There was the ch' ak, or axe-event, where a losing ruler was decapitated. There was hubi, or destruction, probably referring to that of a community. Maya also described a chuc' ak, or capture of an individual, and a "star war," which apparently referred to the major conquest and destruction of another polity.

The Maya historical landscape is populated with several different instances of recorded overlord/subservient relations, as a result of defeat in battle. Yaxchilan over Machaquila in 664 and 729 CE; Piedras Negras over Pomona in 793 CE; Caracol over Ucanal in 800 CE; Caracol over Naranjo in 631 CE; and Caracol over Tikal in 562 CE. While these relationships of dominance and submission are recognized, the actual relationships between these polities were extremely unstable and in a state of constant change. Once a polity conquered another, it could not maintain any dominant control for any period of time. In general it seems that the unequal relationship between these polities was mainly along a political plane. There is no evidence for any of these conquering polities using any economic means to incorporate newly conquered states into a larger polity. The Greek case is helpful here as a comparative window. Because they were not able to economically control elite economic activities outside the polis, Greek polities had poorly developed political economies, which hampered a polis like Athens from seeing how it could economically incorporate its conquered territories in the fifth century BCE. Internally, the Maya were the same and suffered, like the Greeks, from a conceptual inability to see how they could economically incorporate conquered polities. The best they could do was to demand tribute, but tribute is often a one-time payment and differs from actual taxation, which has economic structure and would have come from Mayan ruling lineages having the experience of taxing other powerful lineages in their communities.

This comparison of Greek polities within their networks with that of the Classic Maya has been useful in casting analytical light onto our understanding some of the shortfalls of the Maya. There are several other areas and periods in the world where we could observe people living in similar political and economic circumstances (see papers in Nichols and Charlton 1997). In the New World the basin of Mexico was periodically occupied by small states from shortly before the rise of Teotihuacan (ca. 200 BCE) and shortly after its fall (ca. 700 CE) (Cowgill 2015). The Moche small states (Bawden 1999) spanned the Peruvian coast from 500 BCE to 600 CE. There were various and periodic pre-Incan polities (Janusek 2008) in the Andes from 500 BCE to 1400 CE. In addition to the case of the ancient Greeks, Europe was populated by small polities in Etruscan Italy (Barker and Rasmussen 2000) flourishing from 800 to 300 BCE, and I would also add Anglo-Saxon England, 500–1000 CE. Perhaps the earliest examples of small polities we have come from Mesopotamia (Pollock 1999) in the period 2600–1500 BCE. Harrapan small polities (Wright 2009) lay within the fertile Indus Valley in the centuries from 500 BCE to 500 CE. Preimperial China (Flad and Chen 2013) was fragmented with small polities from 2000 to 200 BCE. And, finally, Egypt (Wenke 2009) was a land of small polities hundreds of years before its unification ca. 3000 BCE. The potential for incorporating ancient Greece into fruitful cross-cultural analysis is great.

Readings

Not much has been published on comparative analysis between ancient Greece and other past cultures, so there are not many further readings to suggest. Those interested in further information on the ancient Maya can turn to such works as Coe (2011) and Sharer and Traxler (2006). An evolutionary perspective on the ancient Maya can be sought in Blanton et al. (1993). The fascinating story of deciphering Maya hieroglyphics is told by Coe (2012).

Glossary

Agora (ai): Principal space within a polis where markets, civic buildings, and honorific statues are often placed.

Akropolis (eis): The fortified high point of an ancient city. The most notable is the akropolis of Athens.

Amphora (ai): Ceramic transport container; most common were those which contained various traded goods, from beans to olive oil to fish sauce. Amphorai on many occasions were stamped on their handles with names of public officials, and are therefore useful to archaeologists for dating. Decorated amphorai were also used as burial urns in the Geometric period.

Andreion: Dining hall on Crete where male citizens of the polis would partake of a common meal.

Andron: Room in many Greek houses where the men of the household would entertain men from the community. This was often the spatial context of the symposion.

Apoikia (ai): "Away settlement"; the polis which hived off a Greek community in the period of fissioning in the eighth and later centuries. Distinguished from an emporion, whose main function was that of a trading post (this distinction, however, is not always clear).

Apsidal: Refers to an apse, the short end of a room or building whose wall is semi-circular.

Archon: Administrator in a Greek polis.

Basileus (eis): Word found in Homeric epic which refers to a ruler, perhaps less than an absolute king. Origin of the word may be from Linear B, "Qa-si-re-u," a possible Bronze Age territorial functionary or leader of a small group.

Boule: Council within a Greek polis, whose main function was to set the agenda for discussion and hence voting, in the ekklesia.

Collared jar: Cycladic suspensory jar with a tall collar often made from marble.

Cuirass: Protective chest armor of a Greek hoplite soldier.

Demos: People who make up the citizenry of a polis. These were men over the age of eighteen, who often held land within the territory of the polis.

Ekklesia: Political assembly of a Greek polis. (See boule.)

Emporion (a): A Greek community in another country whose basic function was that of trade; a trading post. The city of Naucratis in Egypt was one of the most notable Greek emporia.

Ephebe: Male citizen under the age of eighteen, usually undergoing civic and military training.

Ephebeion: Room in a gymnasion building where ephebes received civic education.

Ethnos (e): A definitive people. In a political sense an ethnos was a region in Greece which identified with a particular group of people rather than an individual polis. An ethnos was often administered by a league which met in a sanctuary within the ethnos itself.

Fire basket: Metal basket attached to metal pole, used to roast meat suspended over a fire.

Firedogs: Pair of metal stands used to support small spits over an open fire.

Frying pans: Term used to describe a type of pottery popular in the third millennium in the Cyclades. The vessel's shape resembles that of a low-sided frying pan with a truncated handle. Frying pans often have elaborate decoration on the surface of the bottom of the pan and on the handle.

Hoplite: Name for Greek soldier after the eighth century BCE. Derived from hoplon.

Hoplon: Round shield used by Greek soldier in battle.

Horns of consecration: Stylized bulls' horns used in decoration, e.g., in a tripartite shrine.

Hydria: Water jar with two handles on its side and one at the back for pouring. The jar had a spout and was often decorated with painted scenes, indicating its use in formalized eating and drinking contexts.

Interpolital: Term coined by the author of this book to refer to the interaction of various polities (first used in Small 2010).

Koine: In this book, used to define a region composed of different cultural groups, which share a common material culture.

Koinon: A league or governmental federation, often the principal administrative organization of an ethnos.

Krater: Jar in which water was mixed with wine for drinking parties. Often highly decorated with scenes which would have fit in with discussion at the party.

Lekane: Low, wide bowl with two horizontal handles, often covered by a lid.

Lekythos (oi): Ornamental pitcher, often used to hold olive oil. White-ground (surface) lekythoi were commonly used to hold olive oil to pour over grave monuments, and often left at the monument itself. Many were painted with scenes related to death and funerals.

Lustral basin: Possible religious room in Minoan elite houses. Lower than the rooms around it, it contained a series of steps which led to its floor.

Matt-painted ware: Ware similar in shape to that of Minyan ware, with a matt or dull finish. Appearing in the ceramic record at the same time as Minyan ware, it was once seen as indicative of the arrival of Greek-speaking peoples in the Greek peninsula.

Megaron (a): Distinctive architectural suite in a Mycenaean palace. Design is that of a porch and anteroom which led to a large room with a hearth. At Pylos, Mycenae, and Tiryns this room also contained a possible throne.

Metic: Resident foreigner in a Greek polis.

Minoan Hall: The particular spatial interface between the domestic and non-domestic areas of a Minoan house. The interface was often controlled by a pier-and-door system of doors and windows which could be opened or closed to facilitate or block entrance into domestic space.

Minyan ware: Monochrome burnished pottery made with fine clay. It appears in the archaeological record toward the end of the third millennium BCE. Gray Minyan ware is extremely angular and may well have been based on a metal prototype. Minyan ware was originally thought to signal the arrival of Greek-speaking peoples into the Greek peninsula. See also Matt-painted ware.

Naos: Central room of a Greek temple. It housed votives or gifts to the deity and often the statue of the deity itself.

Obelos (oi): Spit used for the roasting of meat.

Palaistra: Exercise yard, often incorporated into Greek gymnasion buildings.

Panhellenion: A league of Greek cities, established by the Roman Emperor Hadrian in 131–132 CE. Its capital city was Athens.

Peribolos (oi): Architectural feature, often a line of stones or a low wall, marking off the line between sacred and profane ground at a sanctuary.

Phalanx: Greek battle formation of hoplite soldiers, formed of rows of soldiers tightly packed. Each soldier was armed with a sword and javelin and could use his shield in an overlapping arrangement to protect others in the formation.

Pillar crypt: Probable religious room within elite Minoan houses. This room was at a lower level than rooms around it. It also contained a central pillar, which was often decorated with apparently religious symbols.

Pithos (oi): Large storage jar. Standing up to six feet tall, seen in the storerooms at Knossos and later in storerooms in Iron Age Crete.

Poliadic: Refers to the principal cult of a Greek polis. The temple of Athena at Priene housed the poliadic religious institution of the polis.

Polis (poleis): Term close to our concept of a city-state.

Polity: Any organized society with a specific form of government.

Pronaos: Room or porch before the naos in the Greek temple.

Prytaneion: Building where the officials of the polis met. Usually held the city hearth, and often used to house official guests of the polis.

Pyxis (pyxides): Cylindrical jar with a low wall. Often thought to have contained cosmetics.

Rhyton: Ceremonial drinking cup with a pointed end. It had to be held or placed on a special stand.

Sauceboat: Pouring vessel of the early third millennium BCE. The sauceboat resembles the modern "gravy boat," often without a handle. It has a distinctive bird-like spout and was probably used in ritual.

Second Sophistic: Refers to the Greek writers and their writings who flourished from the reign of Nero until the mid-third century CE.

Skyphos (oi): Large two-handled drinking cup, passed from person to person in feasting ceremonies. First appeared in the Early Iron Age.

Strategos (oi): Military leader, similar to our concept of a general.

Stele (ai): Standing stone slab or column. It can be decorated and often used to mark a grave.

Symposion (a): Drinking party attended by men, where politics, sports, art, battle, and sex were discussed. Often held in the andron of the house, where men would recline on couches set along the wall and eat and drink from vessels set on a common table.

Sympotic: Refers to the symposion.

Temenos (oi): Sacred area within a sanctuary, often marked off from profane ground by a low wall (peribolos).

Theoria: Refers to the institution of sending out ambassadors to announce and watch over a truce between warring poleis during a festival period.

Theoros (oi): Sacred ambassador, sent from either a sanctuary or a polis to announce the coming of a festival. The job of the theoros was to observe that a truce was maintained between warring poleis so that people could attend the festival.

Tholos (oi): Round building; in Greek archaeology most often used to describe round tombs.

Tripartite shrine: Shrine within Minoan religion which presents a façade with three divisions. The middle is often higher than those on the ends. The façade is often decorated with columns and horns of consecration.

Tyrant: Ruler who inherited power or seized it through illegal means, often by appealing to lower classes within a Greek polity. Tyrants were most active in the seventh to fifth centuries BCE. Tyranny was one of four types of government in Greece, the others being monarchy, oligarchy, and democracy.

Wanax: Term found in Linear B tablets and in a later form "anax" in Homeric epic, which denotes a king or ruler.

Bibliography

Abell, N. 2014. "Migration, Mobility and Craftspeople in the Aegean Bronze Age: A Case Study from Ayia Irini on the Island of Kea." *World Archaeology* 46 (4): 551–68.

Abulafia, D. 2011. *The Great Sea: A Human History of the Mediterranean.* Oxford: Oxford University Press.

Adrimi-Sismani, V. 2008. "Données Récentes Concernant Le Site Préhistorique de Dimini: La Continuité de l'habitation Littorale Depuis le Début du Néolithique Récent Jusqu'à la fin du Bronze Ancien." In *The Aegean in the Neolithic, Chalcolithic and the Early Bronze Age,* edited by H. Erkanal, H. Hauptmann, V. Sahoglou, and R. Tuncel, 9–34. Ankara: Ankara University Press.

Alcock, S. E. 1993. *Graecia Capta: The Landscapes of Roman Greece.* Cambridge: Cambridge University Press.

Alcock, S. E., A. M. Berlin, A. B. Harrison, S. Heath, J. Spencer, and D. L. Stone. 2005. "The Pylos Regional Archaeological Project, Part VII: Historic Messenia, Geometric through Late Roman." *Hesperia: The Journal of the American School of Classical Studies at Athens* 74 (2): 147–209.

Alden, M. J. 2002. *Well Built Mycenae, 7: Prehistoric Cemetery: Pre-Mycenaean and Early Mycenaean Graves.* Oxford: Oxbow Books.

Ammerman, A. J., and L. L. Cavalli-Sforza. 1984. *The Neolithic Transitions and the Genetics of Populations in Europe.* Princeton: Princeton University Press.

Anagnostis, P. A. 2005. *The Anthropology of Tomb A1K1 of Orthi Petra in Eleutherna. A Narrative of the Bones: Aspects of the Human Condition in Geometric-Archaic Eleutherna.* Rethymnon: University of Crete Press.

Andreadaki-Vlasaki, M. 2002. "Are We Approaching the Minoan Palace of Khania?" In *Monuments of Minos: Rethinking the Minoan Palaces,* edited by J. Driessen, I. Schoep, and R. Laffineur, 157–66. Liège: Histoire de l'art et archéologie de la Grèce antique; Austin: Program in Aegean Scripts and Prehistory.

Antonaccio, C. 1995. *An Archaeology of Ancestors: Tomb Cult and Hero Cult in Early Greece.* Lanham: Rowman and Littlefield.

Antonaccio, C. 2002. "Warriors, Traders, and Ancestors: The 'Heroes' of Lefkandi." In *Images of Ancestors,* 13–42. Aarhus: Aarhus University Press.

Antonaccio, C. 2006. "Religion, Basileis, and Heroes." In *Ancient Greece: From the Mycenaean Palaces to the Age of Homer,* edited by S. Deger-Jalkotzy and I. S. Lemos, 381–95. Edinburgh: Edinburgh University Press.

Antonaccio, C. 2016. "Iron Age Reciprocity." *Journal of Mediterranean Archaeology* 29 (1): 104–11.

Archibald, Z. H. 2000. "Space, Hierarchy, and Community in Archaic and Classical Macedonia, Thessaly, and Thrace." In *Alternatives to Athens: Varieties of Political Organization and Community in Ancient Greece*, edited by R. Brock and S. Hodkinson, 212–33. Oxford: Oxford University Press.

Athanassakis, A. 2004. *Hesiod: Theogony, Works and Days, Shield*. Baltimore: Johns Hopkins University Press.

Atkinson, T. D., R. C. Bosanquet, C. C. Edgar, A. J. Evans, D. G. Hogarth, D. MacKenzie, C. Smith, and F. R. Welch. 1904. *Excavations at Phylakopi in Melos*. Society for the Promotion of Hellenic Studies, Supplementary Paper 4. London: Published by the Council, and sold on their behalf by Macmillan.

Aubet, M. E. 2001. *The Phoenicians and the West: Politics, Colonies and Trade*. Cambridge: Cambridge University Press.

Bandy, M. S. 2004. "Fissioning, Scalar Stress, and Social Evolution in Early Village Societies." *American Anthropologist* 106 (2): 322–33.

Barber, R. L. N. 1987. *The Cyclades in the Bronze Age*. Iowa City: University of Iowa Press.

Barker, E. 2012. *The Political Thought of Plato and Aristotle*. Mineola: Dover Publications.

Barker, G., and T. Rasmussen. 2000. *The Etruscans*. Malden: Wiley-Blackwell.

Barrier, C. R., and T. J. Horsley. 2014. "Shifting Communities: Demographic Profiles of Early Village Population Growth and Decline in the Central American Bottom." *American Antiquity* 79 (2): 295–313.

Bawden, G. 1999. *The Moche*. Malden: Wiley-Blackwell.

Beekman, C. S. 2008. "Corporate Power Strategies in the Late Formative to Early Classic Tequila Valleys of Central Jalisco." *Latin American Antiquity* 19 (4): 414–34.

Beekman, C. S., and W. W. Baden. 2005. *Nonlinear Models for Archaeology and Anthropology: Continuing the Revolution*. Farnham: Ashgate Publishing.

Belletier, M.-P. 2003. "La 'Politique de la Mort': Observations sur les Tombes Attiques aux Epoques Geometriques et Archaique." *Pallas* 61: 71–82.

Bennett, F. M. 1917. "A Study of the Word ΞOANON." *American Journal of Archaeology* 21 (1): 8–21.

Bentley, R., and H. Maschner, eds. 2003. *Complex Systems and Archaeology*. Salt Lake City: University of Utah Press.

Bentley, R., and H. Maschner. 2007. "Complexity Theory." In *Handbook of Archaeological Theories*, edited by R. Bentley, H. Maschner, and C. Chippendale, 245–70. Lanham: AltaMira Press.

Benz, M. 2000. "Die Neolithisierung im Vorderen Orient. Theorien, Archäologische Daten und ein Ethnologische Modell." In *Studies in the Early Near Eastern Production, Subsistence and Environment*. Vol. 7. Berlin: ex Oriente.

Berent, M. 2000. "Anthropology and the Classics: War, Violence, and the Stateless Polis." *The Classical Quarterly* 50 (1): 257–89.

Berent, M. 2006. "The Stateless Polis: A Reply to Critics." *Social Evolution and History* 5 (1): 141–63.

Berg, I. 2007. *Negotiating Island Identities: The Active Use of Pottery in the Middle and Late Bronze Age Cyclades*. New York: Gorgias Press.

Berve, H., G. Gruben, and M. Hirmer. 1973. *Greek Temples, Theatres, and Shrines*. New York: Thames & Hudson.

Betancourt, P. 2004. "Knossian Expansion in Late Minoan IB: The Evidence of the Spirals and Arcading Group." In *Knossos: Palace, City, State*, edited by G. Cadogan, E. Hatzaki, and A. Vasilakis, 295–98. London: British School at Athens.

Betancourt, P., and C. Davaras. 2012. *The Hagia Photia Cemetery II: The Pottery*. Philadelphia: INSTAP Academic Press.

Betancourt, P., and N. Marinatos. 1997. "The Minoan Villa." In *The Function of the "Minoan Villa." Proceedings of the Eighth International Symposium at the Swedish Institute at Athens, 6–8 June 1992*, edited by R. Hägg, 91–98. Stockholm: Svenska Institutet

Bevan, A. 2010. "Political Geography and Palatial Crete." *Journal of Mediterranean Archaeology* 23 (1): 27–54.

Bieber, M. 1961. *The History of the Greek and Roman Theater*. Princeton: Princeton University Press.

Bintliff, J. L. 2012. *The Complete Archaeology of Greece: From Hunter-Gatherers to the 20th Century A.D.* Malden: Wiley-Blackwell.

Blake, M., and J. Clark. 1999. "The Emergence of Hereditary Inequality: The Case of Pacific Coastal Chiapas, Mexico." In *Pacific Latin America in Prehistory*, edited by M. Blake, 55–74. Pullman: Washington State University Press.

Blanton, R. E., G. M. Feinman, S. A. Kowalewski, and P. N. Peregrine. 1996. "A Dual-Processual Theory for the Evolution of Mesoamerican Civilization." *Current Anthropology* 37 (1): 1–14.

Blanton, Richard, Stephen A. Kowalewski, Gary M. Feinman, and Laura M. Finsten. 1993. *Ancient Mesoamerica: A Comparison of Change in Three Regions*, 2nd edn. Cambridge: Cambridge University Press.

Blegen, C. W. 1928a. *Zygouries: A Prehistoric Settlement in the Valley of Cleonae*. Cambridge, MA: Harvard University Press.

Blegen, C. W. 1928b. "The Coming of the Greeks II: The Geographical Distribution of Prehistoric Remains in Greece." *American Journal of Archaeology* 32 (2): 146–54.

Blegen, C.W. 1952. "Two Athenian Grave Groups of about 900 B.C." *Hesperia: The Journal of the American School of Classical Studies at Athens* 21 (4): 279–94.

Blegen, C. W., and M. Rawson. 1966. *The Palace of Nestor at Pylos in Western Messenia I. The Buildings and Their Contents*. Princeton: Princeton University Press.

Blitz, J. 1999. "Mississippian Chiefdoms and the Fission–Fusion Process." *American Antiquity* 64 (4): 577–92.

Blomberg, M., and G. Henriksson. 2005. "Orientations of the Bronze Age Villa Complex at Vathypetro in Crete." *Mediterranean Archaeology and Archaeometry* 5: 51–61.

Blundell, S. 1995. *Women in Ancient Greece*. Cambridge, MA: Harvard University Press.

Boardman, J. 2001. "Aspects of 'Colonization.'" *Bulletin of the American Schools of Oriental Research* 322: 33–42.

Boardman, J. 2006. "Early Euboean Settlements in the Carthage Area." *Oxford Journal of Archaeology* 25 (2): 195–200.

Boggard, A., and P. Halstead. 2015. "Subsistence Practices and Social Routine in Neolithic Southern Europe." In *Oxford Handbook of Neolithic Europe*, edited by C. Fowler, J. Harding, and D. Hoffmann, 385–410. Oxford: Oxford University Press.

Borgna, E. 2004. "Aegean Feasting: A Minoan Perspective." *Hesperia: The Journal of the American School of Classical Studies at Athens* 73 (2): 247–79.

Bouwman, A. S., K. A. Brown, A. J. N. W. Prag, and T. A. Brown. 2008. "Kinship between Burials from Grave Circle B at Mycenae revealed by Ancient DNA Typing." *Journal of Archaeological Science* 35 (9): 2580–84.

Boyd, M. J. 2002. *Middle Helladic and Early Mycenaean Mortuary Practices in the Southern and Western Peloponnese*. Oxford: British Archaeological Reports Publishing.

Bradley, K., and P. Cartledge. 2011. *The Cambridge World History of Slavery*, vol. 1: *The Ancient Mediterranean World*. Cambridge: Cambridge University Press.

Branigan, K. 2001. "Aspects of Minoan Urbanism." In *Urbanism in the Aegean Bronze Age*, edited by K. Branigan, 38–50. Sheffield: Sheffield Academic Press.

Bremmer, J. N. 2012. "Greek Demons of the Wilderness: The Case of the Centaurs." In *Wilderness in Mythology and Religion: Approaching Religious Spatialities, Cosmologies, and Ideas of Wild Nature*, edited by L. Feldt, 25–54. Berlin: de Gruyter.

Brock, J. K. 1957. *Fortetsa: Early Greek Tombs near Knossos*. Cambridge: Cambridge University Press.

Brodie, N., J. Doole, and C. Renfrew, eds. 2001. *Trade in Illicit Antiquities: The Destruction of the World's Archaeological Heritage*. Cambridge: McDonald Institute Monographs.

Brogan, T. M. 2013. "'Minding the Gap': Reexamining the Early Cycladic III 'Gap' from the Perspective of Crete. A Regional Approach to Relative Chronology, Networks, and Complexity in the Late Prepalatial Period." *American Journal of Archaeology* 117 (4): 555–67.

Broneer, O. 1966. "The Cyclopean Wall on the Isthmus of Corinth and Its Bearing on Late Bronze Age Chronology." *Hesperia: The Journal of the American School of Classical Studies at Athens* 35 (4): 346–62.

Broneer, O. 1968. "The Cyclopean Wall on the Isthmus of Corinth, Addendum." *Hesperia: The Journal of the American School of Classical Studies at Athens* 37 (1): 25–35.

Broodbank, C. 1999. "Kythera Survey: Preliminary Report on the 1998 Season." *Annual of the British School at Athens* 94: 191–214.

Broodbank, C. 2002. *An Island Archaeology of the Early Cyclades*. Cambridge: Cambridge University Press.

Broodbank, C. 2004. "Minoanisation." *The Cambridge Classical Journal* 50: 46–91.

Broodbank, C. 2008. "The Early Bronze Age in the Cyclades." In *The Cambridge Companion to the Aegean Bronze Age*, edited by C. Shelmerdine, 47–76. Cambridge: Cambridge University Press.

Broodbank, C. 2013. "'Minding the Gap': Thinking about Change in Early Cycladic Island Societies from a Comparative Perspective." *American Journal of Archaeology* 117 (4): 535–43.

Broodbank, C., and E. Kiriatzi. 2007. "The First 'Minoans' of Kythera Revisited: Technology, Demography, and Landscape in the Prepalatial Aegean." *American Journal of Archaeology* 111 (2): 241–74.

Brown, P. 1993. *The Making of Late Antiquity*. Cambridge, MA: Harvard University Press.

Bruins, H. J., J. A. MacGillivray, C. E. Synolakis, C. Benjamini, J. Keller, H. J. Kisch, A. Klügel, and J. van der Plicht. 2008. "Geoarchaeological Tsunami Deposits at Palaikastro (Crete) and the Late Minoan IA Eruption of Santorini." *Journal of Archaeological Science* 35 (1): 191–212.

Buell, D.M. 2013. "Regional Organization in the Aegean Bronze Age and Near East: A Comparative Study of Three Regions, the Amuq Valley, the Upper Pediada, and Messenia." PhD Thesis, Buffalo, NY: University at Buffalo.

Buell, D. M. 2014. "The Rise of a Minoan City and the (Re)structuring of Its Hinterlands: A View from Galatas." In *Making Ancient Cities: Space and Place in Early Urban Societies*, edited by A. T. Creekmore III and K. D. Fisher, 257–91. Cambridge: Cambridge University Press.

Buell, D. M. 2017. "Of Bulls and Banquets: James Walter Graham's Contributions to Minoan Archaeology and Their Lasting Influence." In *From Maple to Olive: A Colloquium to Celebrate the 40th Anniversary of the Canadian Institute in Greece, Canadian Institute in Greece, Athens, Greece, June 10–11*, edited by D. Rupp and J. Tomlinson, 1–23. Athens: Canadian Institute in Greece.

Bugh, G. R. 2006. *The Cambridge Companion to the Hellenistic World*. Cambridge: Cambridge University Press.

Burke, B. 2005. "Materialization of Mycenaean Ideology and the Ayia Triada Sarcophagus." *American Journal of Archaeology* 109 (3): 403–22.

Burn, A. R. 1984. *Persia and the Greeks: The Defense of the West, c. 546–478 B.C.* Stanford: Stanford University Press.

Cahill, N. 2002. *Household and City Organization at Olynthus*. New Haven: Yale University Press.

Cambitoglou, A., A. Birchall, J. J. Coulton, and J. R. Green. 1988. *Zagora 2: Excavation of a Geometric Town on the Island of Andros*. Athens: Athens Archaeological Society.

Cambitoglou, A., J. J. Coulton, J. Birmingham, and J. R. Green. 1971. *Zagora 1: Excavation of a Geometric Settlement on the Island of Andros*. Sydney: Sydney University Press.

Campbell, L. 2013. "Bronze Age Adyta: Exploring Lustral Basins as Representations of Natural Spaces and Places." *Eras* 14: 1–32.

Carter, J. C. 1983. *The Sculpture of the Sanctuary of Athena Polias at Priene*. London: Society of Antiquaries of London in association with British Museum Publications.

Cartledge, P. 1980. "The Peculiar Position of Sparta in the Development of the Greek City-State." *Proceedings of the Royal Irish Academy: Archaeology, Culture, History, Literature* 80: 91–108.

Cartledge, P. 2002. *Sparta and Lakonia: A Regional History 1300–362 BC*, 2nd edn. London: Routledge.

Cartledge, P. 2003. *The Spartans*. New York: Overlook Press.

Cartledge, P. 2011. *Ancient Greece: A Very Short Introduction*. Oxford: Oxford University Press.

Casson, L. 1951. "Speed under Sail of Ancient Ships." *Transactions of the American Philological Association* 82: 136–48.

Catling, R. W. V., I. S. Lemos, P. G. Calligas, and L. H. Sackett. 1991. *Lefkandi II: The Protogeometric Building at Toumba*. Athens: British School of Archaeology at Athens.

Cavanagh, W. G., and R. R. Laxton. 1981. "The Structural Mechanics of the Mycenaean Tholos Tomb." *Annual of the British School at Athens* 76: 109–40.

Cavanagh, W. G., and R. R. Laxton. 1982. "Corbelled Vaulting in the Late Minoan Tholos Tombs of Crete." *Annual of the British School at Athens* 77: 65–77.

Chadwick, J. 1967. *The Decipherment of Linear B*. Cambridge: Cambridge University Press.

Chaniotis, A. 2005. "La Grande Iscrizione de Gortyna. Centoventi Anni Dopo La Scoperta." In *La Grande Iscrizione de Gortyna. Centoventi Anni Dopo La Scoperta. Atti Del I Convegno Internazionale Di Studi Sull Messara, Athen 2005*, edited by E. Greco and M. Lombardo, 175–94. Athens: Scuola Archeologica Italiana di Atene.

Chase, A. 1998. "Planeación Cívica e Integración de Sitio en Caracol, Belice: Definiendo una Economía Administrada del Periodo Clásico Maya." In *Los Investigadores de La Cultura Maya* 6 (1):26–44.

Chase, A., and D. Chase. 1996. "More than Kin and King: Centralized Political Organization among the Late Classic Maya." *Current Anthropology* 37 (5): 803–10.

Chase, A., and D. Chase. 1998. "Late Classic Maya Political Structure, Polity Size, and Warfare Arenas." In *Anatomia de una Civilizacion Aproximaciones Interdisciplinarias a la Cultura Maya*, edited by A. C. Ruiz, Y. F. Marquinez, J. M. G. Campillo, M. J. I. Ponce de Leon, A. L. Garcia-Gallo, and L. T. S. Castro, 11–29. Madrid: Sociedad Espanola de Estudios Mayas.

Chase, A., and D. Chase. 2001. "Ancient Maya Causeways and Site Organization at Caracol, Belize." *Ancient Mesoamerica* 12 (2): 275–81.

Chase, A., and D. Chase. 2004. "Exploring Ancient Economic Relationships at Caracol, Belize." *Research Reports in Belizean Archaeology* 1: 115–27.

Chase, A., D. Chase, R. Terry, J. Horlacher, and A. Z. Chase. 2015. "Markets among the Ancient Maya: The Case of Caracol." In *The Ancient Maya Marketplace: The Archaeology of Transient Space*, edited by E. King, 226–50. Tuscon: University of Arizona Press.

Chase, D., and A. Chase. 2015. "Ancient Maya Markets and the Economic Integration of Caracol, Belize." *Ancient Mesoamerica* 25 (1): 239–50.

Cheetham, D. 2004. "The Role of 'Terminus Groups' in Lowland Maya Site Planning: An Example from Cahal Pech." In *The Ancient Maya of the Belize Valley: Half a Century of Archaeological Research*, edited by J. F. Garber, 125–48. Gainesville: University of Florida Press.

Cherry, J. F. 1986. "Polities and Palaces: Some Problems in Minoan State Formation." In *Peer Polity Interaction and Socio-Political Change*, edited by C. Renfrew and J. F. Cherry, 19–45. Cambridge: Cambridge University Press.

Childe, V. G. 1983. *Man Makes Himself.* London: Penguin Group.

Chourmouziadis, G. 1971. "Dyo Neai Egatastaseis Tis Archaioteras Neolithikis Eis Tin Dytikin Thessalian." *Archaiologika Analekta Ex Athinon* 4: 164–75.

Chourmouziadis, G. 1973. "Burial Customs." In *Neolithic Greece*, edited by D. R. Theocharis, 201–12. Athens: National Bank of Greece.

Chourmouziadis, G. 1979. *To Neolithiko Dimini.* Volos: Etaireia Thessalikon Ereunon.

Chourmouziadis, G. 1993. *To Neolithiko Dimini: Prospathia Gia Mia Nea Prosengise Tou Neolithikou Ylikou.* Thessalonike: Aristotle University Press.

Christakis, K. S. 2011. "Redistribution in Aegean Palatial Societies. Redistribution and Political Economies in Bronze Age Crete." *American Journal of Archaeology* 115 (2): 197–205.

Cioffi-Revilla, C., and T. Landman. 1999. "Evolution of Maya Polities in the Ancient Mesoamerican System." *International Studies Quarterly* 43 (4): 559–98.

Clark, J., and M. Blake. 1994. "The Power of Prestige: Competitive Generosity and the Emergence of Rank Societies in Lowland Mesoamerica." In *Factional Competition and Political Development in the New World*, edited by E. Brumfiel and J. Fox, 17–30. Cambridge: Cambridge University Press.

Cleveland, J. 2009. "Complexity Theory: Basic Concepts." December 20. www.slideshare.net/johncleveland/complexity-theory-basic-concepts.

Cline, E. H. 2015. *1177 B.C.: The Year Civilization Collapsed*, revised edn. Princeton: Princeton University Press.

Coe, M. 2011. *The Maya*, 8th edn. New York: Thames & Hudson.

Coe, M. 2012. *Breaking the Maya Code.* New York: Thames & Hudson.

Coggins, C. 1975. *Painting and Drawing Styles at Tikal: An Historical and Iconographic Reconstruction.* Vol. 1. Cambridge, MA: Harvard University Press.

Coldstream, J. N. 2000. "Evan's Greek Finds: The Early Greek Town of Knossos, and Its Encroachment on the Borders of the Minoan Palace." *Annual of the British School at Athens* 95: 259–99.

Coldstream, J. N. 2003. *Geometric Greece: 900–700 BC*, 2nd edn. London: Routledge.

Coldstream, J. N., and H. W. Catling, eds. 1996. *Knossos the North Cemetery: Early Greek Tombs.* 4 vols. London: British School at Athens.

Coldstream, J. N., and G. L. Huxley. 1999. "Knossos: The Archaic Gap." *Papers of the British School at Athens* 94: 289–307.

Coleman, J. E. 1985. "'Frying Pans' of the Early Bronze Age Aegean." *American Journal of Archaeology* 89 (2): 191–219.

Coulson, W. D. E. 1998. "The Early Iron Age on the Kastro at Kavousi in East Crete." *British School at Athens Studies* 2: 40–44.

Coulson, W. D. E., and A. Leonard Jr. 1979. "A Preliminary Survey of the Naukratis Region in the Western Nile Delta." *Journal of Field Archaeology* 6 (2): 151–68.

Coulson, W. D. E., and A. Leonard. 1982. "Investigations at Naukratis and Environs, 1980 and 1981." *American Journal of Archaeology* 86 (3): 361–80.

Coulson, W. D. E., M. Tsipopoulou, W. Klippel, L. Little, K. Nowicki, and L. Snyder. 1994. "Preliminary Investigations at Halasmenos, Crete, 1992–93." *Aegean Archaeology* 1: 65–97.

Coulton, J. J. 1982. *Ancient Greek Architects at Work: Problems of Structure and Design*. Ithaca: Cornell University Press.

Cowgill, G. L. 2015. *Ancient Teotihuacan: Early Urbanism in Central Mexico*. Cambridge: Cambridge University Press.

Crielaard, J. P. 2006. "Basileis at Sea: Elites and External Contacts in the Euboean Gulf Region from the End of the Bronze Age to the Beginning of the Iron Age." In *Ancient Greece: From the Mycenaean Palaces to the Age of Homer*, edited by S. Deger-Jalkotzy and I. S. Lemos, 271–97. Edinburgh: Edinburgh University Press.

Crielaard, J. P. 2011. "The 'Wanax to Basileus Model' Reconsidered: Authority and Ideology after the Collapse of the Mycenaean Palaces." In *"The Dark Ages" Revisited. Acts of an International Symposium in Memory of William D. E. Coulson, University of Thessaly, Volos, 14–17 June 2007*, edited by A. Mazarakis-Ainian, 83–111. Volos: University of Thessaly.

Crowther, N. B. 1992. "Second-Place Finishes and Lower in Greek Athletics (Including the Pentathlon)." *Zeitschrift für Papyrologie und Epigraphik* 90: 97–102.

Crowther, N. B. 2014. "Athlete and State: Qualifying for the Olympic Games in Ancient Greece." In *Sport in the Greek and Roman Worlds*, vol. 1: *Early Greece, the Olympics, and Contests*, edited by T. F. Scanlon, 143–57. Oxford: Oxford University Press.

Cucuzza, N. 2011. "Minoan 'Theatral Areas.'" In *Pepragmena Tou I' Kretologikou Synedriou*, edited by M. Andreadaki-Vlazaki and E. Papadopoulou, 153–63. Chania: Christomos Philological Association.

Cunningham, T. 2007. "In the Shadows of Kastri: An Examination of Domestic and Civic Space at Palaikastro (Crete)." In *Building Communities: House, Settlement and Society in the Aegean and Beyond*, edited by R. Westgate, N. Fisher, and J. Whitley, 99–109. London: British School at Athens.

D'Agata, A. L. 1998. "Changing Patterns in a Minoan and Post-Minoan Sanctuary: The Case of Agia Triada." In *Post-Minoan Crete, Proceedings of the First Colloquium on Post-Minoan Crete, Held by the British School at Athens and the Institute of Archaeology, University College London, 10–11 November 1995*, edited by W. Cavanagh and M. Curtis, 19–26. London: British School at Athens.

Dahlin, B. 1984. "A Colossus in Guatemala: The Preclassic Maya City of El Mirador." *Archaeology* 37 (5): 18–25.

Dalby, A. 1996. *Siren Feasts: A History of Food and Gastronomy in Greece*. London: Routledge.

Dalfes, H. N., G. Kukla, and H. Weiss, eds. 1997. *Third Millennium BC Climate Change and Old World Collapse*. New York: Springer.

Davaras, C., and P. Betancourt. 2004. *The Hagia Photia Cemetery I: The Tomb Groups and Architecture*. Philadelphia: INSTAP Academic Press.

Davis, J. L. 1992. "Review of Aegean Prehistory I: The Islands of the Aegean." *American Journal of Archaeology* 96 (4): 699–756.

Davis, J. L. 2008. "Minoan Crete and the Aegean Islands." In *The Cambridge Companion to the Aegean Bronze Age*, edited by C. Shelmerdine, 186–208. Cambridge: Cambridge University Press.

Davis, J. L., and J. F. Cherry, eds. 1979. *Papers in Cycladic Prehistory*. Los Angeles: Cotsen Institute of Archaeology.

Dawkins, R. M., and J. P. Droop. 1910. "Excavations at Phylakopi in Melos, 1911." *The Annual of the British School at Athens* 17: 1–22.

Day, L. 1995. "The Geometric Cemetery at Vronda, Kavousi." In *Pepragmen Tou Z Diethnous Kretologikou A2: Tmima Arxailogikos*, edited by E. Papdogiannakos, 789–810. Rethymnon: Society for Cretan Studies.

Day, L., and L. Snyder. 2004. "The 'Big House' at Vronda and the 'Great House' at Karfi: Evidence for Social Structure in LMIIIC Crete." In *Crete beyond the Palaces: Proceeding of the Crete 2000 Conference*, edited by L. Day, M. Mook, and J. Muhly, 63–79. Philadelphia: INSTAP Academic Press.

Day, L., L. Turner, and N. Klein. 2009. *Kavousi II. The Late Minoan IIIC Settlement at Vronda: The Buildings on the Summit*. Philadelphia: INSTAP Academic Press.

Day, P. M., and D. E. Wilson. 1998. "Consuming Power: Kamares Ware in Protopalatial Knossos." *Antiquity* 72 (276): 350–58.

Day, P. M., and D. E. Wilson. 2002. "Landscapes of Memory, Craft and Power in Prepalatial and Protopalatial Knossos." In *Labyrinth Revisited: Rethinking "Minoan" Archaeology*, edited by Y. Hamilakis, 142–66. Oxford: Oxbow Books.

Day, P. M., and D. E. Wilson. 2004. "Ceramic Change and the Practice of Eating and Drinking in Early Bronze Age Crete." In *Food, Cuisine and Society in Prehistoric Greece*, edited by P. Halstead and J. Barrett, 45–62. Oxford: Oxbow Books.

De Angelis, F. 2003. *Megara Hyblaia and Selinous: The Development of Two Greek City-States in Archaic Sicily*. Oxford: Oxford University School of Archaeology.

De Ste. Croix, G. E. M. 1983. *The Class Struggle in the Ancient World from the Archaic Age to the Arabic Conquest*, 2nd edn. London: Duckworth.

Deger-Jalkotzy, S. 2008. "Decline, Destruction, Aftermath." In *The Cambridge Companion to the Aegean Bronze Age*, edited by C. Shelmerdine, 387–416. Cambridge: Cambridge University Press.

Demarest, A. 1984. "Conclusiones y Especulaciones Acerca de El Mirador." *Mesoamerica* 7: 138–50.

Demarest, A. 1992. "Ideology in Ancient Maya Cultural Evolution: The Dynamics of Galactic Polities." In *Ideology and Pre-Columbian Civilizations*, edited by A. Demarest and G. Conrad, 135–57. Santa Fe: School of American Research Press.

Demarest, A. 1997. "The Vanderbilt Petexbatun Regional Archaeological Project, 1989–1994: Overview, History, and Major Results of a Multidisciplinary Study of the Classic Maya Collapse." *Ancient Mesoamerica* 8 (2): 209–27.

Demarest, A. 2004. *Ancient Maya: The Rise and Fall of a Rainforest Civilization*. Cambridge: Cambridge University Press.

Demetriou, D. 2012. *Negotiating Identity in the Ancient Mediterranean: The Archaic and Classical Greek Multiethnic Emporia*. Cambridge: Cambridge University Press.

Denkers, M. 2012. "The Philippeion at Olympia: The True Image of Philip?" Master's thesis, McMaster University.

Desborough, V. R., R. V. Nicholls, and M. R. Popham. 1970. "A Euboean Centaur." *The Annual of the British School at Athens* 65: 21–30.

Dibble, F., and D. Fallu. 2015. "The Good, the Bad, and the Ugly at the Dark Age Ranch: Taphonomic Reinterpretations of Pastoralism at Nichoria, Messenia." In *116th Annual Meeting of the Archaeological Institute of America*. Cincinnati: Archaeological Institute of America.

Dietler, M. 1996. "Feasts and Commensal Politics in the Political Economy: Food, Power and Status in Prehistoric Europe." In *Food and the Status Quest: An Interdisciplinary Perspective*, edited by P. Wiessner and W. Schiefenhoevel, 87–126. New York: Berghahn Books.

Dietler, M. 2007. "Culinary Encounters: Food, Identity, and Colonialism." In *The Archaeology of Food and Identity*, edited by K. Twiss, 218–42. Carbondale: Southern Illinois University Press.

Dietler, M., and B. Hayden. 2010. *Feasts: Archaeological and Ethnographic Perspectives on Food, Politics, and Power*. Tuscaloosa: University of Alabama Press.

Dietz, S. 1980. *Asine II,2: Results of the Excavations East of the Acropolis 1970–1974. The Middle Helladic Cemetery, the Middle Helladic and Early Mycenaean Deposits*. Stockholm: Skrifter utgivna av Svenska Institutet i Athen.

Dietz, S. 1982. *Asine II,1: Results of the Excavations East of the Acropolis 1970–1974. General Stratigraphical Analysis and Architectural Remains*. Stockholm: Skrifter utgivna av Svenska Institutet i Athen.

Dietz, S. 1991. *The Argolid at the Transition to the Mycenaean Age: Studies in the Chronology and Cultural Development in the Shaft Grave Period*. Copenhagen: National Museum of Denmark, Department of Near Eastern and Classical Antiquities.

Dinsmoor, W. B. 1950. *The Architecture of Ancient Greece: An Account of Its Historic Development*. New York: Biblo and Tannen Publishers.

Docter, R. F., and H. G. Niemeyer. 1994. "Pithekoussai: The Carthaginian Connection. On the Archaeological Evidence of Euboeo-Phoenician Partnership in the 8th and 7th Centuries B.C." *Annali Sezione di Archeologia e Storia Antica* 16: 39–50.

Donlan, W. 1982. "Reciprocities in Homer." *The Classical World* 75 (3): 137–75.

Donlan, W. 1985. "The Social Groups of Dark Age Greece." *Classical Philology* 80 (4): 293–308.

Donlan, W. 1989a. "The Unequal Exchange between Glaucus and Diomedes in Light of the Homeric Gift-Economy." *Phoenix* 43 (1): 1–15.

Donlan, W. 1989b. "The Pre-State Community in Greece." *Symbolae Osloenses* 64 (1): 5–29.

Doumas, C., ed. 1978. *Thera and the Aegean World, I. Papers Presented at the Second International Scientific Congress, Santorini, Greece, August 1978*. London: Thera and the Ancient World.

Doumas, C. 1981. *Thera and the Ancient World, II. Papers and Proceedings of the Second International Scientific Congress, Santorini, Greece, August 1978*. London: Thera and the Ancient World.

Doumas, C. 1983. *Thera, Pompeii of the Ancient Aegean. Excavations at Akrotiri, 1967–79*. London: Thames & Hudson.

Doumas, C. 1988. "EBA in the Cyclades: Continuity or Discontinuity?" In *Problems in Greek Prehistory*, edited by E. French and K. A. Wardle, 21–29. Bristol: Bristol Classical Press.

Doxey, D. 1987. "Causes and Effects of the Fall of Knossos in 1375 B.C." *Oxford Journal of Archaeology* 6 (3): 301–24.

Drennan, R. D., and C. E. Peterson. 2004. "Comparing Archaeological Settlement Systems with Rank-Size Graphs: A Measure of Shape and Statistical Confidence." *Journal of Archaeological Science* 31 (5): 533–49.

Drews, R. 1983. *Basileus: The Evidence for Kingship in Geometric Greece.* New Haven: Yale University Press.

Drews, R. 1988. *The Coming of the Greeks: Indo-European Conquests in the Aegean and the Near East.* Princeton: Princeton University Press.

Driessen, J. 1990. *An Early Destruction in the Mycenaean Palace at Knossos: A New Interpretation of the Excavation Field-Notes of the South-West Area of the West Wing.* Leuven: Leuven University Press.

Driessen, J. 1994. "La Crète mycénienne." *Les Dossiers d'archéologie* 195: 66–83.

Driessen, J. 2002. "'The King Must Die': Some Observations on the Use of Minoan Court Compounds." In *Monuments of Minos: Rethinking the Minoan Palaces. Proceedings of an International Workshop Held in Louvain-La-Neuve, 2001*, edited by J. Driessen, I. Schoep, and R. Laffineur, 1–15. Liège: Histoire de l'art et archéologie de la Grèce antique; Austin: Program in Aegean Scripts and Prehistory.

Driessen, J. 2003. "The Court Compounds of Minoan Crete: Royal Palaces or Ceremonial Centers?" *Athena Review* 3 (3): 57–61.

Driessen, J. 2004. "The Central Court of the Palace at Knossos." In *Knossos: Palace, City, State*, edited by G. Cadogan, E. Hatzaki, and A. Vasilakis, 75–82. London: British School at Athens.

Driessen, J., and C. F. MacDonald. 1984. "Some Military Aspects of the Aegean in the Late Fifteenth and Early Fourteenth Centuries B.C." *Annual of the British School at Athens* 79: 49–74.

Driessen, J., and C. F. MacDonald, eds. 1997. *The Troubled Island: Minoan Crete before and after the Santorini Eruption.* Liège: Histoire de l'art et archéologie de la Grèce antique; Austin: Program in Aegean Scripts and Prehistory.

Eaby, M. 2007. "Mortuary Variability in Early Iron Age Cretan Burials." PhD dissertation, University of North Carolina, Chapel Hill.

Earle, T. 2011. "Redistribution in Aegean Palatial Societies. Redistribution and the Political Economy: The Evolution of an Idea." *American Journal of Archaeology* 115 (2): 237–44.

Eder, B. 2001. "Continuity of Bronze Age Cult at Olympia? The Evidence of the Late Bronze Age and Early Iron Age Pottery." In *Potnia: Deities and Religion in the Aegean Bronze Age*, edited by R. Laffineur and R. Hägg, 201–9. Liège: Histoire de l'art et archéologie de la Grèce antique; Austin: Program in Aegean Scripts and Prehistory.

Efstratiou, N., A. Karetsou, E. Banou, and D. Margomenou. 2004. "The Neolithic Settlement of Knossos: New Light on an Old Picture." *British School at Athens Studies* 12: 39–49.

Efstratiou, N., A. Karetsou, and M. Ntinou, eds. 2013. *The Neolithic Settlement of Knossos in Crete: New Evidence for the Early Occupation of Crete and the Aegean Islands.* Philadelphia: INSTAP Academic Press.

Ellis, S. 1991. "Power, Architecture, and Decor: How the Late Roman Aristocrat Appeared to His Guests." In *Roman Art in the Private Sphere: New Perspectives on the Architecture and Decor of the Domus, Villa, and Insula,* edited by E. Gazda and A. Haeckl, 117–33. Ann Arbor: University of Michigan Press.

Ellis, S. 2007. "Late Antique Housing and the Uses of Residential Buildings: An Overview." In *Housing in Late Antiquity: From Palaces to Shops,* edited by L. Lavan, L. Ozgenel, and A. C. Sarantis, 1–22. Leiden: E. J. Brill.

Erickson, B. 2002. "Aphrati and Kato Syme: Pottery, Continuity, and Cult in Late Archaic and Classical Crete." *Hesperia: The Journal of the American School of Classical Studies at Athens* 71 (1): 41–90.

Erickson, B. 2010. *Crete in Transition: Pottery Styles and Island History in the Archaic and Classical Periods.* Princeton: American School of Classical Studies at Athens.

Errington, R. M. 2008. *A History of the Hellenistic World.* Malden: Wiley-Blackwell.

Erskine, A., ed. 2005. *A Companion to the Hellenistic World.* Malden: Wiley-Blackwell.

Evans, A. J. 1900–1901. "Excavations at Knossos, 1901." *Annual of the British School at Athens* 7: 1–120.

Evans, A. J. 1901–2. "Excavations at Knossos, 1902." *Annual of the British School at Athens* 8: 1–124.

Evans, J. D. 1964. "Excavations in the Neolithic Settlement at Knossos, 1957–60." *Annual of the British School at Athens* 59: 132–240.

Evans, J. D. 1971. "Neolithic Knossos: The Growth of a Settlement." *Proceedings of the Prehistoric Society* 37: 95–117.

Evans, R. K., and C. Renfrew. 1984. "The Earlier Bronze Age at Phylakopi." In *The Prehistoric Cyclades,* edited by J. A. MacGillivray and R. L. N. Barber, 63–69. Edinburgh: Department of Classical Archaeology, University of Edinburgh.

Everitt, A. 2016. *The Rise of Athens: The Story of the World's Greatest Civilization.* New York: Random House.

Fagerstrom, K. 1988. "Finds, Function and Plan: A Contribution to the Interpretation of Iron Age Nichoria in Messenia." *Opuscula Atheniensa* 17: 33–50.

Farmer, J. 2011. "The Megaron at Pylos: A New Interpretation." *University of Maryland Baltimore County Review* 12: 188–90.

Felsch, R., ed. 1996. *Kalapodi I: Ergebnisse der Augrabungen im Heiligtum der Artemis und des Apollon von Hyampolis in der Antiken Phokis.* Mainz am Rhein: Philipp von Zabern.

Felsch, R. 2007. *Kalapodi II. Ergebnisse der Ausgrabungen im Heiligtum der Artemis und des Apollon von Hyampolis in der Antiken Phokis.* Mainz am Rhein: Philipp von Zabern.

Felten, F. 2007. "Aegina-Kolonna: The History of a Greek Acropolis." In *Middle Helladic Pottery and Synchronisms. Ägina-Kolonna Forschungen und Ergebnisse I,* edited by F. Felten, W. Gauss, and R. Smetana, 11–34. Vienna: Österreichische Akademie der Wissenschaften.

Ferla, K., F. Graf, and A. Sideris, eds. 2006. *Priene*. Athens: Foundation of the Hellenic World.

Fields, N. 2004. *Mycenaean Citadels c. 1350–1200 BC*. New York: Bloomsbury.

Finley, M. I. 1957. "The Mycenaean Tablets and Economic History." *The Economic History Review* 10 (1), New Series: 128–41.

Finley, M. I. 1991. *The World of Odysseus*. London: Penguin Group.

Finley, M. I., and B. D. Shaw. 1998. *Ancient Slavery and Modern Ideology*. Princeton: Markus Wiener Publishers.

Fitzsimons, R. 2011. "Monumental Architecture and the Construction of the Mycenaean State." In *State Formation in Italy and Greece: Questioning the Neoevolutionist Paradigm*, edited by N. Terrenato and D. Haggis, 75–118. Oxford: Oxbow Books.

Flad, R. K., and P. Chen. 2013. *Ancient Central China: Centers and Peripheries along the Yangzi River*. Cambridge: Cambridge University Press.

Flannery, K. 1998. "The Ground Plans of Archaic States." In *Archaic States*, edited by G. Feinman and J. Marcus, 15–57. Santa Fe: School of American Research Press.

Forrest, W. G. 1957. "Colonisation and the Rise of Delphi." *Historia: Zeitschrift für Alte Geschichte* 6 (2): 160–75.

Forrest, W. G. 2000. "The Pre-Polis Polis." In *Alternatives to Athens: Varieties of Political Organization and Community in Ancient Greece*, edited by R. Brock and S. Hodkinson, 280–22. Oxford: Oxford University Press.

Forsen, J. 2010. "Mainland Greece." In *The Oxford Handbook of the Bronze Age Aegean*, edited by E. H. Cline, 53–65. Oxford: Oxford University Press.

Fox, J. W. 1987. *Maya Postclassic State Formation: Segmentary Lineage Migration in Advancing Frontiers*. Cambridge: Cambridge University Press.

Fox, J. W. 1989. "On the Rise and Fall of Tuláns and Maya Segmentary States." *American Anthropologist* 91 (3): 656–81.

Fox, R. F. 2012. *Feasting Practices and Changes in Greek Society from the Late Bronze Age to the Early Iron Age*. Oxford: British Archaeological Reports Publishing.

Foxhall, L. 1995. "Bronze to Iron: Agricultural Systems and Political Structures in Late Bronze Age and Early Iron Age Greece." *The Annual of the British School at Athens* 90: 239–50.

Fusaro, D. 1982. "Note di Architettura Domestica Greca nel Periodo Tardo-Geometrico e Arcaico." *Dialoghi de Archeologia* (4), New Series: 5–30.

Gabrielsen, V. 2015. "Naval and Grain Networks and Associations in Fourth-Century Athens." In *Communities and Networks in the Ancient Greek World*, edited by C. Taylor and K. Vlassopoulos. Oxford: Oxford University Press.

Galaty, M., and W. Parkinson, eds. 2007a. *Rethinking Mycenaean Palaces II*. Los Angeles: Cotsen Institute of Archaeology.

Galaty, M., and W. Parkinson. 2007b. "1999 Introduction: Putting Mycenaean Palaces in Their Place." In *Rethinking Mycenaean Palaces II*, edited by M. Galaty and W. Parkinson, 21–28. Los Angeles: Cotsen Institute of Archaeology.

Galaty, M., D. Nakassis, and W. Parkinson. 2011. "Redistribution in Aegean Palatial Societies. Introduction: Why Redistribution?" *American Journal of Archaeology* 115 (2): 175–76.

Galaty, M., D. Nakassis, and W. Parkinson. 2016. "Introduction: Discussion and Debate: Reciprocity in Aegean Palatial Societies: Gifts, Debt, and the Foundations for Economic Exchange." *Journal of Mediterranean Archaeology* 29 (1): 61–70.

Gallant, T. 1989. "Crisis and Response: Risk-Buffering Behavior in Hellenistic Greek Communities." *The Journal of Interdisciplinary History* 19 (3): 393–413.

Gallant, T. 1991. *Risk and Survival in Ancient Greece: Reconstructing the Rural Domestic Economy.* Stanford: Stanford University Press.

Garland, R. 2001. *The Greek Way of Death*, 2nd edn. Ithaca: Cornell University Press.

Garnsey, E., and J. McGlade. 2006. *Complexity and Co-Evolution: Continuity and Change in Socio-Economic Systems.* Cheltenham: Edward Elgar Publishing.

Gauthier, P. 1984. "Les Cites Hellenistiques: Epigraphie et Histoire des Institutions et des Regimes Politiques." In *Praktika tou Ē' Diethnous Synedriou Hellēnikēs kai Latinikēs Epigraphikēs, Athēna, 3–9 Oktōvriou 1982*, 82–107. Athens.

Gerstenblith, P. 2007. "Controlling the International Market in Antiquities: Reducing the Harm, Preserving the Past." *Chicago Journal of International Law* 8 (1): 169–95.

Gesell, G., W. Coulson, and L. Day. 1991. "Excavations at Kavousi, Crete, 1988." *Hesperia: The Journal of the American School of Classical Studies at Athens* 60 (2): 145–78.

Getz-Preziosi, P. 1994. *Early Cycladic Sculpture: An Introduction*, revised edn. Malibu: Getty Publications.

Giddens, A. 1986. *The Constitution of Society: Outline of the Theory of Structuration.* Berkeley: University of California Press.

Gill, D. W. J., and C. Chippindale. 1993. "Material and Intellectual Consequences of Esteem for Cycladic Figures." *American Journal of Archaeology* 97 (4): 601–59.

Gimatzidis, S. 2011. "Feasting and Offerings to the Gods in Early Greek Sanctuaries: Monumentalisation and Miniaturisation in Pottery." In *The Gods of Small Things*, edited by A. Smith and M. Bergeron, 75–96. Toulouse: Presses universitaires du Mirail.

Gimbutas, M. 1974. "Achilleion: A Neolithic Mound in Thessaly. Preliminary Report on 1973 and 1974 Excavations." *Journal of Field Archaeology* 1 (3–4): 277–302.

Glowacki, K. T. 2004. "Household Analysis in Dark Age Crete." In *Crete beyond the Palaces: Proceedings of the Crete 2000 Conference*, edited by L. Day, M. Mook, and J. Muhly, 125–36. Philadelphia: INSTAP Academic Press.

Goffman, E. 1967. *Interaction Ritual: Essays on Face-to-Face Behavior.* New York: Anchor.

Goldman, H. 1931. *Excavations at Eutresis in Boeotia.* Cambridge, MA: Harvard University Press.

Graham, A. J. 2001. "Precolonial Contacts: Questions and Problems." In *Collected Papers on Greek Colonization*, 25–44. Leiden: E. J. Brill.

Bibliography 239

Graham, J. W. 1956. "The Phaistos 'Piano Nobile.'" *American Journal of Archaeology* 60 (2): 151–57.

Graham, J. W. 1957. "The Central Court as the Minoan Bull-Ring." *American Journal of Archaeology* 61 (3): 255–62.

Graham, J. W. 1959. "The Residential Quarter of the Minoan Palace." *American Journal of Archaeology* 63 (1): 47–52.

Graham, J. W. 1960. "Windows, Recesses, and the Piano Nobile in the Minoan Palaces." *American Journal of Archaeology* 64 (4): 329–33.

Graham, J. W. 1961. "The Minoan Banquet Hall." *American Journal of Archaeology* 65 (1): 165–72.

Graham, J. W. 1979. "Further Notes on Minoan Palace Architecture: 1. West Magazine and Upper Halls at Knossos and Malia; 2. Access to, and Use of, Minoan Palace Roofs." *American Journal of Archaeology* 83 (1): 49–69.

Grainger, J. D. 1999. *The League of the Aitolians*. Leiden: E. J. Brill

Graziadio, G. 1988. "The Chronology of the Graves of Circle B at Mycenae: A New Hypothesis." *American Journal of Archaeology* 92 (3): 343–72.

Graziadio, G. 1991. "The Process of Social Stratification at Mycenae in the Shaft Grave Period: A Comparative Examination of the Evidence." *American Journal of Archaeology* 95 (3): 403–40.

Greaves, A. M. 2009. *The Land of Ionia: Society and Economy in the Archaic Period*. Malden: Wiley-Blackwell.

Greco, E. 1994. "Pithekoussai: 'empòrion' o 'apoikìa'?" *Annali di archeologia e storia antica* (1): 11–18.

Green, J. R. 2013. *Theatre in Ancient Greek Society*. London: Routledge.

Green, P. 1990. *Alexander to Actium: The Historical Evolution of the Hellenistic Age*. Berkeley: University of California Press.

Gregory, J. 2008. *A Companion to Greek Tragedy*. Malden: Wiley-Blackwell.

Grove, A. T., and O. R. Rackham. 2003. *The Nature of Mediterranean Europe: An Ecological History*. New Haven: Yale University Press.

Grove, M. 2011. "An Archaeological Signature of Multi-Level Social Systems: The Case of the Irish Bronze Age." *Journal of Anthropological Archaeology* 30 (1): 44–61.

Hägg, R., ed. 1997. *The Function of the "Minoan Villa."* Proceedings of the Eighth International Symposium at the Swedish Institute at Athens, 6–8 June 1992. Stockholm: Svenska Institutet i Athen.

Haggis, D. 1993. "Intensive Survey, Traditional Settlement Patterns, and Dark Age Crete: The Case of Early Iron Age Kavousi." *Journal of Mediterranean Archaeology* 6 (2): 131–74.

Haggis, D. 1999. "Staple Finance, Peak Sanctuaries, and Economic Complexity in Late Prepalatial Crete." In *From Minoan Farmers to Roman Traders: Sidelights on the Economy of Ancient Crete*, edited by A. Chaniotis, 53–85. Stuttgart: Franz Steiner Verlag.

Haggis, D. 2002. "Integration and Complexity in the Late Pre-Palatial Period: A View from the Countryside in Eastern Crete." In *Labyrinth Revisited: Rethinking "Minoan" Archaeology*, edited by Y. Hamilakis, 120–42. Oxford: Oxbow Books.

Haggis, D. 2005. *Kavousi I. The Archaeological Survey of the Kavousi Region*. Philadelphia: INSTAP Academic Press.

Haggis, D. 2007. "Stylistic Diversity and Diacritical Feasting at Protopalatial Petras: A Preliminary Analysis of the Lakkos Deposit." *American Journal of Archaeology* 111 (4): 715–75.

Haggis, D. 2013. "Social Organization and Aggregated Settlement Structure in an Archaic Greek City on Crete (ca. 600 B.C.)." In *From Prehistoric Villages to Cities: Settlement Aggregation and Community Transformation*, edited by J. Birch, 63–86. New York: Routledge.

Haggis, D. 2014a. "Azoria and Archaic Urbanization." In *Cretan Cities: Formation and Transformation*, edited by F. Gaignerot-Driessen and J. Driessen, 119–40. Louvain-la-Neuve: Universitaires de Louvain.

Haggis, D. 2014b. "Excavations at Azoria and Stratigraphic Evidence for the Restructuring of Cretan Landscapes ca. 600 B.C." In *Ein Neues Bild Kretas in Archaischer und Klassischer Zeit: Kulturelle Praktiken und Materielle Kultur im 6. and 5. Jh. v. Chr.*, edited by O. Pitz and G. Seelentag, 11–39. Berlin: de Gruyter.

Haggis, D., and C. Antonaccio, eds. 2015. *Classical Archaeology in Context: Theory and Practice in Excavation in the Greek World*. Berlin: Walter de Gruyter.

Haggis, D., and M. Mook. 2011a. "The Early Iron Age–Archaic Transition in Crete: The Evidence from Recent Excavations at Azoria, Eastern Crete." In *The "Dark Ages" Revisited: An International Symposium in Memory of William D. E. Coulson*, edited by A. Mazarakis-Ainian, 515–27. Volos: University of Thessaly.

Haggis, D., and M. Mook. 2011b. "The Archaic Houses at Azoria." In *Stega: The Archaeology of Houses and Households in Ancient Crete*, edited by K. T. Glowacki and N. Vogeikoff-Brogan, 367–80. Princeton: American School of Classical Studies at Athens.

Haggis, D., M. Mook, T. Carter, and L. Snyder. 2007. "Excavations at Azoria, 2003–2004, Part 2: The Final Neolithic, Late Prepalatial, and Early Iron Age Occupation." *Hesperia: The Journal of the American School of Classical Studies at Athens* 76 (2): 665–716.

Haggis, D., M. Mook, W. D. E. Coulson, and J. Tobin. 1997. "Excavations on the Kastro at Kavousi: An Architectural Overview." *Hesperia: The Journal of the American School of Classical Studies at Athens* 66 (3): 315–90.

Haggis, D., M. Mook, R. Fitzsimons, M. Scarry, L. Snyder, and W. West III. 2011. "Excavations in the Archaic Civic Buildings at Azoria in 2005–2006." *Hesperia: The Journal of the American School of Classical Studies at Athens* 80 (1): 1–70.

Haggis, D., M. Mook, C. M. Scarry, L. Snyder, and W. West III. 2004. "Excavations at Azoria, 2002." *Hesperia: The Journal of the American School of Classical Studies at Athens* 73 (3): 339–400.

Haider, P. 1980. "Zum Frühhelladischen Rundbau in Tiryns." In *Forschungen und Funde: Festschrift B. Neutsch*, 157–72. Innsbruck: Institut für Sprachwissenschaft der Universität Innsbruck.

Haley, J. B., and C. W. Blegen. 1928. "The Coming of the Greeks: I. The Geographical Distribution of Pre-Greek Place-Names." *American Journal of Archaeology* 32 (2): 141–54.

Hall, E. 2006. *The Theatrical Cast of Athens: Interactions between Ancient Greek Drama and Society*. Oxford: Oxford University Press.

Hall, J. 2013. *A History of the Archaic Greek World, ca. 1200–479 BCE*, 2nd edn. Malden: Wiley-Blackwell.

Hallager, E. 1987. "A Harvest Festival Room in the Minoan Palaces? An Architectural Study of the Pillar Crypt Area at Knossos." In *The Function of the Minoan Palaces*, edited by R. Hägg and N. Marinatos, 169–87. Stockholm: Skrifter utgivna av Svenska Institutet i Athen.

Halperin, C., and A. Foias. 2010. "Pottery Politics: Late Classic Maya Palace Production at Motul de San José, Petén, Guatemala." *Journal of Anthropological Archaeology* 29 (3): 392–411.

Halstead, P. 1981. "From Determinism to Uncertainty: Social Storage and the Rise of the Minoan Palace." In *Economic Archaeology: Towards an Integration of Ecological and Social Approaches*, edited by A. Sheridan and G. Bailey, 187–213. Oxford: British Archaeological Reports Publishing.

Halstead, P. 1984. "Strategies for Survival: An Ecological Approach to Social and Economic Change in the Early Farming Communities of Thessaly, Northern Greece." PhD dissertation, Cambridge University.

Halstead, P. 1993. "The Mycenaean Palatial Economy: Making the Most of the Gaps in the Evidence." *Proceedings of the Cambridge Philological Society* 38: 57–86.

Halstead, P. 1995. "From Sharing to Hoarding: The Neolithic Foundations of Aegean Bronze Age Society." In *Politeia: Society and State in the Aegean Bronze Age*, edited by R. Laffineur and W.-D. Niemeier, 11–21. Liège: Histoire de l'art et archéologie de la Grèce antique; Austin: Program in Aegean Scripts and Prehistory.

Halstead, P. 1999. "Neighbors from Hell? The Household in Neolithic Greece." In *Neolithic Society in Greece*, edited by P. Halstead, 77–95. Sheffield: Sheffield Academic Press.

Halstead, P. 2004. "Farming and Feasting in the Neolithic of Greece: The Ecological Context of Fighting with Food." *Documenta Praehistorica* 31: 151–61.

Halstead, P. 2007. "Toward a Model of Mycenaean Palatial Mobilization." In *Rethinking Mycenaean Palaces II*, edited by M. Galaty and W. Parkinson, 66–73. Los Angeles: Cotsen Institute of Archaeology.

Halstead, P. 2011. "Redistribution in Aegean Palatial Societies: Terminology, Scale, and Significance." *American Journal of Archaeology* 115 (2): 229–35.

Halstead, P., and V. Isaakidou. 2011. "Political Cuisine: Rituals of Commensality in the Neolithic and Bronze Age Aegean." In *Guess Who's Coming to Dinner: Feasting Rituals in the Prehistoric Societies of Europe and the Near East*, edited by G. A. Jimenez, S. Monton-Subias, and M. S. Romero, 91–108. Oxford: Oxbow Books.

Halstead, P., and G. Jones. 1989. "Agrarian Ecology in the Greek Islands: Time Stress, Scale and Risk." *The Journal of Hellenic Studies* 109: 41–55.

Hamilakis, Y. 1998. "Eating the Dead: Mortuary Feasting and the Politics of Memory in the Aegean Bronze Age Societies." In *Cemetery and Society in the Aegean Bronze Age*, edited by K. Branigan. Sheffield: Sheffield Academic Press.

Hamilakis, Y. 2002. "What Future for the 'Minoan' Past? Rethinking Minoan Archaeology." In *The Labyrinth Revisited: Rethinking Minoan Archaeology*, 2–28. Oxford: Oxbow Books.

Hammond, N. G. L. 2000. "The Ethne in Epirus and Upper Macedonia." *The Annual of the British School at Athens* 95: 345–52.

Hansen, M. H. 2002. "Was the Polis a State or a Stateless Society?" In *Even More Studies in the Ancient Greek Polis*, edited by T. Nielsen, 17–47. Stuttgart: Steiner Verlag.

Hansen, M. H. 2004. *An Inventory of Archaic and Classical Poleis*. Oxford: Oxford University Press.

Hansen, M. H. 2006. *Polis: An Introduction to the Ancient Greek City-State*. Oxford: Oxford University Press.

Hanson, V. D. 2002. *Hoplites: The Classical Greek Battle Experience*. London: Routledge.

Hayden, B. 1995. "Pathways to Power: Principles for Creating Socioeconomic Inequalities." In *Foundations of Social Inequality*, edited by T. D. Price and G. Feinman, 15–86. New York: Plenum Press.

Hayden, B. 2004. "Sociopolitical Organization in the Natufian: A View from the Northwest." In *The Last Hunter-Gatherer Societies in the Near East*, edited by C. Delage, 263–308. Oxford: British Archaeological Reports Publishing.

Hayden, B. 2009. "Funerals as Feasts: Why Are They So Important?" *Cambridge Archaeological Journal* 19 (1): 29–52.

Hayden, B. 2014. *The Power of Feasts: From Prehistory to the Present*. Cambridge: Cambridge University Press.

Hayden, B., and S. Villeneuve. 2011. "A Century of Feasting Studies." *Annual Review of Anthropology* 40: 433–49.

Heath, M. C. 1958. "Early Helladic Clay Sealings from the House of the Tiles at Lerna." *Hesperia: The Journal of the American School of Classical Studies at Athens* 27 (2): 81–121.

Hendrix, E. A. 2003. "Painted Early Cycladic Figures: An Exploration of Context and Meaning." *Hesperia: The Journal of the American School of Classical Studies at Athens* 72 (4): 405–46.

Herman, G. 2002. *Ritualised Friendship and the Greek City*. Cambridge: Cambridge University Press.

Hertz, R. 2013. *Death and the Right Hand*. London: Routledge.

Higham, C. 2014. "Agricultural Feasting and Social Change in Early Southeast Asia." In *Living in the Landscape Essays in Honour of Graeme Barker*, edited by K. Boyle, R. J. Rabett, and C. O. Hunt, 313–20. Cambridge: McDonald Institute for Archaeological Research.

Hitchcock, L. 2010. "The Big Nowhere: A Master of Animals in the Throne Room at Knossos?" In *The Master of Animals in Old World Iconography*, edited by D. B. Counts and B. Arnold, 107–18. Budapest: Archaeolingua Alapítvány.

Hitchcock, L., J. L. Crowley, and R. Laffineur, eds. 2008. *Dais: The Aegean Feast*. Liège: Histoire de l'art et archéologie de la Grèce antique; Austin: Program in Aegean Scripts and Prehistory.

Hodder, I. 1982. *Symbols in Action: Ethnoarchaeological Studies of Material Culture*. Cambridge: Cambridge University Press.

Hodder, I. 2006. "The Spectacle of Daily Performance at Catalhoyuk." In *Archaeology of Performance: Theaters of Power, Community, and Politics*, edited by T. Inomata and L. S. Coben, 81–102. Lanham: AltaMira Press.

Holkeskamp, K.-J. 1992. "Arbitrators, Lawgivers and the 'Codification of Law' in Archaic Greece: Problems and Perspectives." *Metis. Revue d'anthropologie des monde grec ancien* 7 (1): 49–81.

Hollinshead, M. B. 1999. "'Adyton,' 'Opisthodomos,' and the Inner Room of the Greek Temple." *Hesperia: The Journal of the American School of Classical Studies at Athens* 68 (2): 189–218.

Hölscher, T. 2007. "Urban Spaces and Central Places, the Greek World." In *Classical Archaeology*, edited by S. E. Alcock and R. Osborne. Malden: Wiley-Blackwell.

Horden, P., and N. Purcell. 2000. *The Corrupting Sea: A Study of Mediterranean History*. Malden: Wiley-Blackwell.

Houby-Nielsen, S. 1992. "Interaction between Chieftains and Citizens? VII BC Burial Customs in Athens." *Acta Hyperborea* 4: 343–63.

Houston, S. 2006. "The Problem of Spectacle among the Classic Maya." In *Archaeology of Performance: Theaters of Power, Community, and Politics*, edited by T. Inomata and L. S. Coben, 135–58. Lanham: AltaMira Press.

Humphreys, S. 1978. *Anthropology and the Greeks*. London: Routledge and Kegan Paul.

Hurwit, J. M. 1999. *The Athenian Acropolis: History, Mythology, and Archaeology from the Neolithic Era to the Present*. Cambridge: Cambridge University Press.

Iakovidis, S. 1962. *H Mykenaiki Akropolis Ton Athenon*. Athens: National and Kapodistrian University of Athens..

Iakovidis, S. 1980. *Excavations of the Necropolis at Perati*. Los Angeles: Institute of Archaeology, University of California, Los Angeles.

Iakovidis, S. 2006. "Epilogue: The Acropolis of Athens in Relation to the Other Mycenaean Citadels." In *The Mycenaean Acropolis of Athens*, 248–53. Athens: Archaeological Society of Athens.

Iakovidis, S., and I. Threpsiades. 2001. *Gla and the Kopais in the 13th Century B.C.* Athens: Archaeological Society at Athens.

Ingvarsson-Sundström, A., M. P. Richards, and S. Voutsaki. 2009. "Stable Isotope Analysis of the Middle Helladic Population from Two Cemeteries at Asine: Barbouna and the East Cemetery." *Mediterranean Archaeology and Archaeometry* 9 (2): 1–14.

Inomata, T., and L. S. Coben. 2006. *Archaeology of Performance: Theaters of Power, Community, and Politics*. New York: AltaMira Press.

Isager, S., and J. Skydsgaard. 2013. *Ancient Greek Agriculture: An Introduction*. London: Routledge.

Jacobsen, T. 1976. "17,000 Years of Greek Prehistory." *Scientific American* 234 (6): 76–87.

Jacobsen, T. 1981. "Franchthi Cave and the Beginning of Settled Village Life in Greece." *Hesperia: The Journal of the American School of Classical Studies at Athens* 50: 303–19.

Jacobsen, T. 1984. "Seasonal Pastoralism in Southern Greece: A Consideration of the Ecology of Neolithic Urfirnis Pottery." In *Pots and Potters: Current Approaches in Ceramic Archaeology*, edited by P. M. Rice, 27–43. Los Angeles: Cotsen Institute of Archaeology.

Jameson, M. 1993. "Domestic Space in the Greek City-State." In *Domestic Architecture and the Use of Space*, edited by S. Kent, 92–113. Cambridge: Cambridge University Press.

Jameson, M., C. N. Runnels, T. H. van Andel, and M. H. Munn. 1994. *The Southern Argolid from Prehistory to Today*. Stanford: Stanford University Press.

Janko, R. 2015. "From Gabii and Gordion to Eretria and Methone: The Rise of the Greek Alphabet." *Bulletin of the Institute of Classical Studies* 58 (1): 1–32.

Janusek, J. W. 2008. *Ancient Tiwanaku*. Cambridge: Cambridge University Press.

Jeffery, L. H., and A. W. Johnston. 1990. *The Local Scripts of Archaic Greece: A Study of the Origin of the Greek Alphabet and Its Development from the Eighth to the Fifth Centuries B.C.*, 2nd edn. Oxford: Oxford University Press.

Johnson, G. A. 1977. "Aspects of Regional Analysis in Archaeology." *Annual Review of Anthropology* 6: 479–508.

Johnson, G. A. 1980. "Rank-Size Convexity and System Integration: A View from Archaeology." *Economic Geography* 56 (3): 234–47.

Johnson, G. A. 1982. "Organizational Structure and Scalar Stress." In *Theory and Explanation in Archaeology*, edited by C. Renfrew, M. Rowlands, and B. Segreaves, 389–421. New York: Academic Press.

Jones, A. H. M. 1940. *The Greek City from Alexander to Justinian*. Oxford: Clarendon Press.

Kagan, D., and G. F. Viggiano, eds. 2013. *Men of Bronze: Hoplite Warfare in Ancient Greece*. Princeton: Princeton University Press.

Keesling, K. 2008. *The Votive Statues of the Athenian Acropolis*. Cambridge: Cambridge University Press.

Kelder, J. 2006. "Mycenaeans in Western Anatolia." In *Talanta*, 49–63. Proceedings of the Dutch Archaeological and Historical Society, 36–37.

Kent, S., ed. 1993. *Domestic Architecture and the Use of Space: An Interdisciplinary Cross-Cultural Study*. Cambridge: Cambridge University Press.

Kilian, K. 1986. "The Circular Building at Tiryns." In *Early Helladic Architecture and Urbanization*, edited by R. Hägg and D. Konsola, 65–71. Göteborg: Paul Åströms Förlag.

Kilian, K. 1987a. "Zur Funktion der Mykenischen Residenzen auf dem Griechischen Festland." In *The Function of the Minoan Palaces: Proceedings of the Fourth International Symposium at the Swedish Institute in Athens, 10–16 June, 1984*, edited by R. Hägg and N. Marinatos, 21–38. Stockholm: Svenska Institutet i Athen.

Kilian, K. 1987b. "L'architecture des Résidences Mycéniennes: Origine et Extension d'une Structure de Pouvoir Politique Pendant l'Age du Bronze Récent." In *Le Système Palatial en Orient, en Grèce et à Rome*, edited by E. Lévy, 203–17. Leiden: E. J. Brill.

Kilian, K. 1988. "The Emergence of Wanax Ideology in the Mycenaean Palaces." *Oxford Journal of Archaeology* 7 (3): 291–302.

Killebrew, A. E., and G. Lehmann, eds. 2013. *The Philistines and Other "Sea Peoples" in Text and Archaeology*. Atlanta: Society of Biblical Literature.

Kitts, M. 2011. "Ritual Scenes in the Iliad: Rote, Hallowed, or Encrypted as Ancient Art?" *Oral Tradition* 26 (1): 221–46.

Klein, N. L., and K. T. Glowacki. 2009. "From Kavousi Vronda to Dreros: Architecture and Display in Cretan Cult Buildings." *Hesperia Supplements* 42: 153–67.

Knappett, C., R. Rivers, and T. Evans. 2011. "The Theran Eruption and Minoan Palatial Collapse: New Interpretations Gained from Modelling the Maritime Network." August 22. http://antiquity.ac.uk.ezproxy.lib.lehigh.edu/ant/085/ant0851008.htm.

Koehl, R. B. 1986. "The Chieftain Cup and a Minoan Rite of Passage." *Journal of Hellenic Studies* 106: 99–110.

Kohler, T. 2012. "Complex Systems and Archaeology." In *Archaeological Theory Today*, edited by I. Hodder, 93–123. Cambridge, MA: Polity Press.

König, J. 2005. *Athletics and Literature in the Roman Empire (Greek Culture in the Roman World)*. Cambridge: Cambridge University Press.

Kotsakis, K. 1991. "The Powerful Past: Theoretical Trends in Greek Archaeology." In *Archaeological Theory in Europe*, edited by I. Hodder, 65–90. New York: Routledge.

Kotsakis, K. 2006. "Settlement of Discord: Sesklo and the Emerging Household." In *Homage to Milutin Garasanin*, edited by N. Tasic and C. Grozdanov, 207–20. Belgrade: Serbian Academy of Sciences and Arts and Macedonian Academy of Sciences and Arts.

Kotsonas, A. 2002. "The Rise of the Polis in Central Crete." *Eulimene* 3: 37–74.

Kotsonas, A. 2008. *The Archaeology of Tomb A1K1 of Orthi Petra in Eleutherna: The Early Iron Age Pottery*. Athens: University of Crete Press.

Kotsonas, A. 2017. "Sanctuaries, Temples and Altars in the Early Iron Age: A Chronological and Regional Accounting." In *Regional Stories Towards a New Perception of the Early Greek World: Acts of an International Symposium in Honour of Professor Jan Bouzek Volos, 18–21 June 2015*, edited by A. Mazarakis-Ainian, A. Alexandridou, and X. Charalambidou, 55–66. Volos: University of Thessaly Press.

Kotsos, S., and D. Urem-Kotsou. 2006. "Filling in the Neolithic Landscape." In *Homage to Milutin Garasanin*, edited by N. Tasic and C. Grozdanov, 193–207. Belgrade: Serbian Academy of Sciences and Arts and Macedonian Academy of Sciences and Arts.

Kouka, O. 2013. "'Minding the Gap': Against the Gaps. The Early Bronze Age and the Transition to the Middle Bronze Age in the Northern and Eastern Aegean/Western Anatolia." *American Journal of Archaeology* 117 (4): 569–80.

Kurke, L. 1991. *The Traffic in Praise: Pindar and the Poetics of Social Economics*. Ithaca: Cornell University Press.

Kurke, L. 1992. "The Politics of Habrosune in Archaic Greece." *Classical Antiquity* 11: 91–120.

Kurke, L. 1999. *Coins, Bodies, Games, and Gold: The Politics of Meaning in Archaic Greece*. Princeton: Princeton University Press.

Kurtz, D., and J. Boardman. 1971. *Greek Burial Customs*. Ithaca: Cornell University Press.

Kyriakidis, E. 2006. *Ritual in the Bronze Age Aegean: The Minoan Peak Sanctuaries*. London: Bristol Classical Press.

Kyrieleis, H. 1993. "The Heraion at Samos." In *Greek Sanctuaries: New Approaches*, edited by N. Marinatos and R. Hägg, 125–53. London: Routledge.

La Rosa, V. 1997. "La 'Villa Royale' d'Haghia Triada." In *The Function of the "Minoan Villa." Proceedings of the Eighth International Symposium at the Swedish Institute at Athens, 6–8 June 1992*, edited by R. Hägg, 79–89. Stockholm: Svenska Institutet i Athen.

Lang, F. 1996. *Archaische Siedlungen in Griechenland: Struktur und Entwicklung*. Berlin: Akademie Verlag.

Langdon, S. 2007. "The Awkward Age: Art and Maturation in Early Greece." *Hesperia Supplements* 41: 173–91.

Lawrence, A. W., and R. A. Tomlinson. 1996. *Greek Architecture*. New Haven: Yale University Press.

Lebessi, A. 1974. "Monumento funerario del VII sec. a. C. a Creta." *Antichita cretesi: Studi in onore di Doro Levi*. 2: 120–28.

Lebessi, A. 1991. "Flagellation ou Autoflagellation. Donnes Iconographiques pour une Tentative d'interpretation." *Bulletin de Correspondance Hellénique* 115: 99–123.

Lebessi, A. 2002. *Το Ιερό Του Ερμή Και Τησ ΑΦροδιτής Στη Σύμη Βιάννου, 3, Τα Χαλκινά ανθρωπόμορφα Ειδώλια*. Athens: Archaeological Society at Athens.

Lebessi, A. 2009. "The Erotic Goddess of the Syme Sanctuary, Crete." *American Journal of Archaeology* 113 (4): 521–45.

Lebessi, A., and P. Muhly. 1987. "The Sanctuary of Hermes and Aphrodite at Syme, Crete." *National Geographic Research Reports* 3: 102–12.

Lebessi, A., P. Muhly, and G. Papassavas. 2004. "The Runner's Ring: A Minoan Athlete's Dedication at the Syme Sanctuary, Crete." *Athenaische Mitteilungen* 119: 1–31.

LeCount, L., and J. Blitz. 2010. "A Comment on 'Funerals as Feasts: Why Are They So Important?'" *Cambridge Archaeological Journal* 20 (2): 263–65.

Lefèvre-Novaro, D., A. Pautasso, S. Rizza, and J. Lamaze. 2007. "Les Débuts de la Polis: L'exemple de Phaistos (Crète)." *Ktema, Civilisations de l'Orient, de La Grèce et de Rome Antiques* 32: 467–95.

Legarra Herrero, B. 2009. "The Minoan Fallacy: Cultural Diversity and Mortuary Behaviour on Crete at the Beginning of the Bronze Age." *Oxford Journal of Archaeology* 28 (1): 29–57.

Legarra Herrero, B. 2012. "The Construction, Deconstruction, and Non-Construction of Hierarchies in the Funerary Record of Prepalatial Crete." In *Back to the Beginning: Reassessing Social and Political Complexity on Crete during the Early and Middle Bronze Age*, edited by I. Schoep, P. Tomkins, and J. Driessen, 325–57. Oxford: Oxbow Books.

Leidwanger, J. 2013. "Modeling Distance with Time in Ancient Mediterranean Seafaring: A GIS Application for the Interpretation of Maritime Connectivity." *Journal of Archaeological Science* 40 (8): 3302–8.

Lemos, I. S. 2002. *The Protogeometric Aegean: The Archaeology of the Late Eleventh and Tenth Centuries BC*. Oxford: Oxford University Press.

Lemos, I. S., and H. Hatcher. 1986. "Protogeometric Skyros and Euboea." *Oxford Journal of Archaeology* 5 (3): 323–37.

Lemos, I. S., and D. Mitchell. 2011. "Elite Burials in Early Iron Age Aegean: Some Preliminary Observations on the Spatial Organization of the Toumba Cemetery at Lefkandi." In *The "Dark Ages" Revisited*, edited by A. Mazarakis-Ainian, 634–44. Volos: University of Thessaly Press.

Letesson, Q., and J. Driessen. 2008. "From 'Party' to 'Ritual' to 'Ruin' in Minoan Crete: The Spatial Context of Feasting." In *Dais: The Aegean Feast*, edited by L. Hitchcock, R. Laffineur, and J. L. Crowley, 207–13. Liège: Histoire de l'art et archéologie de la Grèce antique; Austin: Program in Aegean Scripts and Prehistory.

Levy, M. 2005. "Social Phase Transitions." *Journal of Economic Behavior and Organization* 57 (1): 71–87.

Lewis, J. 2013. *Early Greek Lawgivers*. London: Bloomsbury Publishing.

Lintott, A. W. 1982. *Violence, Civil Strife, and Revolution in the Classical City, 750–330 B.C.* London: CroomHelm.

Lomas, K. 2003. "Roman Imperialism and the City in Italy." In *Cultural Identity in the Roman Empire*, edited by J. Berry and R. Laurence, 64–78. London: Routledge.

Lomas, K. 2013. *Rome and the Western Greeks, 350 BC–AD 200: Conquest and Acculturation in Southern Italy*. London: Routledge.

Lyttkens, C. 1997. "A Rational-Actor Perspective on the Origins of Liturgies in Ancient Greece." *Journal of Institutional and Theoretical Economics* 153 (3): 462–84.

Ma, J. 2000. "Fighting Poleis of the Hellenistic World." In *War and Violence in the Greek World*, edited by H. van Wees, 337–76. London: Duckworth and the Classical Press of Wales.

Ma, J. 2003. "Peer Polity Interaction in the Hellenistic Age." *Past and Present* 180 (1): 9–39.

Ma, J. 2013. *Statues and Cities: Honorific Portraits and Civic Identity in the Hellenistic World*. Oxford: Oxford University Press.

MacGillivray, J. A., and R. L. N. Barber, eds. 1984. *The Prehistoric Cyclades*. Edinburgh: Department of Classical Archaeology, University of Edinburgh.

Mackil, E. 2013. *Creating a Common Polity: Religion, Economy, and Politics in the Making of the Greek Koinon*. Berkeley: University of California Press.

MacLachlan, B. 2012. *Women in Ancient Greece: A Sourcebook*. New York: Continuum International Publishing Group.

Malkin, I. 1987. *Religion and Colonization in Ancient Greece*. Leiden: E. J. Brill.

Malkin, I. 1989. "Delphoi and the Founding of Social Order in Archaic Greece." *Métis. Revue d'anthropologie des monde grec ancien* 4 (1): 129–53.

Malkin, I. 2003. "Networks and the Emergence of Greek Identity." *Mediterranean Historical Review* 18 (2): 56–74.

Malkin, I. 2011. *A Small Greek World: Networks in the Ancient Mediterranean*. Oxford: Oxford University Press.

Manson, S. 2001. "Simplifying Complexity: A Review of Complexity Theory." *Geoforum* 32: 405–14.

Manteli, K., and D. Evely. 1995. "The Neolithic Levels from the Throne Room System, Knossos." *Annual of the British School at Athens* 90: 1–16.

Marangou, C. 2001. "Sacred or Secular Places and the Ambiguous Evidence of Prehistoric Ritual." In *The Archaeology of Cult and Religion*, edited by P. F. Biehl, E. Bertemes, and H. Meller, 193–266. Budapest: Archaeolingua.

Marcus, J. 1976. *Emblem and State in the Classic Maya Lowlands: An Epigraphic Approach to Territorial Organization*. Washington, DC: Dumbarton Oaks.

Marinatos, N. 1987. "Public Festivals in the West Courts of the Palaces." In *The Function of the Minoan Palaces*, edited by R. Hägg and N. Marinatos, 135–42. Stockholm: Skrifter utgivna av Svenska Institutet i Athen.

Marinatos, N. 1993. *Minoan Religion: Ritual, Image, and Symbol*. Columbia: University of South Carolina Press.

Marinatos, N. 2010. *Minoan Kingship and the Solar Goddess: A Near Eastern Koine*. Urbana: University of Illinois Press.

Marinatos, N., and R. Hägg, eds. 1993. *Greek Sanctuaries: New Approaches*. London: Routledge.

Marinatos, S. 1936. "Le Temple Géométrique de Dréros." *Bulletin de Correspondance Hellénique* 60 (1): 214–85.

Marston, J. 2011. "Archaeological Markers of Agricultural Risk Management." *Journal of Anthropological Archaeology* 30 (2): 190–205.

Marthari, M. 2001. "Altering Information from the Past: Illegal Excavations in Greece and the Case of the Early Bronze Age Cyclades." In *Trade in Illicit Antiquities: The Destruction of the World's Archaeological Heritage*, edited by N. Brodie, J. Doole, and C. Renfrew, 161–72. Cambridge: Cambridge University Press.

Martin, T. R. 2013. *Ancient Greece: From Prehistoric to Hellenistic Times*, 2nd edn. New Haven: Yale University Press.

Matheny, R. 1980. *El Mirador, Peten, Guatemala: An Interim Report*. Provo: Brigham Young University Press.

Matheny, R. 1986. "Investigations at El Mirador, Peten, Guatemala." *National Geographic Research Reports* 2: 322–53.

Mazarakis-Ainian, A. 1987. "Geometric Eretria." *Antike Kunst* 30 (1): 3–24.

Mazarakis-Ainian, A. 1989. "Late Bronze Age Apsidal and Oval Buildings in Greece and Adjacent Areas." *The Annual of the British School at Athens* 84: 269–88.

Mazarakis-Ainian, A. 1992. "Nichoria in the Southwest Peloponnese. Units IV-1 and IV-5 Reconsidered." *Opuscula Atheniensa* 19: 75–84.

Mazarakis-Ainian, A. 1997. *From Rulers' Dwellings to Temples: Architecture, Religion and Society in Early Iron Age Greece (1100–700 B.C.)*. Goteborg: Paul Åströms Förlag.

McAnany, P. A. 2002. "Rethinking the Great and Little Tradition Paradigm from the Perspective of Domestic Ritual." In *Domestic Ritual in Ancient Mesoamerica*, edited by P. Plunket, 115–20. Los Angeles: Cotsen Institute of Archaeology.

McAnany, P. A. 2014. *Living with the Ancestors: Kinship and Kingship in Ancient Maya Society*, 2nd edn. Cambridge: Cambridge University Press.

McDonald, W. A., W. Coulson, and J. Rosser. 2013. *Excavations at Nichoria in Southwest Greece*, vol. III: *Dark Age and Byzantine Occupation*. Minneapolis: University of Minnesota Press.

McEnroe, J. C. 2010. *Architecture of Minoan Crete: Constructing Identity in the Aegean Bronze Age*. Austin: University of Texas Press.

McInerney, J. 1999. *The Folds of Parnassos: Land and Ethnicity in Ancient Phokis*. Austin: University of Texas Press.

Mee, C. 2011. *Greek Archaeology: A Thematic Approach*. Malden: Wiley-Blackwell.

Milka, E. 2010. "Burials upon the Ruins of Abandoned Houses in the Middle Helladic Argolid." *In Mesohelladika: The Greek Mainland in the Middle Bronze Age*, edited by A. Philippa-Touchais, G. Touchais, S. Voutsaki, and J.C. Wright, 347–55. Supplément Bulletin de Correspondance Hellénique 52. Paris.

Millar, F. 2006. "The Greek City in the Roman Period." In *The Greek World, the Jews, and the East*, edited by H. Cotton and G. Rogers, 106–35. Chapel Hill: University of North Carolina Press.

Miller, S. G. 2006. *Ancient Greek Athletics*. New Haven: Yale University Press.

Minoura, K., F. Imamura, U. Kuran, T. Nakamura, G. A. Papadopoulos, T. Takahashi, and A. C. Yalciner. 2000. "Discovery of Minoan Tsunami Deposits." *Geology* 28 (1): 59–62.

Morgan, C. 1990. *Athletes and Oracles: The Transformation of Olympia and Delphi in the Eighth Century BC*. Cambridge: Cambridge University Press.

Morgan, C. 1999. *Isthmia, Excavations by the University of Chicago under the Auspices of the American School of Classical Studies*, vol. VIII: *The Late Bronze Age Settlement and Early Iron Age Sanctuary*. Princeton: American School of Classical Studies at Athens.

Morris, I. 1986. "The Use and Abuse of Homer." *Classical Antiquity* 5 (1): 81–138.

Morris, I. 1989. "Circulation, Deposition and the Formation of the Greek Iron Age." *Man* 24 (3): 502–19.

Morris, I. 1990. *Burial and Ancient Society: The Rise of the Greek City-State*. Cambridge: Cambridge University Press.

Morris, I. 1997. "The Art of Citizenship." In *New Light on a Dark Age: Exploring the Culture of Geometric Greece*, edited by S. Langdon, 9–43. Columbia: University of Missouri Press.

Morris, I. 1999. "Negotiated Peripherality in Iron Age Greece: Accepting and Resisting the East." In *World-Systems Theory in Practice: Leadership, Production, and Exchange*, edited by P. N. Kardulias, 63–84. New York: Rowman and Littlefield.

Morris, I. 2000. *Archaeology as Cultural History: Words and Things in Iron Age Greece*. Malden: Wiley-Blackwell.

Morris, I. 2004. "Equality and the Origins of Greek Democracy." In *Ancient Greek Democracy: Readings and Sources*, edited by E. Robinson, 45–75. Malden: Wiley-Blackwell.

Morris, I. 2009. "The Eighth-Century Revolution." In *A Companion to Archaic Greece*, edited by K. Raaflaub and H. van Vess, 64–80. Malden: Wiley-Blackwell.

Morris, I., K. A. Raaflaub, and D. Castriota. 1998. *Democracy 2500?: Questions and Challenges*. Dubuque: Kendall/Hunt Publishing.

Mountjoy, P. A. 1995. *Mycenaean Athens*. Jonsered: Paul Åströms Förlag.

Muhly, P. 2008. *The Sanctuary of Hermes and Aphrodite at Syme Viannou IV. Animal Images of Clay. Handmade Figurines; Attachments; Mouldmade Plaques. With a Contribution by Eleni Nodarou and Christina Rathossi.* Athens: Archaeological Society at Athens.

Munro, N. A., and L. Grosman. 2010. "Early Evidence (ca. 12,000 B.P.) for Feasting at a Burial Cave in Israel." *Papers of the National Academy of Sciences* 107 (35): 15362–66.

Murray, O. 1991. "War and the Symposium." In *Dining in a Classical Context*, 83–104. Ann Arbor: University of Michigan Press.

Musgrave, J. H., R. A. H. Neave, A. J. N. W. Prag, R. A. Musgrave, and Danaé I. Thimme. 1995. "Seven Faces from Grave Circle B at Mycenae." *Annual of the British School at Athens* 90: 107–36.

Mylonas, G. E. 1973. *O Taphikos Kyklos B Ton Mykenon.* Athens: Athenian Archaeological Society.

Nafplioti, A. 2008. "'Mycenaean' Political Domination of Knossos Following the Late Minoan IB Destructions on Crete: Negative Evidence from Strontium Isotope Ratio Analysis (87Sr/86Sr)." *Journal of Archaeological Science* 35 (8): 2307–17.

Nakassis, D. 2010. "Reevaluating Staple and Wealth Finance at Mycenaean Pylos." In *Political Economies of the Aegean Bronze Age: Papers from the Langford Conference, Florida State University, Tallahassee, 22–24 February 2007*, edited by D. Pullen, 127–48. Oxford: Oxbow Books.

Nakassis, D., M. Galaty, and W. Parkinson. 2010. "State and Society." In *The Oxford Handbook of the Bronze Age Aegean*, edited by E. H. Cline, 239–50. Oxford: Oxford University Press.

Nakassis, D., W. Parkinson, and M. Galaty 2011. "Redistribution in Aegean Palatial Societies. Redistributive Economies from a Theoretical and Cross-Cultural Perspective." *American Journal of Archaeology* 115 (2): 177–84.

Neer, R. T. 2001. "Framing the Gift: The Politics of the Siphnian Treasury at Delphi." *Classical Antiquity* 20 (2): 273–344.

Neer, R. T. 2004. "The Athenian Treasury at Delphi and the Material of Politics." *Classical Antiquity* 23 (1): 63–93.

Nevett, L. C. 2001. *House and Society in the Ancient Greek World.* Cambridge: Cambridge University Press.

Nevett, L. C. 2010. *Domestic Space in Classical Antiquity.* Cambridge: Cambridge University Press.

Nevett, L. C., ed. 2017a. *Theoretical Approaches to the Archaeology of Ancient Greece: Manipulating Material Culture.* Ann Arbor: University of Michigan Press.

Nevett, L. C. 2017b. "Introduction." In *Theoretical Approaches to the Archaeology of Ancient Greece: Manipulating Material Culture*, edited by L. C. Nevett, 1–14. Ann Arbor: University of Michigan Press.

Nichols, D., and T. Charlton, eds. 1997. *The Archaeology of City-States: Cross Cultural Approaches.* Washington, DC: Smithsonian Institution Press.

Nicholls, R. V. 1958. "Old Smyrna: The Iron Age Fortifications and Associated Remains on the City Perimeter." *The Annual of the British School at Athens* 53/54: 35–137.

Nightingale, G. 2007. "Lefkandi: An Important Node in the International Exchange Network of Jewellery and Personal Adornment." In *Between the*

Aegean and the Baltic Seas: Prehistory across Borders, edited by I. Galanaki, H. Tomas, Y. Galanakis, and R. Laffineur, 421–29. Liège: Histoire de l'art et archéologie de la Grèce antique; Austin: Program in Aegean Scripts and Prehistory.

Nowicki, K. 1994. "Some Remarks on the Pre- and Protopalatial Peak Sanctuaries in Crete." *Aegean Archaeology* 1: 31–48.

Oakley, J. 2004. *Picturing Death in Classical Athens: The Evidence of White Ground Lekythoi*. Cambridge: Cambridge University Press.

Ober, J. 2015. *The Rise and Fall of Classical Greece*. Princeton: Princeton University Press.

Ogden, D. 1994. "Crooked Speech: The Genesis of the Spartan Rhetra." *Journal of Hellenic Studies* 114: 85–102.

Oren, E. D. 2000. *The Sea Peoples and Their World: A Reassessment*. Philadelphia: University of Pennsylvania Press.

Osborne, R. 1985. "Law in Action in Classical Athens." *Journal of Hellenic Studies* 105: 40–58.

Osborne, R. 1998. "Early Greek Colonization? The Nature of Greek Settlement in the West." In *Archaic Greece: New Approaches and New Evidence*, edited by N. Fisher and H. van Wees, 251–70. London: Duckworth and the Classical Press of Wales.

Osborne, R. 2004. "Greek Archaeology: A Survey of Recent Work." *American Journal of Archaeology* 108 (1): 87–102.

Osborne, R. 2009. Greece in the Making, 1200-479 BC. 2nd ed. New York: Routledge.

Overbeck, J. C. 1969. "Greek Towns of the Early Bronze Age." *The Classical Journal* 65 (1): 1–7.

Ozgenel, L. 2007. "Public Use and Privacy in Late Antique Houses in Asia Minor: The Architecture of Spatial Control." In *Housing in Late Antiquity: From Palaces to Shops*, edited by L. Lavan, L. Ozgenel, and A. C. Sarantis, 239–82. Leiden: E. J. Brill.

Pakkanen, J., and P. Pakkanen. 2000. "The Toumba Building at Lefkandi: Some Methodological Reflections on Its Plan and Function. *Annual of the British School at Athens* 95: 239–52.

Palaima, T. 1995. "The Nature of the Mycenaean Wanax: Non-IndoEuropean Orgins and Priestly Functions." In *The Role of the Ruler in the Prehistoric Aegean: Proceedings of a Panel Discussion Presented at the Annual Meeting of the Archaeological Institute of America, New Orleans, Louisiana, 28 December 1992, with Additions*, edited by P. Rehak, 119–42. Liège: Histoire de l'art et archéologie de la Grèce antique; Austin: Program in Aegean Scripts and Prehistory.

Palermo, A., R. Pautasso, and R. Gigli. 2008. "Lo scavo del 2007 sulla Patela di Prinias. Relazione Preliminare." *Creta Antica* 9: 179–209.

Pantou, P. A. 2010. "Mycenaean Dimini in Context: Investigating Regional Variability and Socioeconomic Complexities in Late Bronze Age Greece." *American Journal of Archaeology* 114 (3): 381–401.

Papadatos, Y., and P. Tomkins. 2013. "Trading, the Longboat, and Cultural Interaction in the Aegean during the Late Fourth Millennium B.C.E: The View from Kephala Petras, East Crete." *American Journal of Archaeology* 117 (3): 353–81.

Papadopoulos, J. K. 1997. "Phantom Euboians." *Journal of Mediterranean Archaeology* 10 (2): 191–219.

Papadopoulos, J. K. 2011. "Phantom Euboians: A Decade On." In *Euboea and Athens: Proceedings of a Colloquium in Memory of Malcolm B. Wallace. Athens, 26–27 June 2009*, 113–33. Athens: Canadian Institute in Greece.

Papadopoulos, J. K. 2014. "Greece in the Early Iron Age: Mobility, Commodities, Polities, and Literacy." In *The Cambridge Prehistory of the Bronze and Iron Age Mediterranean*, edited by B. Knapp and P. van Dommelen, 178–95. Cambridge: Cambridge University Press.

Papadopoulos, J. K., and R. Leventhal, eds. 2003. *Theory and Practice in Mediterranean Archaeology: Old World and New World Perspectives*. Los Angeles: Cotsen Institute of Archaeology.

Papakonstantinou, Z. 2014. "Sport, Victory Commenoration and Elite Identities in Archaic and Early Classical Athens." *Classica et Mediaevalia* 65: 87–126.

Parker Pearson, M. 1982. "Mortuary Practices, Society and Ideology: An Ethnoarchaeological Study." In *Symbolic and Structural Archaeology*, edited by I. Hodder, 99–113. Cambridge: Cambridge University Press.

Parkinson, W., and M. Galaty. 2007. "Secondary States in Perspective: An Integrated Approach to State Formation in the Prehistoric Aegean." *American Anthropologist* 109 (1): 113–29.

Pauketat, T. R. 2007. *Chiefdoms and Other Archaeological Delusions*. New York: Rowman AltaMira.

Peatfield, A. A. D. 1987. "Palace and Peak: The Political and Religious Relationship between Palaces and Peak Sanctuaries." In *The Function of the Minoan Palaces*, edited by R. Hägg and N. Marinatos, 89–93. Stockholm: Svenska Institutet i Athen.

Peatfield, A. A. D., and C. Morris. 2012. "Dynamic Spirituality on Minoan Peak Sanctuaries." In *Archaeology of Spiritualities*, edited by K. Rountree, C. Morris, and A. A. D. Peatfield, 227–45. New York: Springer.

Pelon, O. 1992. *Guide de Malia. Le Palais et la Nécropole de Chrysolakkos*. Paris: de Boccard.

Peperaki, O. 2004. "The House of the Tiles at Lerna: Dimensions of 'Social Complexity.'" In *The Emergence of Civilisation Revisited*, edited by J. Barrett and P. Halstead, 214–31. Oxford: Oxbow Books.

Peperaki, O. 2010. "Models of Relatedness and Early Helladic Architecture: Unpacking the Early Helladic II Hearth Room." *Journal of Mediterranean Archaeology* 23 (2): 245–64.

Perlès, C. 2001. *The Early Neolithic in Greece: The First Farming Communities in Europe*. Cambridge: Cambridge University Press.

Peterson, C. E., and R. D. Drennan. 2005. "Communities, Settlements, Sites, and Surveys: Regional-Scale Analysis of Prehistoric Human Interaction." *American Antiquity* 70 (1): 5–30.

Platon, N. 1971. *Zakros: The Discovery of a Lost Palace of Ancient Crete*. New York: Scribner.

Pleket, H. W. 1998. "Political Culture and Political Practice in the Cities of Asia Minor in the Roman Empire." In *Politische Theorie und Praxis im*

Altertun, edited by W. Schuller, 204–16. Darmstadt: Wissenschaftliche Buchgesellschaft.

Plunket, P. 2002. "Introduction" In *Domestic Ritual in Ancient Mesoamerica,* edited by P. Plunket, 1–10. Los Angeles: Cotsen Institute of Archaeology.

Polignac, F. de. 1995. *Cults, Territory, and the Origins of the Greek City-State.* Chicago: University of Chicago Press.

Pollock, S. 1999. *Ancient Mesopotamia: The Eden That Never Was.* Cambridge: Cambridge University Press.

Pomeroy, S., S. Burstein, W. Donlan, J. Roberts, and D. Tandy. 2011. *Ancient Greece: A Political, Social, and Cultural History,* 3rd edn. Oxford: Oxford University Press.

Popham, M. R., P. G. Calligas, L. H. Sackett, J. J. Coulton, and H. W. Catling. 1993. "Lefkandi II. The Protogeometric Building at Toumba. Part 2: The Excavation, Architecture and Finds." *The British School at Athens Supplementary Volumes* 23: 1–101.

Popham, M. R., L. Sackett, and P. Themelis. 1980. *Lefkandi I: The Iron Age.* London: Thames and Hudson.

Poursat, J.-C. 1996. *Fouilles Exécutées à Malia: Le Quartier Mu III: Artisans Minoens: Les Maisons-Ateliers du Quartier Mu.* Paris: École Française d'Athènes.

Powell, B. 1989. "Why Was the Greek Alphabet Invented? The Epigraphical Evidence." *Classical Antiquity* 8 (2): 321–50.

Powell, B. 1996. *Homer and the Origin of the Greek Alphabet.* Cambridge: Cambridge University Press.

Powell, B. 2002. *Writing and the Origins of Greek Literature.* Cambridge: Cambridge University Press.

Powell, B. 2012. *Writing: Theory and History of the Technology of Civilization.* Malden: Wiley-Blackwell.

Prent, M. 2005. *Cretan Sanctuaries and Cults: Continuity and Change from Late Minoan IIIC to the Archaic Period.* Leiden: E. J. Brill.

Prent, M. 2008. "Glories of the Past in the Past: Ritual Activities at Palatial Ruins in Early Iron Age Crete." In *Archaeologies of Memory,* edited by R. M. Van Dyke and S. E. Alcock, 81–103. Malden: Wiley-Blackwell.

Preston, L. 2004. "A Mortuary Perspective on Political Changes in Late Minoan II–IIIB Crete." *American Journal of Archaeology* 108 (3): 321–48.

Preziosi, D. 1983. *Minoan Architectural Design: Formation and Signification.* New York: Mouton.

Preziosi, D., and L. Hitchcock. 1999. *Aegean Art and Architecture.* Oxford: Oxford University.

Price, S. R. F. 1985. *The Roman Imperial Cult in Asia Minor.* Cambridge: Cambridge University Press.

Pullen, D. 1985. "Social Organization in Early Bronze Age Greece: A Multidimensional Approach." PhD dissertation, Indiana University.

Pullen, D. 1986. "A 'House of Tiles' at Zygouries? The Function of Monumental Early Helladic Architecture." In *Early Helladic Architecture and Urbanization: Proceedings of a Seminar Held at the Swedish Institute in Athens, June 8, 1985,* edited by R. Hägg and D. Konsola, 79–84. Göteborg: Paul Åströms Förlag.

Pullen, D. 1994. "A Lead Seal from Tsoungiza, Ancient Nemea, and Early Bronze Age Aegean Sealing Systems." *American Journal of Archaeology* 98 (1): 35–52.

Pullen, D. 2008. "The Early Bronze Age in Greece." In *The Cambridge Companion to the Aegean Bronze Age*, edited by C. Shelmerdine, 19–46. Cambridge: Cambridge University Press.

Pullen, D. 2011a. "Picking out Pots in Patterns: Feasting in Early Helladic Greece." In *Our Cups Are Full: Pottery and Society in the Aegean Bronze Age*, edited by W. Gauss, M. Lindblom, R. A. K. Smith, and J. C. Wright, 217–26. Oxford: Oxbow Books.

Pullen, D. 2011b. "Redistribution in Aegean Palatial Societies. Before the Palaces: Redistribution and Chiefdoms in Mainland Greece." *American Journal of Archaeology* 115 (2): 185–95.

Pullen, D. 2013. "'Minding the Gap': Bridging the Gaps in Cultural Change within the Early Bronze Age Aegean." *American Journal of Archaeology* 117 (4): 545–53.

Pyke, G. 1993. "The Stratigraphy, Structures and Small Finds of Nea Nikomedeia, Northern Greece." MPhil thesis, University of Birmingham.

Pyke, G. 1996. "Structures and Architecture." In *Nea Nikomedeia I: The Excavation of an Early Neolithic Village in Northern Greece 1961–1964, the Excavation and the Ceramic Assemblage*, edited by K. Wardle, 25: 39–53. Supplementary Volume. London: British School at Athens.

Rappaport, R. A. 1968. *Pigs for the Ancestors: Ritual in the Ecology of a New Guinea People*. New Haven: Yale University Press.

Rawlings, L. 2007. *The Ancient Greeks at War*. Manchester: Manchester University Press.

Reents-Budet, D. 1994. *Painting the Maya Universe: Royal Ceramics of the Classic Period*, 2nd edn. Durham: Duke University Press.

Reents-Budet, D., R. Bishop, J. Taschek, and J. Ball. 2000. "Out of the Palace Dumps." *Ancient Mesoamerica* 11 (1): 99–121.

Reese-Taylor, K., and D. Walker. 2002. "The Passage of the Late Preclassic into the Early Classic." In *Ancient Maya Political Economies*, edited by M. Masson and D. Freidel, 87–122. New York: Altamira Press.

Rehak, P., and J. Younger. 1998. "Review of Aegean Prehistory VII: Neopalatial, Final Palatial, and Postpalatial Crete." *American Journal of Archaeology* 102 (1): 91–173.

Reingruber, A. 2011. "Early Neolithic Settlement Patterns and Exchange Networks in the Aegean." *Documenta Praehistorica* 38: 291–305.

Reitsma, F. 2003. "A Response to Simplifying Complexity." www.era.lib.ed.ac.uk/handle/1842/1.

Renfrew, C. 1987. *Archaeology and Language: The Puzzle of Indo-European Origins*. Cambridge: Cambridge University Press.

Renfrew, C. 2010. "Cyclades." In *The Oxford Handbook of the Bronze Age Aegean*, edited by E. H. Cline, 83–98. Oxford: Oxford University Press.

Renfrew, C., and J. F. Cherry, eds. 1986. *Peer Polity Interaction and Socio-Political Change*. Cambridge: Cambridge University Press.

Renfrew, C., and J. F. Cherry. 2011. *The Emergence of Civilisation: The Cyclades and the Aegean in the Third Millennium BC*, 2nd edn. Oxford: Oxbow Books.

Renfrew, C., and J. M. Wagstaff, eds. 1982. *An Island Polity: The Archaeology of Exploitation in Melos*. Cambridge: Cambridge University Press.

Renfrew, C., N. Brodie, C. Morris, and C. Scarre, eds. 2007. *Excavations at Phylakopi in Melos 1974–77*. London: British School at Athens.

Renfrew, C., C. Doumas, C. Marangou, and G. Gavalas, eds. 2007a. *Keros, Dhaskalio Kavos: The Investigations of 1987–88*. Cambridge: McDonald Institute for Archaeological Research.

Renfrew, C., O. Philaniotou, N. Brodie, and G. Gavalas. 2009. "The Early Cycladic Settlement at Dhaskalio, Keros: Preliminary Report of the 2008 Excavation Season." *Annual of the British School at Athens* 104: 27–47.

Renfrew, C., O. Philaniotou, N. Brodie, G. Gavalas, and M. J. Boyd, eds. 2013. *The Sanctuary on Keros and the Origins of Aegean Ritual Practice: The Excavations of 2006–2008*, vol. I: *The Settlement at Dhaskalio*. Cambridge: McDonald Institute for Archaeological Research.

Renfrew, C., O. Philaniotou, N. Brodie, G. Gavalas, and M. J. Boyd. 2015. *The Sanctuary on Keros and the Origins of Aegean Ritual Practice: The Excavations of 2006–2008*, vol. II: *Kavos and the Special Deposits*. Cambridge: MacDonald Institute for Archaeological Research.

Renfrew, C., O. Philaniotou, N. Brodie, G. Gavalas, E. Margaritis, C. French, and P. Sotirakopoulou. 2007b. "Keros: Dhaskalio and Kavos, Early Cycladic Stronghold and Ritual Centre. Preliminary Report of the 2006 and 2007 Excavation Seasons." *Annual of the British School at Athens* 102: 103–36.

Reusch, H. 1958. "Zum Wandschmuck des Thronsaales in Knossos." In *Minoica: Festschrift zum 80 Geburtstag von Johannes Sundwall*, edited by E. Grumach and H. Reusch, 334–58. Berlin: Deutsche Akademie der Wissenschaften zu Berlin.

Rice, P. M. 2008. "Time, Power, and the Maya." *Latin American Antiquity* 19 (3): 275–98.

Rizza, G. 1978. "Gli scavi dei Prinias e Il problema delle origini dell'arte Greca." *Quaderni de "La Ricerca Scientifica"* 100 (1): 3–55.

Rizza, G. 2008. *Priniàs: La Città Arcaica Sulla Patela. Scavi Condotti Negli Anni 1969–2000*. 2 vols. Catania: Consiglio Nazionale Delle Ricerche, Centro di Studio Sull'archeologia Greca.

Rodden, R. 1962. "Excavations at the Early Neolithic Site at Nea Nikomedeia, Greek Macedonia (1961 Season)." *Proceedings of the Prehistoric Society* 28: 267–88.

Rodden, R. 1965. "An Early Neolithic Village in Greece." *Scientific American* 212 (4): 82–88.

Rodden, R. 1996. "Introduction and Acknowledgements." In *Nea Nikomedeia I: The Excavation of an Early Neolithic Village in Northern Greece, 1961–1964, the Excavation and the Ceramic Assemblage*, edited by K. Wardle, 25: 1–8. Supplementary Volume. London: British School at Athens.

Romano, D., and M. Voyatzis. 2010. "Excavating at the Birthplace of Zeus." *Expedition* 52: 9–21.

Roselli, D. K. 2011. *Theater of the People: Spectators and Society in Ancient Athens*. Austin: University of Texas Press.

Runnels, C., C. Payne, N. Rifkind, C. White, N. Wolff, and S. LeBlanc. 2009. "Warfare in Neolithic Thessaly: A Case Study." *Hesperia: The Journal of the American School of Classical Studies at Athens* 78 (2): 165–94.

Rutkowski, B. 1988. "Minoan Peak Sanctuaries: Topography and Architecture" *Aegaeum* 2: 71–99.

Rutter, J. 1983a. "Some Observations on the Cyclades in the Later Third and Early Second Millennia." *American Journal of Archaeology* 87 (1): 69–76.

Rutter, J. 1983b. "Fine Gray-Burnished Pottery of the Early Helladic III Period the Ancestry of Gray Minyan." *Hesperia: The Journal of the American School of Classical Studies at Athens* 52 (4): 327–55.

Rutter, J. 1984. "The Early Cycladic III Gap: What It Is and How to Go about Filling It without Making It Go Away." In *The Prehistoric Cyclades*, edited by J. A. MacGillivray and R. L. N. Barber, 95–107. Edinburgh: Edinburgh University Press.

Rutter, J. 1993. "Review of Aegean Prehistory II: The Prepalatial Bronze Age of the Southern and Central Greek Mainland." *American Journal of Archaeology* 97 (4): 745–97.

Sabin, P., H. van Wees, and M. Whitby, eds. 2007. *The Cambridge History of Greek and Roman Warfare*, vol. 1: *Greece, the Hellenistic World and the Rise of Rome*. Cambridge: Cambridge University Press.

Sallares, R. 1991. *The Ecology of the Ancient Greek World*. Ithaca: Cornell University Press.

Sampson, A. 1985. *Mia Protoelladike Pole Ste Chalkida*. Athens: Etaireia Evoikon Spoudon.

Sampson, A. 1988. *Manika. O Protoelladikos Oikismos Kai to Nekrotapheio II*. Athens: Etaireia Evoikon Spoudon.

Sandars, N. K. 1978. *The Sea Peoples: Warriors of the Ancient Mediterranean, 1250–1150 B.C.* London: Thames and Hudson.

Scheidel, W. 2003. "The Greek Demographic Expansion: Models and Comparisons." *Journal of Hellenic Studies* 123: 120–40.

Schliemann, H. 1878. *Mycenae: A Narrative of Researches and Discoveries at Mycenae and Tiryns*. New York: Scribner.

Schliemann, H., F. Adler, and W. Dörpfeld. 1885. *Tiryns: The Prehistoric Palace of the Kings of Tiryns, the Results of the Latest Excavations*. New York: Scribner.

Schoep, I. 2004. "The Socio-Economic Context of Seal Use and Administration at Knossos." In *Knossos: Palace, City, State. Proceedings of the Conference in Herakleion Organized by the British School at Athens and the 23rd Ephoreia of Prehistoric and Classical Antiquities of Herakleion, in November 2000, for the Centenary of Sir Arthur Evans' Excavations at Knossos*, edited by G. Cadogan, E. Hatzaki, and A. Vasilakis, 283–93. London: British School at Athens.

Schoep, I. 2006. "Looking beyond the First Palaces: Elites and the Agency of Power in EM III–MM II Crete." *American Journal of Archaeology* 110 (1): 37–64.

Schoep, I. 2010. "The Minoan 'Palace-Temple' Reconsidered: A Critical Assessment of the Spatial Concentration of Political, Religious and Economic Power in Bronze Age Crete." *Journal of Mediterranean Archaeology* 23 (2): 219–44.

Scholten, J. B. 2000. *The Politics of Plunder: Aitolians and Their Koinon in the Early Hellenistic Era, 279–217 B.C.* Berkeley: University of California Press.

Schon, R. 2011. "Redistribution in Aegean Palatial Societies. By Appointment to His Majesty the Wanax: Value-Added Goods and Redistribution in Mycenaean Palatial Economies." *American Journal of Archaeology* 115 (2): 219–27.

Shortman, E., and W. Ashmore. 2012. "History, Networks, and the Quest for Power: Ancient Political Competition in the Lower Motagua Valley, Guatemala." *Journal of the Royal Anthropological Institute* 18 (1): 1–21.

Schreiber, T. 1999. *Athenian Vase Construction: A Potter's Analysis*. Malibu: Getty Publications.

Schultz, P. 2009. "Divine Images and Royal Ideology in the Philippeion at Olympia." In *Aspects of Ancient Greek Cult: Context, Ritual, Iconography*, edited by G. Jesper Jensen, B. W. Hinge, and P. Schultz, 125–93. Aarhus: Aarhus University Press.

Scott, M. 2010. *The Spatial Politics of Panhellenism in the Archaic and Classical Periods*. Cambridge: Cambridge University Press.

Seelentag, G. 2014. "An Epic Perspective on Institutionalization in Archaic Crete." In *Cultural Practices and Material Culture in Archaic and Classical Crete: Proceedings of the International Conference, Mainz, May 20–21, 2011*, edited by O. Pilz and G. Seelentag, 121–40. Berlin: de Gruyter.

Séfériadès, M. 2007. "Complexity of the Processes of Neolithization: Tradition and Modernity of the Aegean World at the Dawn of the Holocene Period (11–9 Kyr)." *Quaternary International* 167: 177–85.

Sharer, R., and L. Traxler. 2006. *The Ancient Maya*, 6th edn. Stanford: Stanford University Press.

Shaw, J. W. 1978. "Evidence for the Minoan Tripartite Shrine." *American Journal of Archaeology* 82 (4): 429–48.

Shaw, J. W. 1987. "The Early Helladic II Corridor House: Development and Form." *American Journal of Archaeology* 91 (1): 59–79.

Shaw, J. W. 1989. "Phoenicians in Southern Crete." *American Journal of Archaeology* 93 (2): 165–83.

Shaw, J. W. 1990. "The Early Helladic II Corridor House: Problems and Possibilities." In *L'Habitat Egeen Prehistorique*, edited by P. Darcque and R. Treuil, 183–94. Paris: École française d'Athènes.

Sheehy, J. J. 1991. "Structure and Change in a Late Classic Maya Domestic Group at Copan, Honduras." *Ancient Mesoamerica* 2 (1): 1–20.

Shelmerdine, C. W. 2011. "The Individual and the State in Mycenaean Greece." *Bulletin of the Institute of Classical Studies* 54 (1): 19–28.

Sigurdsson, H., S. Carey, M. Alexandri, G. Vougioukalakis, K. Croff, C. Roman, D. Sakellariou, et al. 2006. "Marine Investigations of Greece's Santorini Volcanic Field." *Eos, Transactions, American Geophysical Union* 87 (34): 337–42.

Sjögren, L. 2007. "Interpreting Cretan Private and Communal Spaces (800–500 BC)." In *Building Communities: House, Settlement and Society in the Aegean and Beyond, Proceedings of a Conference Held at Cardiff University 2001*, edited by R. Westgate, N. Fisher, and J. Whitley, 149–55. London: British School at Athens.

Small, D. 1995a. "Heterarchical Paths to Evolution: The Role of External Economies." In *Heterarchy and the Analysis of Complex Societies*, edited by R. Ehrenreich, C. Crumley, and J. Levy, 71–85. Washington, DC: American Anthropological Association.

Small, D. 1995b. "Monuments, Laws, and Analysis: Combining Archaeology and Text in Ancient Athens." In *Methods in the Mediterranean: Historical and*

Archaeological Views on Texts and Archaeology, edited by D. Small, 143–76. Leiden: E. J. Brill.

Small, D. 1997. "City-State Dynamics through a Greek Lens." In *Cross-Cultural Approaches to City-States*, edited by T. Charlton and L. Nichols, 107–18. Washington, DC: Smithsonian Institution Press.

Small, D. 2002. "Rethinking the Historical Dimensions of Mortuary Practices: A Case from Nisky Hill Cemetery, Bethlehem, Pennsylvania." In *The Space and Place of Death*, edited by H. Silverman and D. Small, 161–66. Washington, DC: American Anthropological Association.

Small, D. 2007. "Mycenaean Polities: States or Estates?" In *Rethinking Mycenaean Palaces II*, edited by M. Galaty and W. Parkinson, 47–54. Los Angeles: Cotsen Institution of Archaeology.

Small, D. 2009. "The Dual-Processual Model in Ancient Greece: Applying a Post-Neoevolutionary Model to a Data-Rich Environment." *Journal of Anthropological Archaeology* 28 (2): 205–21.

Small, D. 2010. "The Archaic Polis of Azoria: A Window into Cretan 'Polital' Social Structure." *Journal of Mediterranean Archaeology* 23 (2): 197–217.

Small, D. 2011. "Contexts, Agency, and Social Change in Ancient Greece." In *State Formation in Italy and Greece: Questioning the Neoevolutionist Paradigm*, edited by N. Terrenato and D. Haggis, 197–217. Oxford: Oxbow Books.

Small, D. 2015. "A Defective Master Narrative in Greek Archaeology." In *Greek Archaeology in Context: Theory and Practice in Excavation in the Greek World*, edited by C. Antonaccio and D. Haggis, 71–86. Berlin: de Gruyter.

Small, D. 2018. "An Explosion, Not Revolution: Recasting Issues in the Greek Iron Age." In *An Age of Experiment: Classical Archaeology Transformed 1976-2014*, edited by L. C. Nevett and J. Whitley, 21–30. Cambridge: MacDonald Institute for Archaeological Research.

Small, D. forthcoming. "Problems with Isolating Rituals of Corporate Power in the Evolution of Archaic States."

Snodgrass, A. M. 1974. "An Historical Homeric Society?" *Journal of Hellenic Studies* 94: 114–25.

Snodgrass, A. M. 1981. *Archaic Greece: The Age of Experiment*. Berkeley: University of California Press.

Snodgrass, A. M. 1986. "Interaction by Design: The Greek City State." In *Peer Polity Interaction and Socio-Political Change*, edited by C. Renfrew and J. F. Cherry, 47–58. Cambridge: Cambridge University Press.

Snodgrass, A. M. 1989. "The Economics of Dedication at Greek Sanctuaries." *Scienze Dell'antichita* 3–4: 287–94.

Snodgrass, A. M. 1998. *Homer and the Artists: Text and Picture in Early Greek Art*. Cambridge: Cambridge University Press.

Snodgrass, A. M. 1999. *Arms and Armor of the Greeks*. Baltimore: Johns Hopkins University Press.

Snodgrass, A. M. 2000. *The Dark Age of Greece: An Archaeological Survey of the Eleventh to the Eighth Centuries BC*. Edinburgh: Edinburgh University Press.

Sommerstein, A. H. 2003. *Greek Drama and Dramatists*. London: Routledge.

Sotirakopoulou, P. 2010. "The Cycladic Middle Bronze Age: A 'Dark Age' in Aegean Prehistory or a Dark Spot in Archaeological Research?" In

Mesohelladika. La Grèce Continentale au Bronze Moyen, edited by A. Philippa-Touchais, G. Touchais, S. Voutsaki, and J. C. Wright, 825–39. Paris: De Boccard.

Sourvinou-Inwood, C. 1993. "Early Sanctuaries, the Eighth Century and Ritual Space: Fragments of a Discourse." In *Greek Sanctuaries: New Approaches*, edited by N. Marinatos and R. Hägg, 1–17. London: Routledge.

Southall, A. 1968. "The Segmentary State in Africa and Asia." *Comparative Studies in Society and History* 30 (1): 52–82.

Souvatzi, S. G. 2007. "Social Complexity Is Not the Same as Hierarchy." In *Socialising Complexity: Structure, Interaction and Power in Archaeological Discourse*, edited by S. Kohring and S. Wynne-Jones, 37–59. Oxford: Oxbow Books.

Souvatzi, S. G. 2008. *A Social Archaeology of Households in Neolithic Greece: An Anthropological Approach*. Cambridge: Cambridge University Press.

Souvatzi, S. G. 2013. "Diversity, Uniformity and the Transformative Properties of the House in Neolithic Greece." In *Tracking the Neolithic House in Europe: Sedentism, Architecture and Practice*, edited by Daniela Hofmann and Jessica Smyth, 45–64. New York: Springer.

Spanakis, S. 1977. "The Ancient Theaters of Crete." *Amaltheia* 8 (30): 35–61 (in Greek).

Spawforth, A. J. 2006. *The Complete Greek Temples*. New York: Thames and Hudson.

Spawforth, A. J. 2011. *Greece and the Augustan Cultural Revolution*. Cambridge: Cambridge University Press.

Spawforth, A. J., and S. Walker. 1985. "The World of the Panhellenion I. Athens and Eleusis." *Journal of Roman Studies* 75: 78–104.

Spawforth, A. J., and S. Walker. 1986. "The World of the Panhellenion: II. Three Dorian Cities." *Journal of Roman Studies* 76: 88–105.

Spivey, N. 2004. *The Ancient Olympics*. Oxford: Oxford University Press.

Stampolidis, N. 1990. "Eleutherna on Crete: An Interim Report on the Geometric-Archaic Cemetery." *Annual of the British School at Athens* 85: 375–403.

Stampolidis, N. 2004. *Eleutherna: Polis, Acropolis, Necropolis*. Athens: Ministry of Culture; University of Crete; Museum of Cycladic Art.

Stewart, D. 2014. "Rural Sites in Roman Greece." *Archaeological Reports* 60: 117–32.

Stocker, S. R., and J. L. Davis. 2004. "Animal Sacrifice, Archives, and Feasting at the Palace of Nestor." In The Mycenaean Feast, edited by J. C. Wright, 2: 179–95. *Hesperia: The Journal of the American School at Athens* 72.

Stockhammer, P. W., ed. 2012. *Conceptualizing Cultural Hybridization in Archaeology*. New York: Springer.

Stone, D. L. 2017. "A Theoretical or Atheoretical Greek Archaeology? The Last Twenty-Five Years." In *Theoretical Approaches to the Archaeology of Ancient Greece: Manipulating Material Culture*, edited by L. C. Nevett, 15–39. Ann Arbor: University of Michigan Press.

Storey, I. C., and A. Allan. 2013. *A Guide to Ancient Greek Drama*. Malden: Wiley-Blackwell.

Strasser, T. 1997. "Storage and States on Prehistoric Crete: The Function of the Koulouras in the First Minoan Palaces." *Journal of Mediterranean Archaeology* 10 (1): 73–100.

Stuart, D. 2005. "Ideology and Classical Maya Kingship." In *A Catalyst of Ideas: Anthropological Archaeology and the Legacy of Douglas W. Schwartz*, edited by V. Scarborough, 257–86. Santa Fe: School of American Research Press.

Swaddling, J. 1999. *The Ancient Olympic Games*. Austin: University of Texas Press.

Symeonoglou, S. 1973. *Kadmeia I. Mycenaean Finds from Thebes, Greece: Excavations at 14 Oedipus St.* Göteborg: Paul Åströms Förlag.

Talalay, L. 1987. "Rethinking the Function of Clay Figurine Legs from Neolithic Greece: An Argument by Analogy." *American Journal of Archaeology* 91 (2): 161–69.

Talalay, L. 2004. "Heady Business: Skulls, Heads, and Decapitation in Neolithic Anatolia and Greece." *Journal of Mediterranean Archaeology* 17 (2): 139–63.

Tambiah, S. 1976. *World Conqueror and World Renouncer: A Study of Buddhism and Polity in Thailand against a Historical Background*. Cambridge: Cambridge University Press.

Tambiah, S. 1977. "The Galactic Polity: The Structure of Traditional Kingdoms in Southeast Asia." *Annals of the New York Academy of Sciences* 293 (1): 69–97.

Tammuz, O. 2005. "Mare Clausum? Sailing Seasons in the Mediterranean in Early Antiquity." *Mediterranean History Journal* 20 (2): 145–62.

Tandy, D. W. 2000. *Warriors into Traders: The Power of the Market in Early Greece*. Berkeley: University of California Press.

Tartaron, T. 2008. "Aegean Prehistory as World Archaeology: Recent Trends in the Archaeology of Bronze Age Greece." *Journal of Archaeological Research* 16 (2): 83–161.

Tartaron, T. 2010. "Between and Beyond: Political Economy in Non-Palatial Mycenaean Worlds." In *Political Economies of the Aegean Bronze Age*, edited by D. Pullen, 161–83. Oxford: Oxbow Books.

Thompson, H. 1982. "Architecture as a Medium of Public Relations among the Successors of Alexander." In *Macedonia and Greece in Late Classical and Early Hellenistic Times*, edited by B. Barr-Sharrar and E. N. Borza, 173–90. Washington, DC: National Gallery of Art.

Thompson, J. G. 1986. "The Location of the Minoan Bull Sports: A Consideration of the Problem." *Journal of Sport History* 13 (1): 5–13.

Thompson, J. G. 1989. "Clues to the Location of Minoan Bull-Jumping from the Palace at Knossos." *Journal of Sport History* 16 (1): 62–69.

Thompson, J. G. 1992. "Clues to the Location of Bull Jumping at Zakro." *Journal of Sport History* 19 (2): 163–68.

Todaro, S. 2005. "EMI–MMIA Ceramic Groups at Phaistos: Towards the Definition of a Prepalatial Ceramic Sequence in South Central Crete." *Creta Antica* 6: 11–46.

Todaro, S., and S. Di Tonto. 2006. "The Neolithic Settlement of Phaistos Revisited: Evidence for Ceremonial Activity on the Eve of the Bronze Age." In *Escaping the Labyrinth: New Perspectives on the Neolithic of Crete*, 177–90. Oxford: Oxbow Books.

Tokovinine, A. 2016. "'It Is His Image with Pulque': Drinks, Gifts, and Political Networking in Classic Maya Texts and Images." *Ancient Mesoamerica* 27 (1): 13–29.

Tomkins, P. 2004. "Filling in the 'Neolithic Background': Social Life and Social Transformation in the Aegean before the Bronze Age." In *The Emergence of Civilisation Revisited*, edited by J. Barrett and P. Halstead, 38–63. Oxford: Oxbow Books.

Tomkins, P. 2012. "Behind the Horizon. Reconsidering the Genesis and Function of the 'First Palace' at Knossos (Final Neolithic IV–Middle Minoan IB)." In *Back to the Beginning: Reassessing Social and Political Complexity on Crete during the Early and Middle Bronze Age*, edited by I. Schoep, P. Tomkins, and J. Driessen, 32–80. Oxford: Oxbow Books.

Tomkins, P., and I. Schoep. 2010. "The Early Bronze Age: Crete." In *The Oxford Handbook of the Bronze Age Aegean*, edited by E. H. Cline, 66–82. Oxford: Oxford University Press.

Torrance, I. C. 2014. "Ways to Give Oaths Extra Sanctity." In *Oaths and Swearing in Ancient Greece*, edited by A. H. Sommerstein and I. C. Torrance, 132–49. Berlin: de Gruyter.

Turner, V. 1957. *Schism and Continuity in an African Society: A Study of Ndembu Village Life*. Manchester: Manchester University Press.

Tsetskhladze, G. R. 1992. "Greek Colonization of the Eastern Black Sea Littoral (Colchis)." *Dialogues d'histoire Ancienne* 18 (2): 223–58.

Tsipopoulou, M., ed. 2012a. *Petras, Siteia. 25 Years of Excavations and Studies: Acts of a Two-Day Conference Held at the Danish Institute at Athens, 9–10 October 2010*. Athens: Danish Institute at Athens.

Tsipopoulou, M. 2012b. "The Kampos Group Pottery from the Cemetery of Petras, Siteia." In *Studies in Honor of Costis Davaras*, edited by E. Mantzourani and P. Betancourt, 213–22. Philadelphia: INSTAP Academic Press.

Tsountas, C. 1908. *Ai Proistorikai Akropoleis Diminiou Kai Sesklou*. Athens: Athens Archaeological Society.

Tsukamoto, K., J. L. Camacho, L. E. C. Valenzuela, H. Kotegawa, and O. Q. E. Olguin. 2015. "Political Interactions among Social Actors: Spatial Organization at the Classic Maya Polity of El Palmar, Campeche, Mexico." *Latin American Antiquity* 26 (2): 200–220.

Twiss, K. 2008. "Transformations in an Early Agricultural Society: Feasting in the Southern Levantine Pre-Pottery Neolithic." *Journal of Anthropological Archaeology* 27 (4): 418–42.

Ubelaker, D., and J. Rife. 2007. "The Practice of Cremation in the Roman-Era Cemetery at Kenchreai, Greece: The Perspective from Archeology and Forensic Science." *Bioarchaeology of the Near East* 1: 35–57.

Urban, P., and E. Shortman. 2004. "Opportunities for Advancement: Intra-Community Power Contests in the Midst of Political Decentralization in Terminal Classic Southeastern Mesoamerica." *Latin American Antiquity* 15 (3): 251–72.

Valmin, M. N. 1938. *The Swedish Messenia Expedition: Malthi Dorion*. Lund: C. W. K. Gleerup.

Van Gennep, A. 2013. *The Rites of Passage*. London: Routledge.

Van Nijf, O. 2006. "Politiek in de Polis." In *Benaderingen van de Geschiedenis van Politiek*, edited by G. Voerman and D. J. Wolffram, 16–22. Groningen: Kossmann Instituut, Rijksuniversiteit.

Van Nijf, O. 2011. "Public Space and the Political Culture of Roman Termessos." In *Political Culture in the Greek City after the Classical Age*, edited by O. van Nijf, R. Alston, and C. G. Williamson, 215–42. Leuven: Peeters.

Van Nijf, O. 2012. "Political Games." In *L'organisation des Spectacles dans le Monde Romain*, edited by K. Coleman and J. Nelis-Clément, 47–88. Geneva: Fondation Hardt Vandœuvres.

Van Nijf, O. 2013. "Ceremonies, Athletics and the City: Some Remarks on the Social Imaginary of the Greek City of the Hellenistic Period." In *Shifting Imaginaries in the Hellenistic Period: Narrations, Practices and Images*, edited by E. Stavrianopoulo, 311–38. Leiden: E. J. Brill.

Van Nijf, O., and R. Alston. 2011. "Political Culture in the Greek City after the Classical Age: Introduction and Preview." In *Political Culture in the Greek City after the Classical Age*, edited by O. van Nijf and R. Alston, 1–26. Leuven: Peters.

Van Wees, H. 2004. *Greek Warfare: Myth and Realities*. New York: Bloomsbury Academic.

Vink, M. 1997. "Urbanization in Late and Sub-Geometric Greece: Abstract Consideration and Concrete Case Studies of Eretria and Zagora c. 700 BC." In *Urbanization in the Mediterranean in the Ninth to Sixth Centuries B.C.*, edited by H. D. Andersen, H. W. Horsnaes, S. Houby-Nielsen, and A. Rathje, 111–42. Copenhagen: Museum Tusculanum Press.

Vitelli, K. D. 1993. *Francthi Neolithic Pottery. Classification and Ceramic Phases 1 and 2. Excavations at Francthi Cave, Greece 8*. Bloomington: Indiana University Press.

Vitelli, K. D. 1995. "Pots, Potters and the Shaping of the Greek Neolithic." In *The Emergence of Pottery: Technology and Innovation in Ancient Societies*, edited by W. K. Barnett and J. W. Hoopes, 55–64. Washington, DC: Smithsonian Institution Press.

Viviers, D. 1994. "La Cite de Dattalla et L'expansion Territorial de Lyktos en Crete Central." *Bulletin de Correspondance Hellénique* 118: 229–59.

Vliet, E. C. L. 2005. "Polis: The Problem of Statehood." *Social Evolution and History* 4 (2): 120–50.

Voskos, I., and A. B. Knapp. 2008. "Cyprus at the End of the Late Bronze Age: Crisis and Colonization or Continuity and Hybridization?" *American Journal of Archaeology* 112 (4): 659–84.

Voutsaki, S. 1998. "Mortuary Evidence, Symbolic Meanings and Social Change: A Comparison between Messenia and the Argolid in the Mycenaean Period." In *Cemetery and Society in the Aegean Bronze Age*, edited by K. Branigan, 41–58. Sheffield: University of Sheffield Press.

Wace, A. J. B. 1921–23. "Excavations at Mycenae IX: The Tholos Tombs." *Annual of the British School at Athens* 25: 283–402.

Walberg, G. 1994. "The Function of the Minoan Villas." *Aegean Archaeology* 1:49–53.

Walberg, G. 2007. *Midea: The Megaron Complex and Shrine Area Excavations on the Lower Terraces 1994–1997*. Philadelphia: INSTAP Academic Press.

Waldbaum, J. C. 1994. "Early Greek Contacts with the Southern Levant, ca. 1000–600 B.C.: The Eastern Perspective." *Bulletin of the American Schools of Oriental Research* 293: 53–66.

Waldbaum, J. C. 1997. "Greeks in the East or Greeks and the East? Problems in the Definition and Recognition of Presence." *Bulletin of the American Schools of Oriental Research* 305: 1–17.

Wallace, S. 2010. *Ancient Crete: From Successful Collapse to Democracy's Alternatives, Twelfth to Fifth Centuries BC.* Cambridge: Cambridge University Press.

Wardle, K., ed. 1996. *Nea Nikomedeia I: The Excavation of an Early Neolithic Village in Northern Greece 1961–1964, the Excavation and the Ceramic Assemblage.* London: British School at Athens.

Watrous, L. V. 1984. "Ayia Triada: A New Perspective on the Minoan Villa." *American Journal of Archaeology* 88 (2): 123–34.

Webster, D., W. Fash, Jr., C. Baudez, B. Riese, and W. Sanders, eds. 1989. *The House of the Bacabs, Copan, Honduras.* Washington, DC: Dumbarton Oaks.

Weiberg, E. 2007. *Thinking the Bronze Age: Life and Death in Early Helladic Greece.* Uppsala: Acta Universitatis Upsaliensis..

Weingarten, J. 1997. "Another Look at Lerna: An EHIIIB Trading Post?" *Oxford Journal of Archaeology* 16 (2): 147–66.

Weingarten, J. 2012. "Minoan Seals and Sealings." In *The Oxford Handbook of the Bronze Age Aegean*, edited by E. H. Cline, 317–28. Oxford: Oxford University Press.

Weingarten, J., S. M. Thorne, M. Prent, and J. H. Crouwel. 2011. "More Early Helladic Sealings from Geraki in Laconia, Greece." *Oxford Journal of Archaeology* 30 (2): 131–63.

Wells, E. C. 2004. "Investigating Activity Patterns in Prehispanic Plazas: Weak Acid-Extraction ICP/AES Analysis of Anthrosols at Classic Period El Coyote, Northwest Honduras." *Archaeometry* 46 (1): 67–84.

Wenke, R. 2009. *The Ancient Egyptian State: The Origins of Egyptian Culture (c. 8000–2000 BC).* Cambridge: Cambridge University Press.

Westgate, R. 2007. "House and Society in Classical and Hellenistic Crete: A Case Study in Regional Variation." *American Journal of Archaeology* 111 (3): 423–57.

Westgate, R. 2015. "Space and Social Complexity in Greece from the Early Iron Age to the Classical Period." *Hesperia: The Journal of the American School of Classical Studies at Athens* 84 (1): 47–95.

Whitelaw, T. 2004. "The Development of an Island Centre: Urbanization at Phylakopi on Melos." In *Explaining Social Change: Studies in Honour of Colin Renfrew*, edited by J. F. Cherry, C. Scarre, and S. Shennan, 149–66. Cambridge: McDonald Institute for Archaeological Research.

Whitelaw, T. 2018. "Recognising Polities in Prehistoric Crete." In *From the Foundation to the Legacy of Minoan Society*, edited by M. Relaki and Y. Papadatos. Oxford: Oxbow Books.

Whitley, J. 1991. "Social Diversity in Dark Age Greece." *The Annual of the British School at Athens* 86: 341–65.

Whitley, J. 2001. *The Archaeology of Ancient Greece.* Cambridge: Cambridge University Press.

Whitley, J. 2003. *Style and Society in Dark Age Greece: The Changing Face of a Pre-Literate Society, 1100–700 BC.* Cambridge: Cambridge University Press.

Whitley, J. 2017. "The Material Entanglements of Writing Things Down." In *Theoretical Approaches to the Archaeology of Ancient Greece: Manipulating Material Culture,* edited by L. C. Nevett, 71–103. Ann Arbor: University of Michigan Press.

Wiencke, M. H. 1989. "Change in Early Helladic II." *American Journal of Archaeology* 93 (4): 495–509.

Wiencke, M. H. 2000. *Lerna IV: The Architecture, Stratification, and Pottery of Lerna III.* Princeton: American School of Classical Studies at Athens.

Wijnen, M. 1981. *The Early Neolithic I Settlement at Sesklo: An Early Farming Community in Thessaly, Greece.* Leiden: Faculty of Archaeology, Leiden University.

Wilk, R. 1983. "Little House in the Jungle: The Causes of Variation in House Size among Modern Kekchi Maya." *Journal of Anthropological Archaeology* 2 (2): 99–116.

Wilkinson, T. J., and S. T. Duhon. 1990. *Franchthi Paralia: The Sediments, Stratigraphy, and Offshore Investigations.* Georgetown: Georgetown University Press.

Willetts, R. F. 1965. *Ancient Crete: A Social History from Early Times until the Roman Occupation.* New York: Routledge.

Wilson, D. E. 1999. *Keos IX: Ayia Irini: Periods I–III. The Neolithic and Early Bronze Age Settlements.* Mainz am Rhein: Philipp von Zabern.

Wilson, D. E. 2007. "Early Prepalatial (EM I–EM II): EM I Well, West Court House, North-East Magazines, and South Front Groups." In *Knossos Pottery Handbook,* 49–77. Athens: British School at Athens.

Wilson, D. E. 2008. "Early Prepalatial Crete." In *The Cambridge Companion to the Aegean Bronze Age,* 77–104. Cambridge: Cambridge University Press.

Wilson, D. E. 2013. "Ayia Irini II–III, Kea: The Phasing and Relative Chronology of the Early Bronze Age II Settlement." *Hesperia: The Journal of the American School of Classical Studies at Athens* 82 (3): 385–434.

Wilson, D. E., and P. M. Day 2000. "EM I Chronology and Social Practice: Pottery from the Early Palace Tests at Knossos." *The Annual of the British School at Athens* 95: 21–63.

Wilson, D. E., and M. Eliot. 1984. "Ayia Irini, Period III: The Last Phase of Occupation of the EBA Settlement." In *The Prehistoric Cyclades,* edited by J. A. MacGillivray and R. L. N. Barber, 78–87. Edinburgh: Department of Classical Archaeology, University of Edinburgh.

Wrenhaven, K. L. 2012. *Reconstructing the Slave: The Image of the Slave in Ancient Greece.* New York: Bloomsbury Academic.

Wright, J. C. 1994. "The Mycenaean Entrance System at the West End of the Akropolis of Athens." *Hesperia: The Journal of the American School of Classical Studies at Athens* 63 (3): 323–60.

Wright, J. C. ed. 2004. *The Mycenaean Feast.* Princeton: American School of Classical Studies at Athens.

Wright, J. C. 2006. "The Formation of the Mycenaean Palace." In *Ancient Greece: From the Mycenaean Palaces to the Age of Homer,* edited by S. Deger-Jalkotzy and I. S. Lemos, 7–52. Edinburgh: Edinburgh University Press.

Wright, J. C. 2010. "Towards a Social Archaeology of Middle Helladic Greece." In *Mesohelladika: The Greek Mainland in the Middle Bronze Age, Actes du Colloque International Organise par l'Ecole Francaise d'Athens, en Collaboration avec l'American School of Classical Studies at Athens et Le Netherlands Institute in Athens, Athenes, 8–12 Mars 2000*, edited by A. Philippa-Touchais, S. Voutsaki, and J. C. Wright, 803–15. Bulletin de Correspondance Hellénique: Supplément 52. Paris: De Boccard.

Wright, R. 2009. *The Ancient Indus: Urbanism, Economy, and Society*. Cambridge: Cambridge University Press.

Yasur-Landau, A. 2010. *The Philistines and Aegean Migration at the End of the Late Bronze Age*. Cambridge: Cambridge University Press.

Yoffee, N. 2005. *Myths of the Archaic State: Evolution of the Earliest Cities, States, and Civilizations*. Cambridge: Cambridge University Press.

Younger, J. 2005. "Some Similarities in Mycenaean Palace Plans." In *Autochthon: Papers Presented to O. T. P. K. Dickinson on the Occasion of His Retirement*, edited by A. Dakouri-Hild and E. S. Sherratt, 185–90. Oxford: British Archaeological Reports Publishing.

Younger, J., and P. Rehak. 2008. "The Material Culture of Neopalatial Crete" and "Minoan Culture: Religion, Burial Customs, Administration." Both in *The Cambridge Companion to the Aegean Bronze Age*, edited by C. Shelmerdine, 140–64 and 165–85. Cambridge: Cambridge University Press.

Zalloua, P. A., D. E. Platt, M. El Sibai, J. Khalife, N. Makhoul, M. Haber, Y. Xue, et al. 2008. "Identifying Genetic Traces of Historical Expansions: Phoenician Footprints in the Mediterranean." *The American Journal of Human Genetics* 83 (5): 633–42.

Zuchtriegel, G. 2018. *Colonization and Subalternity in Classical Greece: Experience of the Nonelite Population*. New York: Cambridge University Press.

Zuiderhoek, A. 2008. "On the Political Sociology of the Imperial Greek City." *Greek, Roman and Byzantine Studies* 48 (4): 417–45.

Index

Achaean (Akhaian) League, 176
Aetolian (Aitolian) League, 176
agora
    Hellenistic context for status display,
        179
Akrotiri, 75, 78
Alexander the Great, 174
Alexandria, 175
Alkmaionidai, 169
Alur, 129
andron, 165, 169, 195, 219, 222
Antonaccio, C., 117, 119–20, 126
Archanes, 45, 50
Argolid, 70, 74, 76, 79
Asine, 71–72, 102
aspects of emergence
    post-phase transition in the Iron Age,
        167–69
Athens, 82, 102, 113, 115, 117, 123,
        125, 131–32, 136, 140, 143, 145,
        149, 152, 155–58, 160, 163, 170,
        181, 221, 227, 255
athletics
    post-phase transition in the Iron Age,
        145–49
    pre-phase transition in the Iron Age,
        145
Ayia Irini, 39, 47, 70, 75
Ayia Photia, 45
Azoria, 185
    "Andreion", 193–95
    cult building, 188
    household institutions, 195
    internal institutional structure, 194–95
    kitchens, 194
    lack of open public assembly, 188
    as model of institutions of a Cretan
        Iron Age community, 187–92

basileus, 93, 120, 219
Berent, M., 171
Bintliff, J. L., 28
Blegen, C. W., 16, 35, 71, 82–83
Broodbank, C., 13, 18, 47, 67, 70, 75
Buell, D. M., 50, 67

centaur, 114
Chase, A., 216–17
Chase, D., 216–17
Cherry, J. F., 47, 55, 66, 89, 167
Coldstream, J. N., 101, 191–92, 198,
        203
community fissioning in the Iron Age,
        126–29
complexity theory
    application to emergence of Cretan
        palaces, 51–52
    application to emergence of
        Mycenaean polities, 79
    application to Iron Age Crete,
        198–203
    application to Iron Age Greece
        without Crete, 106–7
    application to Mesopotamia, 4–5
    application to transegalitarian
        societies, 6
    connection to feasting and
        aggrandizers, 6
    definition, 3
corridor house, 35, 38
councils and assemblies
    post-phase transition in the Iron Age,
        156
    pre-phase transition in the Iron Age,
        121
Cretan Iron Age storage pithos as display
        item, 191

Crielaard, J. P., 120, 125
culture
    archaeological, 31–32

Daskaleio-Kavos, 69
Delphi, 111
Dhimini, 20–21, 24, 26, 28, 95
    defensive features, 27
Dietler, M., 5, 8
drama, 160–61
Driessen, J., 58, 60, 76, 78, 96

economic institutions
    post-phase transition in the Iron Age,
        162–63
    pre-phase transition in the Iron Age,
        121–22
El Mirador, 209
ethnos, 166–67
    in the Hellenistic period, 176
Eutresis, 32, 35, 72

feasting
    in Cyclades 2400–2200 BCE, 67
    elaborate in 8th century, 102
    funeral feasting and emergence of
        Mycenaean polities, 79–82
    funeral feasting in Messara 2100–1900
        BCE, 49–50
    impetus for the emergence of Cretan
        palaces, 51–52
    Kastri/Lefkandi assemblage,
        67–69
    in Keros-Syros culture, Cyclades, 44
    Mycenaean kylix cup, 102
    in the Neolithic, 21
    new feasting institutions after fall of
        Mycenaean polities, 102
    as a window in complexity theory,
        5–6
Finley, M. I., 8, 89, 120
Fitzsimons, R., 82, 197
funeral lekythos, 153
funerals
    post-phase transition in the Iron Age,
        155
    pre-phase transition in the Iron Age,
        118
    sumptuary legislation, 155

Galatas, 50, 66, 75
Galaty, M., 51, 58, 91, 95, 119, 208
Gallant, T., 15–16
Giddens, A., 1
Glowacki, K.T., 188, 196
Gournia, 49–50, 66–67, 78
Graham, A. J., 128
Graham, J. W., 58–59
Greek alphabet, 104–6
Greek sculpture, 141–43
gymnasion, 162

Haggis, D., 8, 21, 46, 53, 76, 185, 203
Hagia Triadha, 63
Halstead, P., 5, 16, 21, 27–28, 37, 55,
    91–92
Herodotos, 9, 129, 131, 167
Hesiod, 104, 112, 120
Hodder, I., 2, 31
Homer, 104, 112, 120
household institutions
    in Korakou culture, 35
    mid-second millennium at Eutresis
        and Asine, 72
    in Minoan communities, 65–66
    Minoan hall system, 72
    Minoan houses and villas, 63–65
    Myrtos, 45–46
    in the Neolithic, 21–25
    Neolithic Sesklo, 20
    post-phase transition in the Iron Age,
        163–66
    pre-phase transition in the Iron Age,
        107–10
    in third century CE and later, 179
Humphreys, S., 2, 162

Iakovidis, S., 82, 98, 124
institutional evolution in Iron Age Crete,
    196–98

Kalapodi, 111–12
Kato Zakro, 50, 55, 59, 65
Kavousi region, 187
Knossos, 26, 44, 46, 50–52, 54–55,
    59–62, 65–66, 74, 76, 78–79, 87,
    91–92, 95–97, 113, 189, 191, 196,
    198–202, 222
    Neolithic, 29

koine, 185
koinon, 167
Korakou culture, 32
Kythera, 70–71, 95

Lebessi, A., 192–93
Lefkandi, 67, 71, 102, 113–16, 122,
    124–25, 132, 198
    elite funeral pavilion, 115–17
Linear A, 63–65
Linear B, 121
liturgy, 157

Ma, J., 177, 179
Macedon, 173
Malia, 46, 49–50, 52, 55, 59, 65, 74, 78,
    87
Malkin, I., 9, 14, 128, 130
Maya
    benefits of structural comparison to
        Classic Greece, 216–17
    Caracol, 216
    characteristics of Classic period elite
        networks, 210–11
    El Palmar, 211
    internal instability in Classic period,
        213–16
    Preclassic elite networks, 209–10
    Skyband use by non-royals, 213
Mazarakis-Ainian, A., 101, 108, 110,
    120, 135
McEnroe, J. C., 50, 53, 58, 76
McInerney, J., 111, 172
Megara Hyblaia, 133
Melos, 18, 26, 39, 47, 69
Messara, 45, 49, 52, 198
Mook, M., 185
Morgan, C., 111–12, 150
Morris, I., 101, 113, 120, 122, 125, 135,
    155, 166, 169, 172
Mount Lykaion, 111–12
Muhly, P., 193
Mycenae, 74, 79, 81–82, 87, 96–97, 221
Mycenaean, problem of ethnic
    identification, 95
Myrtos, 45–46, 49

Nakassis, D., 58, 91, 99
Nea Nikomedeia, 20

Neolithic, possible hierarchy in,
    27–29
networks in the Iron Age, 129–30
Nevett, L. C., 8, 132, 164, 166
Nichoria, 102, 107, 109, 112

Olympia, 111–12
Oropos, 107–8
Osborne, R., 8, 71, 123, 128

Palaikastro, 45, 50, 65, 67, 78, 192
Panhellenion, 182
Panionion, 131
Parkinson, W., 51, 91, 95, 208
periods of chaos
    at Iron Age Eleutherna, 201
    at Iron Age Knossos, 201
    at Iron Age Prinias, 202
    Middle-Minoan Knossos, Phaistos,
        and Peak sanctuaries, 53
    in middle Minoan Messara, 49
    middle second Millennium in
        Mycenae, 79
    as seen in complexity theory, 5
    toward end of the Iron Age, 126
Petras, 45, 50, 53, 78
Phaistos, 46, 50, 52–55, 59, 62–63, 65,
    74, 78
Philippeion, 180
Phoenician settlements, 127
Phylakopi, 39, 47, 69–70, 75
Pithekoussai, 128
politics
    in Hellenistic and Roman periods,
        176–79
    post-phase transition in the Iron Age,
        156–57
    pre-phase transition in the Iron Age,
        119–21
post–Iron Age phase transition temple,
    136–37
Powell, B., 104
Priene
    agora, 178
    sanctuary of Athena Polias, 137–40
public assembly
    post-phase transition Iron Age
        theatrical, 158–62
Pullen, D., 38–39, 46, 71

Pylos
  palace, 83
  territorial integration, 93–95

Quiche Maya, 129

Reents-Budet, D., 211
Renfrew, C., 16, 41, 43–44, 47, 69, 89,
  167

sanctuaries
  Delphi, 149–50
  function of, in Cretan Iron Age,
    195–96
  Hera at Samos, 143–44
  honorific statues, 140–41
  Idaean cave, 192
  incorporation of Imperial Cult, 179
  Olympia, 145–49
  post-phase transition in the Iron Age
    economic functions, 150–51
  Syme, 192–93
Scheidel, W., 101, 123
Schoep, I., 46–47, 76
Second Sophistic, 183
Sesklo, 20, 24, 26, 29
  defensive features, 27
Shaw, J. W., 35, 62, 202
Small, D., 58, 79, 94, 106, 132, 151,
  155, 162, 170–71, 177, 220

Snodgrass, A. M., 100–1, 104, 106,
  119–20, 148, 167, 172
social structure as an analytical frame, 3
social war, 174
Souvatzi, S. G., 20, 22, 28, 120
Sparta, 149, 158
Spawforth, A. J., 137, 182, 184
Symposion, 165

Talalay, L., 26
Tartaron, T., 58, 97, 208
Termessos, 176–78
Theoroi, 130
Tokovinine, A., 211
Tsipopoulou, M., 45, 50

underdeveloped political economy in
  Classical Greece, 170–72

van Nijf, O., 177, 182

warfare
  post-phase transition Iron Age,
    151–52
  pre-phase transition Iron Age, 118–19
warrior grave, 117
Whitley, J., 7, 101, 104, 113, 125
Wright, J. C., 8, 74, 82–83

Yoffee, N., 4–6, 52, 106, 123